D1031816

STUDIES IN NON-DETERMINISTIC
PSYCHOLOGY

A Publication of the National Institute for the Psychotherapies

STUDIES IN NON-DETERMINISTIC PSYCHOLOGY

EDITED BY
GERALD EPSTEIN, M.D.

with

James L. Fosshage, Ph.D.
Kenneth A. Frank, Ph.D.
Henry Grayson, Ph.D.
Clemens A. Loew, Ph.D.
Henry Lowenheim, Ph.D.

VOLUME V IN THE SERIES
NEW DIRECTIONS IN PSYCHOTHERAPY
Series Editor
Paul Olsen, Ph.D.

 **HUMAN SCIENCES PRESS**
72 Fifth Avenue   3 Henrietta Street
NEW YORK, NY 10011 ● LONDON, WC2E 8LU

812145

Library of Congress Cataloging in Publication Data
Main entry under title:

Studies in non-deterministic psychology.

   (New directions in psychotherapy; v. 5)
   "A publication of the National Institute for the Psychotherapies."

   Bibliography
   Includes index.
   1. Phenomenological psychology.   2. Psychology
—Philosophy.   3. East and West.   4. Psychotherapy.
I. Epstein, Gerald, 1935-   II. National Institute for the Psychotherapies.   III. Series.   [DNLM:
1. Psychological theory.   2. Psychotherapy.
W1 NE374FE v. 5 / WM420 S933]
BF204.5.S75   150.19'2   LC 80-13820

ISBN 0-87705-654-4

CONTENTS

CONTRIBUTORS

DAVID BOHM, PH. D., is Professor of Theoretical Physics at Birkbeck College, London University. He holds a Ph.D. in physics from the University of California at Berkeley, where he has taught. He has done research at Princeton University, in Israel, and in Brazil. He is the author of *Causality and Chance in Modern Physics, Quantum theory,* and *The Special Theory of Relativity.* A monograph on the meaning of physics and consciousness called *Fragmentation and Wholeness* has been published by the VanLeer Foundation. His new book, *Wholeness and the Implicate Order* was published this year. His main interest is in the philosophical aspects of quantum and relativity theory.

SWAMI DAYANANDA is a sanyassin (Hindu monk), a teacher of Vedanta, and a scholar of the sanskrit language and literature. He is the head of Sandeepany Sadhanalaya, a traditional Vedic institute in Bombay, India. He has lectured extensively in India for the past 20 years and at many universities in the United States. He is currently conducting a course of study

in Vedanta and Sanskrit at Sandeepany West in Piercy, California.

SANDRA EISENSTEIN is a sculptor. She has taught fine arts
at various universities including Montclair State College, N.J.,
and the University of Wisconsin. From 1976–1978 she attended
a course in Vedanta at Sandeepany Sadhanalaya in Bombay,
India, studying under Swami Dayananda. She is currently
teaching Vedanta in New York.

BETH GORDON is currently an active student of the Tibetan Rinpoche Choygam Trungpa in New York City, and is a
student of Buddhist psychology.

GEORGE HOGBEN, M.D., received his medical education
at the State University of New York at Buffalo, and his psychiatric training at the Payne Whitney Psychiatric Clinic and
Cornell University Medical Center. He spent two postdoctoral
years studying research concepts and methods at New York
University. Dr. Hogben is applying Waking Dream technique
to the investigation and treatment of psychotic disorders. He
has conducted several linguistic studies, most recently involving syntactic processing in schizophrenia. His other research
interests are the impact of political process on mental health;
traumatic neurosis, especially war neuroses; and the nutritional
aspects of mental health.

PAUL OLSEN, PH.D., is Director of Intern Training and of
Publications at the National Institute for the Psychotherapies,
in New York City. He is general editor of the series, *New
Directions in Psychotherapy,* and editor of the journal *Comprehensive Psychotherapy,* soon to appear. He has also published
a number of novels, short stories, and nonfiction books, and is
currently coauthor of a work on the mother–son relationship
to be published by Harper and Row.

KENNETH L. PHILLIPS, M.A., is a practicing psychotherapist in New York City. He is also a physicist for Citicorp, an international corporation based in New York City. He has trained at the New York Psychoanalytic Institute and the C.G. Jung Institute in New York where he currently serves on the faculty. He has traveled widely in the Orient where he learned I Ching and has authored numerous articles on the subject while also teaching it in New York and elsewhere in the United States. Currently he is completing a major book on I Ching.

CARL RINZLER, M.D., is a practicing psychiatrist in New York City. He received his psychiatric training at Mt. Sinai Hospital in New York. He is a student of Buddhist psychology and is a student of Choygam Trungpa, Rinpoche in New York City.

CHARLES SCOTT, PH.D., is professor and chairman of the Department of Philosophy of Vanderbilt University. He is a specialist in the area of phenomenological philosophy and is an expert in the writings of Martin Heidegger. He has written over 37 articles and several books, many pertaining to the philosophy of Heidegger. He is also a practicing psychotherapist having studied and worked closely with the noted Swiss analyst Medard Boss.

DAVID SHAINBERG, M.D., is Training and Supervising Analyst at the Postgraduate Center for Mental Health in New York City. He is the author of *The Transforming Self: New Dimensions in Psychoanalytic Process* published by Intercontinental Medical Books, New York.

DIANE SHAINBERG, M. A., C.S.W., is a faculty member, teacher, and supervisor at the Postgraduate Center for Mental Health in New York City, the National Institute for the Psychotherapies, and the Center for Non-Deterministic Studies, also in New York. She is in private practice, and is currently finishing a book: *The Treatment of the Person Named Border-line.* She is a student and practitioner of Zen Buddhism. She has studied the process of Waking Dream with Madam Colette Muscat in Jerusalem, Israel, and has published in this area. She has also studied Vedanta and Tai Chi. Her practice and study of Eastern philosophy has indicated new ways to practice psychotherapy in keeping with the findings in modern Western science, the world in which we live, and the patients whom we see.

JACOB STATTMAN, PH.D., is founder and present Director of the Institute of Unitive Psychology of the Netherlands, a postgraduate center for training and clinical practice in the fields of humanisitic, bioenergetic, and transpersonal psychology and psychotherapy. He developed his concepts of unitive psychology after extensive background in Oriental and Western studies, and has been influenced by the existential psychotherapies of the European tradition, the transformation schools of Tibetan and Zen Buddhism, and the somatic therapies of the Reichian tradition.

KEN WILBER is editor of *Re-Vision,* a journal devoted to transpersonal concerns. He is author of *The Spectrum of Consciousness, The Atman Project, No Boundary, Up From Eden,* and is widely regarded as one of the foremost authorities on transpersonal psychology.

WARREN WILNER, PH.D., is a clinical psychologist and psychoanalyst in private practice in New York City. He is a graduate and supervisor of psychotherapy at the William Alanson White Institute of Psychiatry, Psychoanalysis, and Psychology. He is a faculty member and supervisor of psychotherapy at The Center For Non-Deterministic Studies in New York City.

About the Editor

Dr. Gerald Epstein is founder and Director of The Center For Non-Deterministic Studies, a psychotherapy training center sponsored by The National Institute for The Psychotherapies in New York City. He received his psychiatric training at Kings County Hospital in Brooklyn, N.Y., and his psychoanalytic training from The New York Psychoanalytic Institute from which he graduated in 1972. He is assistant clinical professor of psychiatry at Mount Sinai Hospital in New York. His interests are wide ranging, varying from being cofounder and editor-in-chief of *The Journal of Psychiatry and Law* to developing a new system of psychotherapy called Waking Dream Therapy. He has published on this latter topic (see the first chapter of this book) and has recently completed a book titled *Waking Dream Therapy: Dream Process as Imagination.* The present volume, *Studies in Non-Deterministic Psychology,* is his effort to present to the professional audience the broad vista of phenomenological thought of which Waking Dream is a part. Much of what is explicated in the pages of this book is taught at the Center for Non-Deterministic Studies at 330 West 58 St., New York, NY 10019.

INTRODUCTION

The pace of science and its discoveries has quickened considerably over the past decade. Part of the impetus has come form the fresh insights afforded to scientific investigation in general, and psychological investigation in particular, by the discoveries of holography, left–right cerebral hemispheric specialization, and the infusion of oriental meditative practices into western culture. These discoveries have prompted a new way of looking by scientists into the field, which itself has been embedded in a matrix of causal deterministic thinking. Along with these new perceptions one cannot forget the transformative work of Einstein and Heisenberg in the areas of relativity and uncertainty, respectively. The findings of current science, inspired by the genius of the two men just mentioned (along with Kurt Godel), has tended to find uncanny correspondence with the doctrines of oriental thought; so much so that the underpinnings of the present foundations of western science have been shaken. What we have taken for granted before as clear-cut distinctions between what was real and unreal is currently undergoing radical revision. The reverberations have been felt as well in the region of the behavioral sciences. The paradigm of Freudian dynamics in psychology, and its many offshoots within and without the Freudian movement, has stood as the standard out of which has been fashioned the many therapeutic approaches that now adorn the horizon.[1] The impact of the new physics from the West and the acausal, non-deterministic point of view from the East is forcing us to seriously question the present fundamental principles upon which modern western psychology and psychotherapy rests—especially since the current techniques have not made a significant contribution toward stemming the tide of human mental suffering. This investigation began in a serious way when Abraham Maslow introduced his "third force" or humanistic psychology into the American scene. In Europe Medard Boss, basing his work on the phenomenological philosophy of Martin Heidegger, called his form of therapy Daseinsanalysis (the analysis of the being of the there). He created a profound transformation of psychoanalytic method in the process and has made fundamental contributions to the fields of schizophrenia, psychosomatics, dreams, and therapeutic process, among others. Of course there have been other currents that, almost presciently, have emerged nearly or exactly at the time the surge of oriental thought and new western science made their appearance in a meaningful way. It is the intent of this book to present the major outstanding streams of an integrated non-deterministic psychological approach together with its therapeutic application which will address itself to the transformation going on in science of which non-deterministic psychology is a part. It is my feeling that perhaps this way may turn out to be an efficacious one for treating human mental suffering.

The book is divided into three parts. Part I deals with the ground of the new paradigmatic shift. Interestingly, our readers will be surprised to find that not only does the impact of western science assert itself, but also that it speaks in a manner that is close to human experience, as does the wisdom of the East. For the former Dr. David Bohm presents his concept of the implicate and explicate order of the universe. He points us to the unitary nature of the universe, and to the ongoing flow of human existence within this unitary process. Set off against the scientific perspectives, and at the same time buttressing it, are the bases of the doctrines offered by Indian Vedanta and Tibetan Buddhist teaching. Vedanta asks the question: "what is self?" and "what is the relation of desire to self?". Buddhism discusses the fundamental issue of pain, its relationship to self, and putting an end to self. I have added another dimension by introducing another aspect of nonrational thinking having its source in the ancient wisdom of the Mediterranean region—the realm of imagination—and as such serves as a bridge between eastern and western thought.

Part II represents the therapeutic application of what has been outlined in Part I. The readers will become acquainted with the various ways in which they can engage their patients in a rich and meaningful therapeutic encounter. Much of what is outlined in this section has been concretely applied in terms of teaching this entire approach to clinicians through a training center established in New York City in 1978, called *The Center For Non-Deterministic Studies*.

Part III comprises contemporary thinkers, all of whom have clinical experience and who are trying to weld a philosophical understanding to our understanding of the clinical situation. The variety of thought encountered in this part is remarkable, the more so because the starting points are different but ultimately they meet and are all traveling the same road at the end. I think the movement toward a unitary purpose, arrived at from different directions, and by different roads, underscores the fundamental oneness and wholeness that the new paradigm encompasses which has served as the inspiration for this book.

Judging by what has been stated above, the timeliness of this book cannot be stressed enough. Whether we are aware of it or not, the direction of science is changing. Sir James Jeans said as far back as 1937 that "the stream of knowledge is heading toward a non-mechanical reality; the universe begins to look more like a great thought than like a machine. Mind no longer appears as an accidental intruder into realms of matter."[2] The words of Jeans seem almost prophetic now considering the advances that have been made in modern science that seem to be moving in the direction that bear out Jeans' words, especially in physics. The new understanding of holography has been a development that has captured the imagination of some modern scientists, and has ushered in a new consideration of the universe and our place in it. The discovery of specialized cerebral hemispheric functioning throws new light on the relationship of brain to mind and on the functioning of the brain itself. These shifts have forced, and will continue to force psychotherapists to reconsider their appreciation of what constitutes reality for them and their patients. It is the intention of this book to provide a direction for the reader to begin to think of other paradigms that may have at least as much relevance to the understanding and treating of emotional suffering as those currently available. At the same time the reader may be stimulated to continue his search in a serious way along the lines indicated in these pages. Perhaps he will find out for himself how meaningful such a search might be.

G.E.

NOTES

1. No matter what technique or variant presently offered by "neo" schools, or various analytic movements—viz. object relations—the fundamental principles of causality and determinism as enunciated by natural science inform them.

2. Jeans, J., *The Mysterious Universe,* Cambridge Eng., Cambridge University Press, 1937, p. 122.

Part I

PRINCIPLES

The importance of this book for western psychological thinking and for psychotherapists of whatever stripe—psychoanalysts, psychiatrists, psychologists, social workers, and all other lay therapists—is that the direction of modern western science is drawing our attention to another way of looking at the most important phenomenon we know in psychological life —reality. It is essential that we be cognizant of these developments because the prevailing psychological model takes its direction from the formulations of the prevailing scientific paradigm. This was certainly true for Freud and for most of those following. The impact of psychodynamic thinking is the single most influential one for most psychotherapists practicing today. This model derives from the natural scientific one that emphasizes the causal deterministic point of view. Most psychotherapists are not acquainted with this fact, nor do they consider the relevance of it for their treatment of emotional disorders. If they did consider the relevance and influence on their clinical practice we might begin to see a radical shift take place in how therapy is conducted. The major point to consider here is that, recognize it or not, each and everyone of us approaches our work with a preconceived philosophical view of how the world is constructed. In other words, everyone has a world view about what constitutes reality. That world view is applied to how and what we consider to be an individual's relationship to "reality," its supposed aberrations, and to what is considered to be the way to help someone adapt to "reality." In speaking of the way to help, I refer primarily to the insistence that the analytic, interpretive, logical mode is the best course to follow in understanding, figuring out, and making sense of the world. Our making-sense capacity seems to have failed us in making sense out of "man's inhumanity to man" over these past 10,000 years. It seems that all attempts to make sense through commonsense have not succeeded in ending the suffering of mankind, and in some cases has fostered this suffering. Why should this be so? Those of us who have engaged the emerging paradigm of western scientific thought have begun to recognize that the content of thought has been self-deceptive in permitting us to gain access to the depths of our being and to the sources of our suffering. Linear thought has as its tendency the grasping of fixed nodal points where it can come to rest as it were. These nodal points are experienced as certainty, sureness, memory, explanation, and predicting the future as examples. Our linear thought is *always* telling us what the explanation is for some event or some experience we encounter; or at least it is trying to do so. Our linear thought does what its tendency pushes it to—it tries to make sense out of the world. This making sense often occurs as an interpretation of experience wherein the interpretation is *mistakenly perceived* as an objective truth about encountered experience. We are, thereby, deceived, albeit not maliciously or purposefully. This sort of thinking tends to objectify what is fundamentally subjective. This notion of the deceptiveness of the objectification of subjective thought has gained support from the researches of modern science, for example, in the realm of quantum and subatomic physics. Whereas before it was held that the atom—the particulate entity—was the fundamental reality, it now appears more likely that the fundamental reality is a process or stream of energy flowing incessantly out of which particulate matter, like atoms, is abstracted. It seems that these force fields of energy are without form, but that appearances are contained within them in a virtual state, much the same as a tree is contained, virtually, in a seed. The atomistic model has held sway for hundreds of years, and is now seriously challenged by the force-field theory. This challenge holds significant consequences for the fields of psychiatry and psychology. The reason for this is that, unbenownst to most psychotherapists, their work is derived from the prevailing scientific model. In other words, the work of psychotherapy now carries on the atomistic theory into the domain of human mental functions and interpersonal relationships. Translated into more familiar terms the emphasis of most psychotherapeutic activity centers on the contents of one's thought processes, and using that content to figure out one's relationship to the world. The contents of thought in the form of words are analogous to the atoms as the fundamental building blocks of psychological life. Words as building blocks led immediately to the primacy of causal thinking. Causal thinking is the method by which the words are tied together. Words built upon words lead to linear logical thinking causally determined and atomically inspired. In psychology, as in atomistic science, analogously speaking, material units (words) are the "fundamental" elements out of which human experience is built. From the psychotherapeutic perspective the emphasis has always been on the unfolding of words via thought, which are the contents of consciousness. These thoughts are then given meaning via interpretation, which support the causal presuppositions: something that was (the cause) produces what is (the effect).

The force field paradigm addresses our attention to the flow or stream of energy. On the psychological level we may begin to look at something other than the contents of consciousness. We can begin to look then at that from which the contents of consciousness comes. That is, *we can look at consciousness itself.* This is what non-determinism addresses itself to—the richness of the movement of the mind. Hopefully the turning of attention to this possibility will enable psychology to strike a balance between the contents and the movement of consciousness. So far the overwhelming weight of psychological interest has been on the contents, creating an imbalance that may not permit a total therapeutic experience.

The principles expounded in the chapters of this part attest to the viability of another way of looking that balances the deterministic view and may promote healing as a result of this balancing.

Gerald Epstein tries to underscore the importance of imagination for the healing process. The importance of this work for the context of the present book is to show not only the connection of healing to imagination, but also to emphasize the necessity for reintroducing imagination into the stream of western therapeutics where it held an exceedingly prominent role before the reign of Cartesian thought came to dominate western scientific thinking.

Swami Dayananda, through his translator Sandra Eisenstein, concerns himself with the fundamental problem of human existence, that of *wanting.* Everyone wants something or other existing outside of oneself to complete oneself. That is, man's fundamental error is that he believes himself to be incomplete and that his completeness can only be gained by acquiring that which is not part of oneself. No wanting can result in effecting man's completeness since the resolution of any particular want engenders another want. What all men really want is to be free from want. Such freedom is possible and is a fundamental principle of Vedantic thought.

Carl Rinzler and Beth Gordon make a very important distinction that is significant for the development of psychiatry and psychology. They do so through the explication of the major Buddhist principles, themselves a very profound psychological system. They begin by showing that both psychology and Buddhism emerge as a response to the suffering of the world. They point out that whereas therapy assumes that the individual can be changed so that his pain is minimized and happiness increased, Buddhism regards the *very notion of "individual" itself as the cause of pain.*

David Bohm wants to show the unbroken wholeness of the totality of existence as an undivided flowing movement without borders. Implied is the inadequacy of the pervading general commitment to analyze everything into independently existent but interlacing parts each having a more or less fixed nature.

G.E.

chapter 1

THE RELATIONSHIP OF HEALING TO IMAGINATION

Gerald Epstein, M.D.

The etymology of the word "healing" comes from the root that also means holy. We define ourselves as members of the healing arts if we are engaged in the work of therapy. Yet, in the realm of our traditional therapeutic approaches, scant if any, reference is made to the inclusion of what is holy into the process. Psychology, as it is generally organized within our cultural context, derives its guiding principles from the natural scientific application of what originally was discovered as the principles underlying the operation of machines and of the material world in general. When philosophical materialism dominates the value system of a society there tends to be a diminishing emphasis on the holy. This situation might occur as a consequence of the elevation of the material thing to a revered status, while feelings about religious or spiritual life are relegated to the realm of the aberrant and the pathological; or what might be worse, not taken seriously at all. This trend has been followed in the field of psychology and the dominant modes of western therapy that have developed thus far in this century, namely, behaviorism and dynamic psychology. The term "behaviorism" speaks for itself; it has increasingly been demonstrated as a dehumanizing form of therapy, contemptuous of the finer nuances of human existence. Dynamic psychology has represented an attempt to break out of destructive life patterns and to provide a method which would help individuals to achieve some measure of psychological freedom. Here was a way of counteracting the crushing influence imposed by industrial and technological society, with its concommitant movement toward mediocrity and conformity. However, by opting to work within the framework of the technological culture and the tenets of natural science, dynamic psychology has severely restricted itself. Defining its goals according to the prejudices of contemporary culture, dynamic psychology has come to regard the expression of religious feeling and experience—the latter necessarily nonmaterial and often beyond verbal explanation—as unreal and aberrant. With regard to the "holy," it appears that the movement of psychology has paralleled that of the culture. If healing is intimately related to the holy (as etymology suggests) then our current approaches to therapy are inadequate. Any psychology that aligns itself with a purely materialistic view of the world cloaks its theories in terms based on the image-making tendency of linear thought and erects theoretical structures on purely empirical foundations, cannot, by its own tenets, allow for the admittance of what is nonmaterial and qualitative. Dynamic psychology is inherently prejudiced against that which stands outside of concrete reality.

In order for a meaningful healing to take place within the context of our current therapeutic procedures, psychology must develop tolerance toward *all* experience, including the holy, which is fundamentally a non-rational phenomenological event. Indeed, psychology must pave the way for opening human beings to this dimension within themselves. It can be questioned as to whether the purely materialistic philosophy implied in the theories underlying the technique of free association in current psychotherapeutics can permit an individual to find those spiritual sources—often apprehended as non-rational experience—that are necessary for man to achieve a totality of fulfillment. Free association, as performed and interpreted by the patient and conceived of by the therapist, is derivative of the analytic and rational function of the mind. Free association is geared to addressing not what presents itself to us immediately in the phenomenological openness of our perception, but rather toward discerning through analysis what lies "behind" what appears to our perception.

What would provide a link between healing, the holy, therapeutics, and science? At the outset we could say that the attributes of this link would have to include its accessibility to man living in everyday life, while at the same time permitting him to experience that which is transcendental. This link must not be fraught with an aura of mystification or cultism and it must allow human beings to grow by finding possibilities for change that can be fulfilled experientially. Such a link is to be found in the revitalizing influence and application of the creative imagination in our everyday existence. For centuries the imaginal has been held in disrepute in western life simply because the growth of natural science and technology would not permit the "visionary" element into common life. The rise of capitalism and industrial society, rationalism, and formalized religion in the post-renaissance period all formed pieces of a whole which was constituted to exploit the natural wealth of the western world in order to satisfy economic and expansionistic needs. The powerbrokers, therefore, developed the conglomerate of organized church, industry, and the military, which has continued to consolidate its grip on western society. One overriding aim of these groups was to stamp out whatever appeared to run counter to their attempts to restrict imaginative and spiritual freedom; another was to assimilate all discoveries of the new science within a utilitarian framework. With the leveling of culture and the promulgation of an orderly mediocrity came the sacrifice of those idealists and seers who posed a threat to the established order of material "reality." Empirical philosophy became the rationale for investing the world of gross matter with exaggerated significance; only that which was graspable by the five senses was "real." All other experience incapable of quantitive measurement or calculation was, therefore, consigned to the realm of the "unreal." Imagination, fantasy, and intuition became members of that unreal fraternity. Prior to the removal of the imaginal from the province of "reality," this faculty was so acceptable in daily life that it was an essential part of medical care.

In the late medieval and early renaissance period, the human imagination flourished in movements like alchemy, Christian mysticism, and Kabbalah, all of which emphasized an active connection between man and God by exercising the vehicle of imagination. The organ of imagination, was thought to be located in the ventricles of the brain, serving as a regulator of visual phenomena like dreams and hallucinations. Individuals were encouraged to enter the imaginal realm where they would often discover some object that seemed to have healing properties. The patient was then told to obtain an amulet or talisman that corresponded to that which he had found in the imagination, a reminder of what he discovered about himself in the imaginal realm and which he was to carry out in his everyday life. In this way an attempt was made to establish a unity of experience between interior and exterior life.

The imaginal realm is an accepted reality in traditions like Sufism, Tibetan Buddhism, Kabbalah and in American Indian lore. Although the imaginal is accepted as a genuine realm of existence, the physical body is not accepted as the locus of what constitutes the essential "I" or mind. The body is the vehicle for the manifestation of mind in the world of concrete reality. But the world of concrete reality is not the only one available to human beings; it is rather that which happens as in linear time. In the imaginal reality—as in the creative process—events are lived outside of linear time; in fact, it is here that time is reversed and entropy decreased. Entropy by definition occurs as the linear movement of time in a unidirectional manner. This is the movement of time in concrete waking reality. Any event lived in linear time, such as everyday life, must participate in an entropic movement in which entropy is increased. As time progresses, entropy increases. However, in an event experienced as occurring outside of linear time, entropy by definition in that event is decreased. Therefore, in the creative process of imaginal existence entropy perforce is decreased and the breaking down process is stilled. The inaugurators of the disciplines alluded to above were well aware that this process of attaining to such "timelessness" initiated the event of healing, for it is only outside of linear time, in a field of totality, that the fragmentation that is characteristic of linear thought disappears. At this moment of insight the verbal, actional, and imaginal modes of existence are harmonized. The verbal is used here only to describe the event while it is seen and explored in the imagination. A common occurrence in connection with practices involving extension into the immaterial reality is an immediate sense of connection with a spiritual dimension. One often experiences a feeling that is described as holy, and this experienced connection is part of the healing process which eliminates the fragmentation brought about by identification with the objects of our perception. Since linear thinking constantly manages to deceive us in this way, healing can only occur when we abandon the habit of linear thinking, even if momentarily. Paradoxically, psychological healing takes place, outside the intellectual process.

Scholars of eastern philosophy point out that Mahayana Buddhists posited the notion of a "storehouse consciousness" comprised of realms of images, which were both a barrier and a pointer to the level of no-mind. The adepts of Kabbalah knew this as well, and they transformed such knowledge into a method of meditational practice that quickly surpassed ratiocination and dependence on habitual mental fabrications in favor of the unqualified present experience and the phenomonology of the moment. These methods stand as phenomenological systems that are essentially opposed to the speculations of dynamic psychology, which proposes that appearances are less significant than that which remains unmanifest. As an instance, of the latter, Freud (1916) stated:

> We do not merely seek to describe and classify phenomena but to comprehend them as indications of a play of forces in the psyche, as expressions of goal-directed tendencies which work in unison or against one another. We are striving for a dynamic conception of psychic phenomena. *Perceived phenomena must in our conception recede behind the assumed, posited tendencies.* (my emphasis)

Simply put, in order to illustrate the opposing points of view, and borrowing a little from Freud: dynamics = *sometimes* a cigar is a cigar; phenomenology = a cigar is *always* a cigar. The further elaboration of this phenomenology as it has been modified to meet our western psychological needs, combines the spheres of verbal description, imagination, and action (experience) and will be described below by a method called Waking Dream (Epstein, 1978, 1981).

A fundamental problem that has pervaded the psychological field has been that of understanding fantasy as part of the mental life of the individual. Harking back to what I said previously about what has evolved out of the Cartesian fallout, namely the elevation of the material to a central position in life experience, fantasy also falls into the domain of the unreal. Fantasies are not quantifiable nor graspable within measurable limits. As a result, psychology (explicitly) and all natural science (implicitly) have come to regard fantasy as "unreal," products of a person's psyche (itself an unproven speculation) that when revealed are to be understood by the sense that can be made out of them by linear logic so they can be dispensed with rather than played around with, or indulged in. Even more tolerant psychotherapists who will be quick to point out that they accept fantasies as realities will invariably interpret fantasies in line with a dynamically oriented point of view or *Weltan-*

schauung. To put it simply, fantasies will be seen by therapists and patients alike as either causing some difficulty or conflict or caused by some difficulty or conflict. The result is always the same—a deterministic picture *must* be appended to fantasy life. It can be no other way if one's world image is preconceivedly brought to bear, by therapist and patient alike to the phenomenon (in this case fantasy) that stands before them.

What would the situation be otherwise, that is, without applying the deterministic world view? The immediate effect would be a distinct experience of openness and acceptance of the event called fantasy. Once the event is accepted, *without having to fit it into an explanatory framework,* it can be allowed to stand on its own ground without having to be immediately devalued by being translated into another framework—namely, linear logical thought. Once this habit of translation is stopped then the person is automatically given permission, for the first time, to play *in* in the event, to explore it, to treat it as a reality of sensory veracity that can reveal information *albeit in its own language, not necessarily linear logical.* No longer does one have to disown an important content in the chain of mental life but instead can come to take a less critical and more tolerant view of one's own experience.

Fantasy can be seen as the first step on the road to imagination. These two events differ in many important ways. Although the terms fantasy and imagination are used interchangeably they, are in fact, different and should not be lumped together. The grouping of the two probably came about as a result of Cartesian influence which caused all nonmaterial events to be viewed as unreal and so came under one heading. Fantasy can be understood as perhaps the raw material for the imaginative process. This latter process utilizes an organ of perception, the imagination, to apprehend a nonmaterial reality behind sensory reality, which has noetic value. These imaginal realms of existence are ever changing, not controlled by an individual's personal bidding as in the case of fantasy. Whereas fantasy is easily identifiable in relation to one's concerns in everyday life which one is trying to master, imaginal experience transcends the conflictual by permitting a new action to take place within the framework of a usually unique encounter that could never be ordinarily drummed up by a person's waking thoughts. Let me give an example to concretize these points.

A subject experiencing imagery work reported that she is

> . . . in a garden. I see a tree and it and the garden are white. I see a chrysanthemum that is white and has ancient Aramaic letters on it. The center is red and gold. The stem is long and green. I look at the flower's reddish gold center and I go down into it finding myself in a cave or a series of caves by the sea. I hear a murmuring of music—like ooooo, echoing through the caves. Beyond, through the openings I can see and smell the blue sea. I listen to the music and I hear the words, "Where are you going?" I notice that there are lovely sea nymphs in white, hair streaming, dancing and singing barefoot on the rocks. I realize that the nymphs are sirens. I crouch beneath a rock and watch them. I am a small, dark child—barefoot, but keen and brave. Suddenly, the sirens take small boats and paddle out to sea through the cave opening with their long paddles standing up in their boats. I wish to follow them and have no boat. But suddenly a white feather falls down and serves as a boat for me. I float out to sea after them but can't really hear what they are saying. I return from this trip through the stem of the flower and as I gaze at the chrysanthemum after emerging I see the letters DHRV in Hebrew in the center.

One can note several distinctions between this event and the fantasy activity in which we ordinarily engage. Fantasies, as constructs of the linear thought process, always have logical threads running through them that help to tie up the various events. They also pertain, in the overwhelming majority of instances, to what one feels to be deficient in one's life and conversely what one would like to get—often supplied in the fantasy. As can be noted by the above imaginal experience, one enters a new world where transformations take place and laws other than those governed by linear logic are operative. These laws are nondeterministic and acausal and are those that essentially inform the world of imagination—the world of nonconcrete, immaterial reality.

One other matter seems worthy of taking up in the context of the direction of this book as it applies to imagination. The subject to which I allude is that of narcissism. Simply put, narcissism, as it is used in psychological circles, refers to an overabundance of self-interest, self-preoccupation, or self-absorption. Such self-absorption can manifest in a variety of ways that are seemingly unrelated yet bespeak a similar process. For example, the vanity of a show business star, the power urge of a dictator, the inward retreat of a schizophrenic. All of these behaviors are termed narcissistic although one form may bespeak excessive self-love whereas another may bespeak excessive self-hate. Regardless of the motive, there is one commonality of purpose that binds all the forms together and that is: *the elevation of the personal I or personal self to the center of experience.* Regardless of the supposed reason for doing so, what one observes is an inordinate concern with one's personal interest, with the attendant feeling that all that goes on in the world revolves around that individual's personal existence on this earth. This affectation is analogous to the older astronomical notion that the sun revolved around the earth, therefore, the earth was the center of our solar system. In human experience one can observe a similarly held notion with respect to certain people's relationship to the world. We tend to encounter the exaggerations of Ptolemaic propositions in human garb in the clinical situation. However, we are lulled often into counting such expression as an aberration having clinical meaning only rather than recognizing that what we are observing is a gross manifestation of a cultural phenomenon existing everywhere in the world. If one begins to look at areas of one's life either in relation to one's individual existence or to one's communal existence, the same narcissistic processes, socially sanctioned, would be observed. A casual glance at the world's political and economic situations reveal the essential divisiveness and unlovingness engendered in people's relationships to one another powered by overwhelming self-interest—in short by individual and collective narcissism. What is germane to my discussion is to take a look at what might fuel these predominant narcissistic trends that are manifested by all of us to some degree. It is only when it becomes to a greater degree, and beyond a certain point, that this attitude is considered intolerable, such as criminal or pathological behavior (for example, schizophrenia), that it is no longer socially sanctioned. What I mean to say is that such a pervasive world view must be based on some important factor or factors (I am of the opinion that the narcissistic orientation of whatever degree outweighs the selfless, altruistic orientation). To begin with, the perpetuation of self-interest is a characteristic of social conditioning, particularly within a cultural context that promotes individualism and success based on acquisitiveness and competitiveness. In an environment of this sort one must maintain an attitude of self-importance and come to regard others as objects of need who are there mainly to be used to supply whatever is needed. Relationships are built up then on creating the other in one's image, so to speak. By that I mean one sees the other according to a preconceived idea of what the other ought to be or do. This a prevailing mode of relatedness in which most of us participate. The outcome of such relationships is that any of the positive feelings people may have for each other often come crashing down and evaporate once one of the participants fails to conform to the image that has been set up. In effect, what this means is that people rarely ever relate to each other as they really are, free of preconceived prejudice imposed on them. A common example of this is the relationship of husband and wife. I select this one out of the myriad possibilities of relationships because of the enormous divorce rate in our culture. In the typical husband and wife situation, the partners come to the relationship with expectations of and for each other. These expectations are, in effect, images, something in the mind's eye, that, when they are not met, lead to discord and the withdrawl of affection and love.

Once that situation ensues, the rest of the relationship goes downhill, extramarital affairs take place, the marraige vows ("for better or for worse") are forgotten and divorce becomes a fact.

What prompts us to create images in this way? I think it is the same process that deceives us into believing that the fragment of reality that we see represents the whole of reality. This act of taking the part to be the whole in this way[1] is the same process of which narcissism is a part. This process is causal thinking or linear thought. This sort of thinking tends toward analyzing the world into bits or fragments. It can not do otherwise and once one is conditioned—as social conditioning continues to perpetuate—to see the world only through what one can glean via linear thought, one is forced to have to construct his relationship to reality through what the fragments tell him. The task, in this instance, always seems to be for the person to try and devote his energy into taking the fragments and piecing them together in order to make sense out of the world. This piecing together is the movement of linear logic. I won't go into the pitfalls of this process (as often happens, one mistakes logic for reality—the logic may be perfect but the reality quite faulty) but it is this fragmenting action that continuously presses one to have to create for himself what reality is out of very little information. One has no other choice under these circumstances. Since one is relying on a part, believing it to be the whole, one has a great deal of difficulty in accepting anyone else's reality construction, unless it conforms to one's own (obviously everyone who follows the same belief in linear thought's ability to apprehend reality is going through the same process). From this vantage point, and without having to go into lengthy exposition, one can get a beginning appreciation of why narcissism is such an ubiquitous problem. One is quite committed to preserving one's image or construction of reality hewed out of a fragment in which one takes oneself (that fragment) to be the whole, and will do so at any cost. Hence one can begin to understand the *necessity for self-absorption* engendered by such thinking. As long as this type of thinking remains dominant in the cultural context fostered by the cultural conditioning (accepting the equation that success = competitiveness = "getting ahead") there is no chance for any therapeutic modality as long as it derives its fundamental principles from the same linear thinking that has just been mentioned—to ever combat the difficulties posed in human relationships by the problems of narcissism.

Is there a way to see the whole rather than the fragment? I think yes, and I think that one can via the function of imagination. Imagination is a process occurring as an analogical function which operates as a process that sees the whole of something. It tends toward binding or bringing to unity rather than toward breaking apart as is the case with linear logic. Imagination is a realm of reality, as well as an organ of perception. This realm lies behind that ordinarily perceived by our senses and is a world as real as the one we usually refer to as objective reality. It is here that one can see the whole since in the act of apprehending imaginal reality linear logic is suspended and gestaltic perception is opened up. Furthermore, rather than creating images, as is the case in linear thinking, the brain *duplicates* images that are apperceived in imaginal reality. In other words, here what is received is a real event, a direct concrete experience, the information of which is sent back to the brain and is processed there, i.e., given name and meaning by the linear thought process. So we come to see that there are two types of images that must be distinguished: the created one and the duplicated one. The latter belongs to an experience of wholeness that, when experienced by one, does carry with it a recognition of one's unity or wholeness. The effect of such an experience is to give one a sense, not only of one's wholeness but of one's connection with that of which he's a part—other people, nature, the creatures, and the environment of this world in general. Once such a recognition occurs it is likely that one's self-absorption and self-preoccupation diminishes considerably and is replaced by a more selfless concern for the creatures and environment of this world. In my clinical work with imagination, utilizing a particular form called Waking Dream, as illustrated in the example presented earlier, I have found this to be so: that in wholeness healing is to be formed and fragmentation and its offspring, narcissism, is replaced (never eliminated) to the extent that one's life becomes richer and more full of hope and joy with the development of sharing and caring for others.

One final note: it is my contention that without the presence of the dimension of imagination in human existence one cannot grasp the presence of the holy—that which is transcendent and immanent. The holy is related to the wholeness of experience and cannot be comprehended by a process that fragments. The holy is an experience not a logical proposition. Many people who open their imagination experience some connection with holiness, and somehow, and we have seen this to be true etymologically as I have stated at the outset, there is an organic connection between holy and healing, and imagination is the catalyst.

The hopeful quality about imaginal work and imagination in general is that it is a potential of practically all human beings, meaning that it can be experienced by most everyone and in doing so one can make his life into a creative work.

NOTES

1. There is an instance where the part does contain, rather than stands for the whole and occurs within a framework related to imagination called holography, which will be discussed by Dr. David Bohm in chapter four.

REFERENCES

Epstein, G. The experience of waking dream in psychotherapy in *Healing: implications for psychotherapy,* Eds. J. L. Fosshage and P. Olsen. New York: Human Sciences Press, 1978, pp. 137–184.

Epstein, G. *Waking dream therapy: dream process as imagination.* New York: Human Sciences Press, 1981. (in press)

Freud, S. "Introductory Lectures on Psychoanalysis." *Standard edition,* Vol. XV, p. 67. See also *A general introduction to psychoanalysis* (Transl. Joan Riviere). New York: Liveright, 1935; p. 60.

chapter 2

DISCERNING THE FUNDAMENTAL PROBLEM ACCORDING TO ADVAITA VEDANTA

by Swami Dayananda Saraswati as told to Sandra Eisenstein

The request was for an article on Vedanta with relevance to western psychotherapy. I posed that question to Swami Dayananda and he said,

> Vedanta is not a technique, nor a theory, nor a system that one can learn and apply to the ways of the mind. It is a teaching that changes your understanding . . . your vision, in fact, of the nature of all problems that the mind comes up with. Thus, the very nature of problem-solving is altered by seeing that when one solves a specific or topical problem it is only a temporary resolving. Vedanta discerns the fundamental problem which is the very basis of all topical problems and goes about *solving* that. It takes the individual off the endless circle of problem solving by unfolding the very root cause of all problems.

The article Swami Dayananda presented for this book goes about explaining exactly what that fundamental problem is and how Vedanta, as a teaching, solves it.

S.E.

There is a word in Sanskrit, "Moksa," which means liberation. And one who is desirous of liberation is called a "Mumukshu." To seek liberation is different from seeking a solution to a specific problem. Liberation essentially is putting an end to all problems (by the knowledge of the truth of the problem).

In the Upanishads it is said, "Jnanam eva Moksah," that is, knowledge alone is liberation. The knowledge it speaks of is knowledge of oneself which is unfolded by the very teaching of these Upanishads, also known as Vedanta. If this is true, that is, if such a thing is there as total liberation from all the problems and sorrows of life and one need not do anything but simply know something, why isn't everyone a Mumukshu?

Being a Mumukshu requires a certain recognition (which one can arrive at on one's own or can be led to see by another) of one's situation in the world. It entails a certain objective insight into a problem that is universal. We always tend to think in terms of our specific situation, in terms of *a* situation. A mumukshu is one who has begun to discern and inquire into *the* situation. This drastically changes his vision of the ends he wishes to achieve and of problem solving.

There are two ways to approach a situation in which I wish to achieve a result: (1) to know (determine) the end I wish to gain and thereby adopt an adequate and appropriate means, (2) to know the nature of the problem and thereby know the nature of the solution. This is not great wisdom but common sense. If I want to go to China, I know there are a series of means I must fulfill to gain that end. I cannot get there by sitting still unless I only want to go there in my dreams. Then, upon achieving my goal I am satisfied that I have reached the desired end. There is no question that I wanted to be in China and now I am in China. In a similar way, my problem that I am cold is known to me and the solution is thereby clear that I require some thing or setup which will provide heat.

Once these things are known, my life takes on a direction. The problems or yearnings, no matter how unpleasant and distracting, are reduced to means and ends. There is a clarity about it.

But then, one does not find the situation in life so clear cut. That is, I want to gain something, an object, a place, a situation, a state of mind, an achievement, etc., or I want to rid myself of a particular state of mind or situation. I adopt what seems to be the proper means and even achieve the sought-after end but I do not seem to get the desired result. The desired being some form of satisfaction. That is, if I am hungry and fulfill it by eating, I should gain the satisfaction of having my hunger satiated for that is the end sought, not the food. In the same way, if any one end or series of ends desired are attained I should be the satisfied person. My desire should be satiated. If I find a solution to a problem that is troubling me, I should be the satisfied person. For it is only because of that problem or that unattained end that I am dissatisfied. At some point, after putting forth proper efforts I should cease being dissatisfied. If that is not the case, two reasonable questions to ask would be:

Is the end I wish to attain clear to me? Is the problem I want to solve clear to me?

It is from this very simple standpoint that we start a Vedantic enquiry, and that is to first ascertain the nature of the problem that is to be solved and that, in turn, will reveal the nature of the solution. Or we can approach it from the standpoint of ascertaining what end one is actually after and that will determine the necessary means. And so, we begin by simply stripping away the particulars and looking at the very urge for seeking ends and problem solving in man.

All of man's problems and seeking originate in his mind. When he is in deep sleep, he is not conscious of any struggles. There is nothing he wants to change, nothing to do. But when awake or dreaming, his peace of mind is constantly being challenged by thoughts and situations. And his urge is to resolve all disturbances, to make things better.

This is the glory of the human mind, that is, its unique capacity to inquire into the nature and meaning of things, to reason out, to analyze, to appreciate subtleties, to imagine, to conceptualize, to come to conclusions, to make choices.

An animal makes minimal choices governed by its inborn

instinct and the urge to survive. For example, a cow instinctively fulfills the need to nourish its body by eating grass. It does not deliberate and then choose to be a vegetarian. It does not insist, either, that the only way to prepare grass is with a special gourmet sauce. An animal's instincts allow it to perpetuate its life and part of that urge for survival is the attraction to that which supports and enhances its survival and a retreat from that which is painful and threatens the survival of its body. Similarly, man wants his body and its various systems to survive and function without pain and disease or situations which threaten it. And these natural urges of the body must be fulfilled in order for the system to continue thriving. Everything that is born goes naturally toward sustaining its life and away from terminating it. But then man has an intellect, a thinking faculty and mere bodily survival does not make his life. He not only wants to go on living but to live in a particular way.

If man naturally seeks to protect his body by sustaining its life force, he also seeks to fulfill the natural urges of the mind. And his mind being an instrument of reason seeks a certain modicum of clarity. It moves, shifts, and changes but still it does not like confusion or ignorance. It wants to make sense of things, to understand, it wants to know, it wants to feel at ease with its thoughts and moods at home in its environment. This mind of man makes him self-conscious and self-aware. And being aware of himself he cannot but be a desirer, a seeker. That is, the very essence of man's life is that he is after ends. They may be lofty, profound, or profane. Nevertheless, at any moment in a man's life we find that the life he leads is but an expression of the desires entertained by him till and at that point. Although the specific want varies from person to person and from time to time in one person, what does not vary is "I Want." In every sought after end is an "I want something that will make me different than I am now." That is, although one may want to attain a particular thing or situation or rid oneself of the same, what one actually wants is something pervasive and elusive. It is an unqualified want. All one knows is the one

one is now is not the one one wants to be. Having a mind that is self-conscious one is appreciative of a lack, something that one misses in oneself and that mind being an instrument of reason, one looks into this unqualified want and according to one's knowledge and values qualifies it.

What man really wants is to be free from want. That "I want" is exactly what one does not want. To fulfill a desire is actually to get rid of it. Therefore, to say "I want" is really to say "I don't want to have any want."

But one cannot help but want because being self-aware one is conscious of one's incompleteness. That is, if one does not take oneself to be incomplete one would not want to be different than what one is. And this sense of incompleteness expresses itself through the seeking of different ends. This is not something one cultivates or learns in time. An infant is also a desirer. It may not know exactly what it wants, but in addition to merely wanting to live, it also wants that which will make it feel good, happy, secure, etc. As one grows, one's desires become defined, refined, and constantly renovated according to one's cultivated likes and dislikes, ethics, values, and one's whims and moods of the moment.

Thus, we find that in addition to the basic urge to survive, there seems to be another basic urge that manifests in the mind and that is "to have things be well with me." It can be expressed by saying "I want to be full, complete, adequate, fulfilled, happy, self-possessed." However one says it, it means the same thing. And unlike all the cultivated desires for specific ends that one picks up in time, this one seems to come along with being born. It is a desire the forefathers had. No one has to be told that being full, happy, etc. is a desirable thing.

In order to satisfy that urge one seeks something, be it an object, a situation, etc., believing that or hoping that a change of some condition will result in or bring man closer to the full person he wants to be.

The water buffalo does not want to live in Brooklyn, to go to the Himalayas for a vacation, to change its hairstyle, to be a cow. But man always wants to change some aspect of his situation. Man is aware of his incompleteness and cannot stand it. And this urge to be full, complete, etc., is not a peculiar trait of some men but is common to all human beings of all time. It is implicit in any action that extends beyond mere instinctual bodily survival. It is, in fact, *the desire* behind all topical desires, the fundamental desire, the mother desire, for it is that which gives birth to all desires and motivations.

One may choose to dress a particular way, buy a summer house, get a better job, have a meaningful relationship, rid oneself of bad habits . . . etc, etc. Why? Not for the sake of the thing itself but for one's own sake, for what it will invoke in one upon the gain of it.

It is important that this be seen, for this is *the end* one is really after.

Having determined *the end* we should now be able to arrive at the appropriate and adequate *means.* But first let us see what is meant when we say one wants to be complete, full, adequate, etc. This particular "state of mind" or experience we seek is known to all of us. And it is because it is known that we justify all our searches and struggles for it. For when I was happy at a particular time—I was free of all my limitations, I was myself. It is that self I love to be, I live to be, and seek to be in all my desired for ends. Could I call that completeness I seek as something limited, something relative? If what I am seeking is actually that specific object, then I am, in fact, seeking a limited end. For all such things are limited by their own boundaries which define it as an object or condition in time and space.

If what one really seeks is to rid oneself of imcompleteness, that completeness one seeks cannot be limited because a completeness that is limited is dependent on other factors for its sustenance and is therefore incomplete. At the present moment, one is dependent upon a number of things and situations for the sense of well-being. And it is this very dependency which sustains one's incompleteness. What one wants is freedom from this kind of dependency. Otherwise one's well being is at the mercy of conditions which themselves are subject to change based on other conditions. Thus, if behind all one's seeking and struggles, what one actually sought was only another state—incomplete—just like the one that at present obtains—there would be no sense or strength to any pursuit.

Completeness or fullness is not a measurable entity. It is not a finite sum in the sense that I continue adding things and one day I am *full* and *complete.* That is like saying 1000 units of achievements will make me full and minus one I am incomplete. It is fallacious and certainly not even within the realm of experience. For we find that the person with name, fame, and fortune is not necessarily the fulfilled person. In fact, he continues seeking more.

If in every desire one has, what one really wants is to put an end to the wanting person . . . it is clear that the wanting person will not go unless the person is complete, without limit, lacking nothing. Then alone can one say "enough." Is it realistic and reasonable to say I want to be free from want? For what one finds is that no matter what the gain, no matter how rewarding it may be for the time being, one does not cease being a seeker, a desirer after ends. No end satisfies that urge for completion. In fact, there is the expression "that's life" in commiseration with the fact that built into the nature of every gain is a quality that makes it fall short of its intended mark. One either laughs or cries at that fact and goes on to the next pursuit as though it will bring him closer. In addition to the temporariness of all ends gained is the fact that I, as the gainer, am constantly changing my values, my moods, and the one who is receiving the sought-after end is not exactly the one who was seeking it. So even the impact of the gain loses its potency or meaning. Then, too, the gain itself is a limited thing. For every gain there is always an investment, there is always a loss. If nothing else, there is the loss of the prior condition. And even as one is reading these pages, one is losing the opportunity to watch television which may be equally appealing. One has to decide. Under no circumstances can I physically be here and there at the same time. But then any choice has to necessarily involve a negation, an elimination and we always hope we've chosen the better one.

Thus all that we find in the world are only limited ends. What we have discerned both logically and experientially is that what a man seeks in his heart is to be free of limitation, he wants an end that does not come to an end. Perhaps we do not know of such an end because we have not employed the proper means. Can there be a means which would result in a limitless end? For gaining those ends one has not yet achieved there are a spectrum of means available in the world. Between any end to be accomplished and the one who wants to accomplish it there is always a distance, a gap in terms of time or space. And to bridge that gap one must put forth the proper effort, be it physical or mental. But then what one can produce by effort will always be limited, because the very effort itself is limited.

An action cannot produce a result that is not inherent therein. I cannot walk lying down. An action can only produce a result which is appropriate to that action. So by the very laws inherent in any action—in the world—we find what we gain is limited. Yet what we seek is not. It is really what you call a Catch-22. And it is all mathematics. I am limited and I go after something which is limited through limited means. Insecure plus insecure (i.e., it being bound by time) equals insecure. Incomplete plus a million equals the same incomplete because that is logical and it is also our experience. A finite sum like one and a finite sum like a million both have the same distance between themselves and infinity. So, in discovering the end, one is really seeking what we have done to arrive at the problem one is really facing. And that is: I cannot help but seek completion, yet there is nothing available by which I can gain it.

This is the realization of a *Mumukshu.* And although

there may be a despair to this realization, it is not a position of self-condemnation but of self-appreciation, for that is the nature of the solution.

At the moment, though, there still seems to be one remaining alternative. We seem to have gotten ourselves into a corner and the only solution left which one can conceive of is to give up this desire for completeness and accept the fact that life consists only of limited and relative gains. After all, we know that any desire that one picks up in time can also be given up in time by growing out of it through a change in values, education, outlook, or by simply being willing to drop it, knowing it is an impossibility. Although fulfillment of this urge seems to be an impossibility, as we have said, it is not something one picks up in time. Just as one cannot give up the urge to nourish the body, one cannot give up the urge for completeness, happiness. Try! This is what makes it *the fundamental problem.* It is natural and what is natural is meaningful. As a natural problem it must have a solution as even other natural urges, like hunger or thirst have. And, whatever is natural about ourselves is always gladly accepted. For example, no one complains that "my eyes see." No one is irritated because there are eyeballs in the eye sockets. But if there is a small speck of dust in the eye, naturally, you cannot stand it. Even the physical system itself cannot stand those bugs that do not belong to the system. In fact, there is a big fight leading to your running a temperature because these are all intruders and must be rejected. Similarly, no one wants to feel inadequate, unhappy, incomplete. All these are conditions the mind cannot accept. I want to shake them off. Why? Because they are intruders. If these are unnatural it would follow then that I am the opposite of what I cannot stand. That is, it is natural for me to be without them. Therefore, I naturally go about working for that which is my own nature and ridding myself of the intruders.

What this means is: if I cannot stand sorrow and agitation, then my nature must be happiness and peacefulness. Otherwise why should I not stand sorrow? I should be quite at home with sorrow if it is my nature. But like a virus it is an intruder.

Thus, all I seek is my own nature. Whatever beautiful thing I seek in all my seeking, I am. (This is like saying that what I want is the head on my shoulders.) But then, if it is so, why do I miss it? One cannot miss oneself. Still, if I keep missing it and begin searching for it, having countless plans and schemes, doing endless things to gain it, the search I would say stems from *self-disowning, self-ignorance.*

The problem is now complete. And it is a problem of a different nature for the end is of a different nature. That is, what I want to gain is not something away from me, not something different from me, not something yet to be achieved. What I want to gain is what I want to be. What I want is myself. Thus the means for such an end must be of a different nature than putting forth effort however great that effort be.

If no going after, nor getting away from something is involved does that mean that without any motion one will become complete? Yes, but then the word "become" has no meaning here for every becoming involves change and change involves limitations. If without becoming I am to "become," then clearly what we are after is the *gain of the already gained.*

It is because of this that this search always seems to be shrouded in mystery. That is because what one seeks is hidden in the most secretive of hiding places, in the very seeker himself. So, in the very act of seeking, one is denying the sought, for all one can seek is that which is different from the one who seeks.

If what one seeks is already gained but one is ignorant of the fact, the only means for gaining it is *knowledge.* For example, I seek to be the possessor of my eyeglasses which I have absentmindedly placed on the top of my head and I go about searching for it. All efforts are fruitless. I simply do not *know* that I own them at present. That knowledge will make me the possessor of the glasses.

The seeker and the end sought are identical. The problem is nothing but ignorance. Therefore the solution can only be *knowledge.*

If there is such a thing as self-disowning and self-igno-rance, then there is such a thing as self-knowledge. That is what the Mumukshu comes to seek—and that is Vedanta.

When we talk about self-knowledge, we have to identify who is that self-that I am. What do we mean when we say "I"? It is an irony that the word "I," which I use constantly through-out the day and from which standpoint I view and judge the world has no definite object for it in my mind. Just to think, every word I use elicits a known object or concept in the mind. I say the word "pot" and a corresponding thought form of the object pot is there. This is how language functions. If I hear the word "pot" and see "cot" you would say that my knowledge is erroneous. If I see nothing you would say I am totally igno-rant of the object "pot." If I use the word gagaboogai—a mean-ingless, nonsense word—I use it as just that but definitely not to connote something in the world. Every word has its corre-sponding object. Nevertheless I say I—I—I—I—I—I hundreds of times a day. Who is this I? Who is this one I experience so intimately, who is myself? For it seems to be this I who is unhappy, who can't get his life together, who wants to fulfill his potential, his capacities, who wants a meaningful relationship, who does not want to suffer, and now wants to know himself. I want to address this I. I want to see this I. Who is he?

Upon inquiring into who I am, it is my experience that I am here as a conscious being and everything else is the world. That is, we can reduce the entire creation into two factors: the subject and the other, the object. Anything I can objectify is an object and the one who objectifies it is the subject. In an object one does not have the "I" notion, the "I" sense. I am not there in an object because it is something I know. The "I" is always the subject. And when I say object it need not always be a tangible object but includes even intangible things we appreci-ate and come to know. I am aware of time and space, for example which are not tangible things but which are still in my knowledge and objectifiable.

Although it is quite an acceptable fact that I am the subject and as the subject am not anywhere in the world as an object of my knowledge, one tends to conclude that I, the subject am the physical body. That is, it is the intimate experience of everyone that "I" is within the extremities of the physical body and that the world exists outside its boundaries. I do not exist, for example, between my fingers. And there is certainly no remote feeling about a pain that is taking place in some far corner of the body. When my toe is hurt, I am hurt.

But then we tend to overlook the fact that the physical body is as well an object for everybody elses knowledge. Not only is it an object for everyone else but for oneself too. I know my body and all its corners and crevices. But then the subject and object are always two distinctly different entities. The knower of anything is distinct from the thing he knows. Therefore, I cannot be the physical body. Similarly, if I try to attribute the identity of "I" to any function or system of the body, it resolves in the same subject—object, knower—known relationship. For example, my sense organs are known to me as are their functions. And although I say "I am tall," "I am short," with reference to the body, or I say "I am hungry" with reference to the physiological system, or I say "I am blind" with reference to a sense organ, it is all *with reference to.* Just as one says I am uncle, I am cousin, I am father, etc., with reference to different people. Clearly, "I" is not any of these nor a composite of these. In each case, one is looking at oneself only from a particular standpoint, all of which is objectifiable. Every situation, from moment to moment naturally invokes in you a person relevant to that situation (i.e., when I see my son, I am father, etc.). It is this relative "I" that we are confronting all the time. And it is this relative "I" that has all the problems. "I" as daughter have a problem. "I" as short person have a problem, etc. Never do we confront the "I" that is there in all these relative roles. That is, if there is an absolute "I," a central "I", an "I" as such, there is no occasion in which that "I" is known.

If I commit an error, taking myself to be other than the complete self, that error is not going to be beneficial to me.

Therefore, naturally, this error becomes a great loss for me. For "I" is free from limitations and I have concluded I am the body taking onto myself all of its limitations. If I am neither the physical body nor the sense organs nor the physiological system nor any relative role I play, then what is left? It must be the mind. Mind means what? You do not mean that you are the tangible brain. The brain itself is an object. Then, too, the functions of the brain are known. That is, the thoughts of the mind are as well-known to me as any object. Each perception, conclusion, doubt, etc., is known. Restlessness, depression, agitation are all known to me. Furthermore, any one thought cannot be "I" because when the thought goes, somehow "I" remains. Thus, although I say "I am restless," "I am agitated," I am speaking only of conditions that belong to the mind. I am not the mind for I am the one who is aware of all thoughts. The thoughts come and go and I am still here. Before the thought arrives, while the thought is there and after it goes away, I am very much present, which means I am independent of thought.

In Sanskrit we call the total mind with its various functions Antah karana. Karana means instrument. So the mind is an instrument capable of giving me knowledge, imaginations, memories, emotions, problems. Being an instrument, it must necessarily be in the hands of something else that is different from it, like any other instrument (the telescope does not see through itself.) Therefore, "I" cannot be the mind. You could say perhaps that what is different from all this is ignorance, but even ignorance is known to me. What I know I know, and what I do not know I also know. (I know, for example, that I am ignorant of Russian.)

Therefore, if you analyze you would have to say: I am . . . I am . . . I am . . . I ammm. I exist and I know. I am but a knower of all things. Things I know vary, but I am the one who knows all the time. But here, we have to go one more step. For, if I am the knower of all this, I am the knower only when I come to know something. That is, with reference to things known, I am the knower. If I reduce the identity of "I" to knower, know

means what? The one who is *aware* of. I am the awarer. Awar-
er and know*er* are functional words. The *er* is added with
reference to a function like driv*er,* speak*er* meaning "the one
who" and is again a relative name. The "I" I want to know is
the one who is unrelated to anything. And that can only be the
content of the knower, the awarer, which is *awareness.* This
unqualified awareness is the meaning of the word "I." If you
place "I" anywhere else but in the subject, the ultimate subject
—awareness, you commit a mistake.

In the body awareness is. In the thought, awareness is. But
awareness is also independent of both. Both depend on awareness for their existence. Awareness depends on nothing. It is
self-existent, self-evident.

Once I see that I am this awareness, which is independent,
on which depend all thoughts and the objects thereof, I am free
from all possible limitations that I can ever suffer. Our lives are
spent seeking happiness. We consider happiness or fullness to
be a state of mind . . . an experience . . . and so it comes and
goes. Once gained it does not stay for long and even at that, it
has to be worked for and hoarded for its brief moment of glory.
What is this happiness and where is it? In the Vedantic teaching
the self is said as being *Ananda* which means fullness. If the self
is pure Awareness it is thus formless and having no characteristics to circumscribe it - it is free from all limitations. It is the
very fullness, the very happiness one seeks. It must be clear that
fullness is not the quality of an object outside . . . nor is it
somewhere inside the physical body. Because happiness usually
coincides with the gain of a desired end or condition we attribute it to the very thing itself. Whereas at that moment the
mind is no longer wanting nor projecting; and it is a wonderful
moment for I am simply with my self. And so the happiness/-
fullness which seems to come and go, dependent on various
conditions, is really there all the time as the nature of one's own
self. I am that fullness always but because of ignorance about
my self I take myself to be other than I am. The truth about
myself is covered by ignorance just like the sun, which does not

change nor cease shining but appears otherwise when covered by clouds.

The self which is said to be *Chit* (awareness) and *Ananda* (fullness) is also said to be *Sat* which means that which always is, which never gets negated.

We showed in the beginning that all man's urges and pursuits thereupon, if reduced to their fundamental forms would be expressed in the desire to live and live happily and to be free from ignorance. When the teaching properly unfolds the nature of the self, its identity is revealed as

Sat = existence which never gets negated,

Chit = awareness, the basis of all that is known, and

Ananda = fullness, without limit.

All one seeks is exactly oneself. It is ironic.

If awareness is the real meaning of "I," then "I" is no more an historical person. All the problems one suffers from belong to the historical I, the relative I, the falsely identified I, to the role one plays at any given moment. It is something like an actor who, playing the part of a beggar, takes the hunger and poverty of the beggar home with him after the show. And then, again, in saying "I am restless," I am depressed, I am fat, I am lean, all of these problems belong in fact to the object of one's knowledge; not to the subject who witnesses them. It is something like watching a congested traffic scene and saying "I am congested." Yet we watch the traffic flow of our thoughts and take its various conditions as belonging to ourself. It is true, the mind is agitated, the body is fat. These problems belong to the mind and the body, not to I. This knowledge puts one's immediate problems in the proper perspective. The problems belong to the object not to the subject. That is true objectivity.

A wise man, a liberated being (whatever you call him) knowing himself to be full and complete is thus always full and complete in spite of his situation and is not dependent on a situation or thing or condition to be full. You could say he is a master of himself because he knows the truth of himself.

In knowing the truth of oneself one naturally comes to know the truth of the world of the objects of his knowledge. (We have not even begun to touch this subject in this article.) The problem that he originally took as being real and thus in dire need of resolution he now sees as belonging to a false fellow. He knows, "I am the one who gives reality to that fellow," "I have no problem," "I am so full and complete nothing can add to me or take from me." That is seeing oneself and one's life as they are. Only then can a topical problem be tackled for what it really is. There is a total release in that, for I am no longer a creature in the world. All I have said here are mere words on paper and Vedanta has always been an oral tradition of teaching passed from teacher to student. It is said to be a "Pramana," that which is instrumental to giving rise to knowledge and it is taken by those who come to it as serious dedicated students to be a means of knowledge as true as the eyes are a means of knowledge for knowing the color and form of a physical object. Thus, two things are there: the type of teacher and the attitude of the student. As an oral tradition, it requires a teacher who handles the words, unlocks the meaning behind the words. To say "you are full, you are limitless" is one thing. To make the student *see* what that actually means is another. If that is not done, the words just evolve into another conditioning.

There is a reason for the need for this methodology and it rests in the very nature of the subject matter. What I want to know is what I want to be is what I am. And this "I" is not available for any objectification and thus is not available for any known means of knowledge. All available means of knowledge involve some sensory data, be it perception, presumption, inference, or illustration. The only means of knowledge which has the scope to reveal the self is the *word.* But even the word, producing thoughts in the mind, generally reveals but an object. As we said, a concept is an object, which means it is different from the subject. To gain any knowledge that knowledge must necessarily take place in the mind. But anything that can be objectified by the mind is other than the subject. Furthermore, all I have available to communicate with are known words, but known words can only produce knowledge of that which is known. If I say to you "You are Brahman" the meaning of the word "Brahman" is unknown to you. So I say: Brahman means "the limitless." The "limitless" has no correlative object in the known world and so all I can really communicate is a vague notion or subjective concept (i.e., what you take the word to mean.)

Thus, the subject matter being so unique, it being neither an object nor a concept, yet undeniably there, the communication of it requires very special handling. Words must be elaborately defined so that what is meant by them is what is received. Paradoxes must be juggled, illustration handled, contexts set up so that the implied meaning of words can be seen. For this a teacher is necessary, one who knows the truth as well as the methodology for revealing it.

Secondly, the one who comes to this teaching, comes to it with a particular attitude. Being a Mumukshu, he has discerned *to a degree* the nature of the problem and so there is a receptivity, an openness to what the teacher teaches. Because what is being sought is not the solution to a relative problem, is not the opinion of one man which may or may not be confirmed by additional information, it is not a speculative philosophy or system or school of thought which may be usurped at a later date by a greater intellect. What is sought is very simply *The Truth*. This really distinguishes it from all other types of learning and problem solving. And we find that in the very learning process is a love and a trust that comes from the relief of discovering the means for what you really want to gain. The teacher is not an authority but is more akin to a candle who is going to light another candle.

Thus, this knowledge gives man the end that he was seeking in all his pursuits and solves all problems in the sense that the true nature of the "owner" of the problem and the true nature of the problem itself is seen.

chapter 3

BUDDHISM AND PSYCHOTHERAPY

Carl Rinzler, M.D.
Beth Gordon

Most attempts to join psychotherapy and Buddhism have seemed like shotgun weddings. Since both have rich and sophisticated views of the human mind, there is a powerful temptation to compare them, but attempts to find similarities seem somewhat strained, and efforts to contrast them often portray psychotherapy as naive and clumsy. Trying to see either discipline through the eyes of the other does justice to neither. For some reason, writers seem unwilling to acknowledge that psychotherapy and Buddhism view human existence so differently that drawing parallels or achieving a synthesis is almost impossible.

Both Buddhism and psychotherapy began as a response to human suffering. Psychotherapy assumes that the individual can be changed so that his pain is minimized and his happiness increased. Buddhism regards the very notion of individuality as the cause of pain. From this perspective, pain results from a tendency to solidify energy into a barrier that separates "I" and "other." Fixation on this barrier is transformed through the practice of meditation. Since Buddhism is not concerned with the individual changing but with changing the experience of individuality itself, its aim and outlook is totally different from that of therapy. In challenging the underlying assumptions of Western psychology, Charles Tart (1975) points out that:

> . . .as long as an assumption is *implicit* . . . you are unlikely ever to question it, and so you are totally in the power of that assumption.

By discussing the differences between Buddhism and psychotherapy, some of the assumptions that we make may become clearer.

BACKGROUND

Central to the basic teachings of Buddhism are the *Four Noble Truths:* the truth of suffering, the origin of suffering, the cessation of suffering, and the path to this cessation.

Ego is described in terms of five aggregates (*skandhas*); the teaching of non-self (*anatman*) states that in the five aggregates no independently existent, immutable self, or soul can be found. There is no first cause, prime mover, or God. All phenomena arise in interrelation to others. They are dependent on transitory causes and conditions and thus subject to inevitable decay and disintegration.

Buddhism today is divided into three major schools. The Hinayana Buddhism of Ceylon and Southeast Asia adheres closely to the early teachings; the practitioner hopes to attain individual liberation through the realization of egolessness. Mahayana Buddhism, practiced in India, China, and Japan goes beyond the idea of personal salvation to a commitment to others' sanity. The experience of egolessness is extended as well, that is, all phenomena are seen as empty, devoid of concept. Vajrayana Buddhism of Tibet is predicated on the insights of the Hinayana and Mahayana schools. When the practitioner no longer relies on concepts, experience is open and full, and the dynamic quality of energy is apparent.

Although student of Vajrayana Buddhism employ a variety of meditative techniques, the basic practice is sitting meditation (*Shamata-Vipashyana*). At least in form, it is the simplest type of meditation. The meditator is instructed to turn his awareness to breathing. Although his mind may wander, he is told not to evaluate anything that comes up during meditation. The discipline of meditation is to return to the simplicity of the situation.

BUDDHIST VIEW OF HUMAN EXISTENCE

Buddhism teaches that there are three marks of human existence: pain, impermanence, and egolessness. The marks should not be understood as Buddhist doctrine, but as a description of all human experience. They refer to subtleties of experience that often cannot be expressed until they take the form of concrete symptoms, which psychotherapy may attempt to treat. The description of the three marks, then, is not a different view of life—it is an articulation of what most people feel, are unable to express, and try to remedy. It is a bittersweet picture—it tells us that our experiences of life's discontinuities are not symptomatic of our own malfunctioning, but that what we experience is inescapable and true.

Pain

We live our lives in a context of pain. Our suffering takes several different forms. There is a background of pain that is so much a part of our lives that we take it for granted. It occurs on a moment-to-moment basis. No matter where we are or what we are doing, we find ourselves on edge, itchy, and tense, feeling vaguely irritated and off balance. We try to relax in our free time and find ourselves wanting something to do. Even in moments of pleasure we are not completely content—we worry about how long they will last or how to make them better, or our mind races ahead to plan the next good time. This kind of pain is so amorphous and diffuse, so woven into the fabric of our lives, that we cannot locate it or even be sure it exists. It is something like the way we feel before an attack of flu-our body feels strange but there is no fever, cough, or nausea; we go about our business feeling ill and wondering if our mind is playing tricks. We almost welcome the onset of fever for its tangible physical misery. There is a pervading sense of confusion and oppression; so although there are moments when our minds seem clear and we relax, they are fleeting; and the alternation of hope and disappointment is painful.

Sometimes awareness of this pain becomes sharper. Philosophers refer to "existential angst" or "mal de siecle"— a sense of isolation or alienation or a feeling that there must be more to life. Crystallized, these experiences become borderline psychiatric symptoms—depression, insomnia, or chronic anxiety.

Superimposed on this vague background of pain is the task of just getting through life. Each new situation leaves us feeling uncertain and vulnerable; sickness disrupts the habits we depend on. As we grow older, we feel that new experiences would be repetitious or not worth the effort. And finally we face death —the total loss of ourselves and everything we cherish.

All this is just preface to what we focus on as our "real pain"—the frustration or disappointment we experience in our attempts to find happiness. We tend to regard happiness as our birthright, and the human potential movement in psychotherapy has augmented this conviction. We think finding happiness is an easy matter—"I'd be happy," we say, "if only I could have *this,*" and we set off in search of it. But *this* remains out of reach; or worse, we actually obtain it and discover it is not what we wanted or not enough—we want *that* as well. After repeating this pattern again and again, we realize we do not even know what we want; so bewildered, we start all over again with a new strategy. Our unwavering belief in the imminence of a solution makes us react to frustration by speeding up our efforts. As we do so, we lose what little clarity and precision we had and become clumsy and inept. Disappointed in love, we decide that buying new clothes will make us feel better, so we rush off to the store forgetting our money. Arriving there, desperate for comfort, we make our purchase with a check. When notified that our account is overdrawn, we become irritated and insult our best friend. One could continue this scenario endlessly, but the point is clear—we never stop believing in a solution and compound our difficulties by our efforts to find one.

Impermanence

Our experience and everything around us is constantly changing—this is self-evident, but we go to extraordinary lengths to avoid acknowledging it. We would like to believe that our world is fixed, stable, and secure, and we find our recognitions of impermanence alarming. We try to freeze everything, even the present moment. We are so busy holding onto a memory or thought that we trip or stumble over something new. We are afraid to remain in transit, so our mind moves on to something that feels certain—we might think about tonight's dinner menu or the movie we will see. The content of the thought, whether it is pleasureable or painful, is much less important than its solidity. This is a moment-to-moment description of how we structure our lives as a whole. We try to see our situations and our world as permanent and unchanging, to arrange things so that whatever we value will always be available to us. We expect our jobs, our lovers, and our families to predictably reward us and are shocked and dismayed when they do not.

The peculiarity of our perspective is accented by the fact that a Zippo lighter is the only thing in this society that carries a lifetime guarantee. We live in a world of planned obsolescence and disposable products; one in which attitudes, material things, and even laws of nature are changing faster than ever before. The inevitable decay of material things and the constant mutation of human feelings has always existed—today we accelerate them. Confronted by impermanence on every level— from the subtlest fleeting experience to the glaring changes in environment and culture, we continue to behave, although uneasily, as if we can still find a way out—write our own insurance policy.

Egolessness

We take it for granted that our sense of self, or ego, is as real and continuous as our heartbeat and tend to ignore messages to the contrary. Buddhism focuses on the discontinuities of our experience and describes our constant flickering doubts as egolessness. Like pervasive pain, the experience of egolessness is difficult to articulate. In reflective moments we may wonder who we are and what we are doing with our lives, but these questions make us uneasy and we try to push them away. Yet the uneasy feeling persists; it is as though we were being haunted: there's a vague sense of hollowness or insubstantiality, of not being able to quite "get it together." The very way we operate seems odd. Our thoughts feel disjointed and disorderly; our bodies clumsy and out of "sync" with our minds. Our words lag behind our thoughts and our tongue behind our words, so there is no fluidity in what we do or think. This sort of concern becomes a private embarrassment, and we feel transparent, as if acting out a part and doing it poorly. Simple activities that should be routine become self-conscious and awkward; so no matter what credentials we possess, we feel fraudulent and unequal to the task.

Although we make attempts to tidy up our act, the doubts still remain; and we fear our secret will be exposed. Although people still relate to us as perfectly normal, we ourselves are not so sure. We suspect they are better equipped to handle life, without realizing that they feel just the same about us.

The Buddhist description of human existence poses a question for psychotherapy. Although these experiences could easily be dismissed as neurotic feelings of insecurity and anxiety, we would be remiss to explain them away so simply. And if they truly portray the human situation, then what is psychotherapy attempting to treat?

METHOD

The basic problem in any discussion of Buddhism and psychotherapy is that it is difficult to look at Buddhist teaching and practice from a dualistic point of view. A discussion of scientific method illuminates the vast differences between the two approaches.

When Freud entitled his first tentative description of mind, "Project for a Scientific Psychology," he implicitly expressed an axiom of psychotherapy stated herein:

> It is the thrust of the scientific mode of inquiry and the scientific
> adjudication of data that encompasses and gives a crucial stamp
> to an array of activities we call psychiatric. (Offer & Freedman,
> 1972)

A distinctive method characterizes this: in essence, the scientist separates himself from the object of inquiry. He observes it from different perspectives, using his own senses and specialized tools to measure its qualities. He then steps back to form an abstract composite of the object's features. The more complete his descriptions, the more he is convinced that the object has been fully understood.

This method of understanding things is alien to a nondualistic point of view. Indians, as is evident from their language, approach subject and object quite differently. They speak of the "apprehender" and "apprehendable" to convey that both are part of the same process. The approach is not to remove oneself from phenomena and observe them from some reference point, but rather to identify with them completely. D. T. Suzuki (1960) illustrates these very different perspectives by comparing two poems about flowers, one a haiku by the Japanese poet Basho and the other by Tennyson. Tennyson's is the well-known verse:

> Flower in the crannied wall,
> I pluck you out of the crannies:—
> Hold you here, root and all, in my hand,
> Little flower—but if I could understand
> What you are, root and all, and all in all,
> I should know what God and man is.

Tennyson's approach is familiar to us. He plucks the flower from the ground. Feeling separate from his world, he becomes more concerned with asking questions than with the living flower. He thinks that by standing apart from what he wants to know, he might learn something important. Contrast this to Basho's poem:

> When I look carefully
> I see the *nazuna* blooming
> by the hedge.

There is no need to pluck the flower or to question it. The experience of the flower is immediate and direct; the flower speaks for itself.

We return to our assumption that stepping back from something, questioning, and analyzing, is the best way of understanding it. Science and the scientific investigation of mind are attempts to codify this method so that it will be uniformly employed, but scientific method is basically just another expression of our approach to all of life. We constantly back away from our experience, examining and speculating about it in an effort to make it logical and consistent, to ensure that it is reliable and certain. The simplicity of meditation can cut through these complicated circumventions and returns us to direct and simple experience. Like Basho seeing the flower, experience becomes sufficient in itself.

Keeping in mind this difference in perspectives, we can now look at how it shapes our whole approach to our lives— to pain, ego, emotions, and awareness.

PAIN

Psychotherapy treats pain as a problem: "Pain is bad and should be avoided," (Tart, 1975) and symptoms are seen as expressions of an avoidable underlying affliction. A patient in distress summons the therapist to war—he explores the symptoms in detail, exhaustively investigates their causes, and uses empathy or intuition to understand what the patient is experiencing. He tries as far as he can to open himself to the patient's suffering and then steps back to draw conclusions. This is a perfectly good scientific method, but it has some interesting effects on the patient. As his pain is described, defined, and lamented, it takes on increasing solidity and his sense of identity is augmented in the process. He varies the Cartesian "I think, therefore I am" to "I feel pain, therefore I am," and also gains the credential of being neurotic. Pain becomes something separate and irritating—like a cast on a broken arm. The more he feels separate from his problem, the more likely he is to blame it on his environment or his past. Although his symptom may seem annoyingly intractable, the search for its solution forms a delightful emotional and intellectual exercise.

Buddhism does not see pain as a problem to be solved or eliminated but instead as inspiration. Disappointment and frustration lead us to question the basic assumptions that guide our lives. Pain is a message that someting is wrong and provokes our intelligent inquiry.

The real issue is the manner in which we elaborate our pain into suffering. Suffering originates in the mind's attempt to secure itself, to hold onto a sense of uniqueness and solidity. To do this we struggle to maintain our fixation of "I" and "other," trying to inflate our sense of separate identity. Our existence turns into one prolonged attempt to stop life from puncturing this balloon. When we manage to find pleasure, we feel powerful and substantial, so we try to make sure it is predictably available. Our lives then become a struggle to make our situations totally secure; we work diligently to have things safe, orderly, and permanent. Unfortunately the world is not always cooperative, and when our illusions are threatened we panic and try harder to maintain them. It's as though we were building a sandcastle against an incoming tide. We know we have a certain amount of time before the next wave threatens, so we scurry around trying to erect barriers to protect our castle, never allowing ourselves to realize that the waves are not going to stop.

Given the situation in which our struggle just creates more suffering, Buddhism would not analyze details or symptoms. Instead the approach would be to directly connect with the process and actually experience mind's grasping for territory. This is what happens in meditation. Because ego[1] is insubstantial it finds reference points to make it feel real. A problem will come up which seems terribly important, and there is a tendency to nurture it rather than return to the breath. We try to hold onto it, yet it slips away. For a tiny fraction of a second, there is a gap in our thoughts, our minds are blank. There are no reference points in this blankness, and the ego goes into total panic desperate to fill the void. As the merest flicker of thought occurs, the ego grabs it and tries to expand it and soon we have a whole new drama. Since ego is intrinsically flimsy, its appetite for solid territory is insatiable, so we find ourselves grinding out problem after problem.

In the simple context of just sitting and breathing, our endless complaints sound like hollow chatter, and at some point we tire of our churning. Boredom becomes refreshing—a relief from mind's struggle and speed. As the clutter of thoughts and feelings dissipates, there is a sense of open space. The mind becomes calmer and gravitates toward the simplicity of that space, rather than the claustrophobic quest for a personal solution. We begin to appreciate the mind's capacity for neurotic embroidery and the fickle quality of mind itself. Experiencing the constant replay of our struggle for something solid to hang onto, we develop a sense of humour about how we create our situations and become more gentle with ourselves.

EGO

"Ego" began as a Freudian concept and "ego psychology" still forms a major part of the framework of psychiatric theory today; it has influenced all existing therapies to some degree. In general use, the term has lost its specificity and is used almost synonymously with "personality" or "self-image." Therapists tend to view the ego of a symptomatic patient as defective or not working at its full capacity. In general, it is seen as an embattled fortress; as a tenuously compensated, fragile structure. Neurosis occurs when "the impoverished ego is unable to keep up its defensive work," (Greenson, 1967).

Freudians speak of helping the patient achieve "new ego strengths"; others prefer terms like "cognitive reorganization" or "better adaptive capability." The basic idea is the same: the individual can rebuild and restructure his mental apparatus into something trustworthy and reliable, something that he likes and that will function in his best interests. Inherent in this concept of a dependable ego is the idea of an integrated self-image. There are variations on this assumption:

> A sense of personality, personal identity, is vital and its loss is
> pathological. An individual's personality is what makes him
> unique, skilled, worthwhile, and gives him his sense of identity.
> (Tart, 1975)

However expressed, the theme is that ego has solidity and can
be adapted to serve the individual.

> . . . the patient's ego is expanded and freed. . . . The patient can
> make his decisions and live his life more with his ego, the organ
> of reason, of adaptation, of grasp of reality, and of unemotional
> objective thinking. (Saul, 1972)

Unlike psychotherapy, Buddhism sees the solidity of ego as a
myth we try to maintain:

> The sense of continuity and solidity of self is an illusion. There
> is really no such thing as ego, soul or *atman.* It is a succession
> of confusions that create ego. The process which is ego actually
> consists of a flicker of aggression, a flicker of grasping—all of
> which exist only in the moment. Since we cannot hold onto the
> present moment, we cannot hold onto me and mine and make
> them solid things.
>   The experience of oneself relating to other things is actually
> a momentary discrimination, a fleeting thought. If we generate
> these fleeting thoughts fast enough, we can create the illusion of
> continuity and solidity. It is like watching a movie, the individual
> film frames are played so quickly that they generate the illusion
> of continual movement. So we build up an idea, a preconception,
> that self and other are solid and continuous. And once we have
> this idea, we manipulate our thoughts to confirm it and are afraid
> of any contrary evidence. (Trungpa, 1975)

Ego's insubstantial nature can be experienced in meditation, where constant shiftingness of the mind and fragmented,
discontinuous thought is characteristic. Although Freudian
psychology tends to view discontinuity of ego function with
alarm, Buddhism recognizes it as an existing state of affairs.

The Buddhist idea is not to patch up an imperfect ego—this would be a temporary, piecemeal solution. It seems wiser to ask why constant repair is necessary.

Understanding the insubstantial nature of ego clarifies the common misconception that Buddhism regards it as some sort of villain to be eradicated or destroyed. It seems obvious that approaching such a flimsy, disjointed structure with an all-out assault would be like attacking a heap of toothpicks with an ax. We should also understand that egolessness is not absence of all personality. There is nothing wrong with being what we are, with having our own characteristics and idiosyncrasies.

> Our particular style with its particular energies runs through all the processes of psychological evolution ... but this is not a hangup at all. It is our wealth. (Trungpa, 1975)

Our individual styles become problematic only when used in service of ego's search for territory.

> The whole idea of Buddhist meditation is therefore to work with the core of neurotic clinging to territory, rather than to try to change a person's style of relating to the world. Individual differences in energy flow, and in cultural and historical circumstances, are not problems. Released from the distortions caused by territorial clinging, the styles manifest as sane expressions of intelligence. (Casper)

Buddhism, then, does not attempt to change our ego structure, but questions the nature of the structure itself. Through meditation the transparency of ego's grasping, and eventually the transparency of the dualistic barrier itself, becomes apparent. Where therapy tries to equip ego better for its struggle for security, meditation provides the space to realize that there is no hope, no need for the struggle at all.

At this point we can question again what psychotherapy is treating. As long as we conceive of ego as some tangible and important section of our mind, it makes perfect sense to try to rebuild it. If, though, it has the gossamer quality that Buddhism describes, then the therapist is addressing his talents to thin air.

EMOTION

It is impossible to generalize about a psychotherapeutic view of emotion since there have been so many different ones at different times. Freud's view that emotion should be subservient to intellect was welcomed at first. As Tart has put it:

> Emotions interfere with logical reason and make man irrational; therefore they should be suppressed or eliminated except for recreational purposes. (Tart, 1975)

This assumption went unchallenged for nearly 50 years and excessive emotional expression was regarded as "acting out," as avoidance of basic conflicts. In the last two decades, this assumption has been vehemently attacked. Recognition and expression of emotion have assumed increasing importance; and for some, freedom to shout, scream, or be angry is regarded as the *sine qua non* of therapy. This trend seems to have reached its peak and the pendulum is again swinging toward renewed respect for intellectual functions. Since most therapists view thought and emotion as quite different, there is no forseeable end to this controversy.

No such controversy exists in Buddhism. Neither thought nor emotion has special status. Instead, thought is seen as part of a process that gives emotions their power:

> The emotions are composed of energy, which can be likened to water, and a dualistic thought process, which could be likened to pigment or paint. When energy and thought are mixed together, they become the vivid and colorful emotions. Concept gives the energy a particular location, a sense of relationship,

> which makes the emotions vivid and strong. Fundamentally, the
> reason why emotions are discomforting, painful, frustrating, is
> because our relationship to the emotions is not quite clear.
> (Trungpa, 1975)

Generally, we are afraid of our emotions. We fear that they will overwhelm us, and that we will lose our center of command. Meditation is a way of confronting this fear by relating directly to the emotions as they are.

Relating directly to emotions, identifying with them, is antithetical to our usual way of dealing with them as external and problematic—our warfare approach. Psychotherapy concerns itself with issues of suppressing or "acting out" emotions. In either case, the emotion is treated as problematic. Suppression helps one imagine that emotions are awesome and terrible and must be hidden away; emotion is actually being fed in this process. Acting out or becoming involved in some emotional display is just the opposite side of the coin—the emotion is treated as something disturbing that has to be discharged. Both strategies involve an unnecessary attempt to escape, rather than relate to and skillfully employ the energy.

In meditation, the practitioner first begins to see the transparent quality of emotions and thoughts, and then experiences them in their actual context—the open expanse of mind.

> Even though waves arise, the essence of your mind is pure; it is
> just like clear water with a few waves. . . . To speak of waves
> apart from water or water apart from waves is a delusion. Water
> and waves are one. . . . A mind with waves in it is not a disturbed
> mind, but actually an amplified one. (Suzuki, 1970)

When we experience the real nature of emotions, they lose their terrifying quality. The battle between "me" and my emotions, "me" and my thoughts abates. The barrier set up by concepts has been removed—one has identified completely with the energy of emotions.

It should be clear that there is no desire to eradicate emotions but to allow their energy to function spontaneously and, appropriately, unfettered by the mind's usual panic to secure itself. The emotional upheavals of life become opportunities to see through this panic and so they are very much a part of the practitioner's path.

AWARENESS

Recently there has been a growing number of new therapies, each promoting its own brand of awareness. Some approaches attempt to have patients relive their earliest traumas whereas others dwell on becoming more in touch with bodily sensations. Analytical therapies, of course, tend to prefer cerebral awareness. But all share the common denominator of encouraging consciousness of self in one form or another and often creating a special almost hallowed, reference point for the patient to relate to. If a patient seems unwilling to keep returning to the kind of awareness his therapist thinks important, he is considered "resistant"—it is assumed he is suppressing upsetting feelings or thoughts. If he shares the therapist's enthusiasm for a certain kind of insight or experience, then it is felt that he has some special tool—his awareness takes on solid quality and often becomes a doctrine, something to guide him securely through life.

The meditator starting out has the same tendency to make something special out of his experience, to think of it as a credential or tool. Meditation practice, though, seems to be self-correcting. Dwelling on awareness is so universally human that it is taken for granted that the practitioner will constantly have to clear away this kind of hangover from his practice as he develops. For example, beginning practitioners tend to become conscious of precision in everyday life. After a while they feel tremendously impressed with their meticulous devotion to detail and need encouragement to loosen up. All through the Buddhist path, the practice is presented as to undercut any kind of dwelling on anything whatsoever.

A practitioner dwells on his awareness for the same reasons that patients do—the ego seizes any new experience to confirm itself. But as the practice repeatedly frustrates his attempts to make doctrine out of experience, he eventually begins to trust that he can exist without a reference point to secure him. The need to keep track of how he is doing, to constantly check back with himself, becomes less heavy-handed, and awareness shifts from the usual self-consciousness to what is actually going on all around.

The caricature of the yogi contemplating his navel is really antithetical to Buddhist awareness, which constantly expands outward, away from any notion of a centralized self. Once self-confirmation is no longer a question, the world can be approached on its own terms—without expectation or demands. Then every situation is interesting and can be welcomed with inquisitiveness and often delight.

CONCLUSION

Psychotherapy assumes that ego is solid and can be equipped with tools to help it function better for our well-being. Buddhism sees ego as manipulating perceptions, emotions and thoughts to maintain the illusion of solidity, and states that sanity is self-existing when ego stops struggling to become secure.

One way we confirm our sense of security is by fitting any new idea into our existing system of belief. For example, the reader probably takes it for granted that (1) the contents of this article can be evaluated by scientific method, and (2) psychotherapy is flexible enough to incorporate and utilize almost any idea or technique.

However, since psychotherapy and Buddhism have very different visions, it should be clear that any attempt to adapt a Buddhist idea or technique would be foolish. Out of context, it would just be another toy for ego to play with and no longer Buddhist at all. As for applying scientific method to Buddhist teachings, however hard one tries to understand them intellectually, they are meaningless without direct experience. The transparency of ego, for example, is not an idea we can study but an experience which becomes apparent in meditation. We can easily experience the process of ego's securing itself just by being aware of our temptation to draw conclusions from this article. We would like to take little bits and pieces of Buddhism and fit them into our own world view—or if that cannot be done, to accept or reject Buddhism on the spot. Our impulse is to cover up the irritating quality of the questions posed by quickly deciding where we stand. At the very same time, though, we could see through our attempts to find solid ground. Then the situation is open.

Notes

1. Some semantic clarification is needed here. The Sanskrit word for "ego" obviously carried none of the specific connotations that Freud added; it is close to the Latin "self" and is used in this sense here.

References

Casper, M. *Space awareness.* Unpublished text

Greenson, R. *The technique and practice of psychoanalysis.* New York: International Universities Press, 1967.

Offer, D., & Freedman, D. X. *Modern psychiatry and clinical research.* New York: Basic Books, 1972.

Saul, L. *Psychodynamically based psychotherapy.* New York: Science House, 1972.

Suzuki, D. T. In *Zen Buddhism and psychoanalysis.* ed. Erich Fromm New York: Harper and Row, 1960.

Suzuki, S. *Zen mind, beginner's mind.* New York: Weatherhill, 1970.

Tart, C. T. In *Transpersonal psychologies.* ed. Charles Tart New York, Harper and Row, 1975.

Trungpa, C., *The myth of freedom.* Berkeley, Ca.: Shambala, 1975

chapter 4

THE ENFOLDED ORDER AND CONSCIOUSNESS

David Bohm, Ph.D.

Introduction

It may be said that the basic theoretical notions in physics have been in a state of serious and sustained confusion over the past 40 years or so, and that fundamental changes are needed in these, which are, indeed, long overdue. In various other publications (Bohm, 1971, 1973, 1975, 1978, 1980) a certain new approach to these questions is proposed which meets many of the conceptual difficulties encountered in current theories and shows promise of being capable of further developments that can coherently assimilate the present general body of fact in physics in new ways. In this new approach, what is most essential is the notion of the unbroken wholeness of the totality of existence, as an undivided flowing movement without borders. This implies, of course, the inadequacy of the prevailing general commitment to analyze everything into independently existent but interacting parts, each having a more or less fixed nature.

Inseparable from this approach is the proposal of a new fundamental order for description of the universe, and comprehending its basic relationships. This is the *implicate* or *enfolded* order. Its essential feature is that everything is *enfolded* into everything. In contrast, in the traditional mode of thought, all the basic elements in any theory (which are those in terms of which the world is analyzed) must lie outside of each other, and are connected only in external relationships. Such elements are in an *explicate* or *unfolded* order (a simple example of which is furnished by the Cartesian grid).

In accordance with the current generally accepted terminology, one could perhaps say that these notions constitute proposals for a new "paradigm" in physics. It is my feeling, however, that the term "paradigm" signifies something that is both static and relatively separate, so that it may be expected to apply in a fairly constant way over a rather long time and to some limited field (such as physics), which is also distinct from other fields (such as psychology). This very term is therefore not in harmony with our notion of unbroken wholeness which implies that not only is the universe of this nature, but also our *ideas* concerning the universe. So it would be disharmonious to propose a new but fixed set of ideas concerning a universe in flowing movement, as well as permanently to restrict our ideas concerning a universe of unbroken wholeness to a certain field of study. We will therefore not use the term "paradigm" to describe the new notions suggested in this paper. Rather, they are *proposals* that are relevant to the nature of everything, and that refer to an over-all order. Such proposals have commonly been called *metaphysical* and *cosmological.*

If we now turn our attention to psychology, we can see that this field is currently dominated by a metaphysics and cosmology close to that which has generally prevailed in physics. Thus, there has been a very strong tendency to analyze mankind into independently existent but interacting individuals, and to analyze the consciousness of each individual into separately existent but interacting parts. The basic order for description and understanding of relationships has been the explicate order, in which, in some sense, each part lies outside the other parts and is connected with them by external relationships. Thus, Freud, who set the main features of the general metaphysical and cosmological attitudes in modern psychology, tended to regard each person as a separate "atom," with an internal mental constitution (e.g., Ego, Id, Superego) whose parts were modified in a causally determined interaction with each other, and with other individuals in society. The parallel between these ideas and the physics of Freud's day is strikingly evident.

As has happened in physics, the field of psychology appears to have developed an ever-growing confusion. Many incompatible theories have been adopted by various mutually exclusive groups, which have included even some that tend to move against the prevailing commitment to analysis.

Among the earliest of these were the views of Jung, with his "collective unconscious' and his reference to qualities such as "synchronicity," which transcend the explicate order of time and space, as well as the kind of causal connnection that is also characteristic of the explicate order. His principal suggestions are, however, based largely on myths, imagery, poetry, etc., and as such are not generally considered to be properly scientific. As will become clear in this paper, a key question is whether psychology can *scientifically* go beyond the prevailing analytic metaphysics and cosmology.

It is being suggested here that the time may be ripe for psychologists to give serious attention to some of the new metaphysical and cosmological notions that are now being proposed in this paper, in connection with the attempt to bring greater order into the general concepts of physics. Indeed, as has already been indicated, these new notions contain within themselves the implication that they cannot be restricted to a definite and separate field, such as physics, but that their very essence is to "unfold," so as to apply in new ways to new fields. In this paper, we shall attempt to sketch a few lines along which one can see how such a process may begin to take place.

THE IMPLICATE ORDER

The development of the implicate order had its germ in the observation that relativity and quantum theory (the two most fundamental structures of physical law now known) both imply, though each in its own way, the need for a notion of unbroken wholeness in flowing movement (see Bohm 1971, 1973, 1975, 1978, 1980). One can give here as an illustrative example of such movement the image of a vortex in water. Here, we have a relatively constant, recurrent, stable form (the vortex). Such a form has no independent existence, but it is derived from the movement of a whole (the water) from which it has been abstracted. Two such vortices coming near each other merge to give rise to a single undivided form, which once again is derived from the underlying movement in a deeper and more inward whole.

One might suppose (as was indeed widely done during the 19th century) that space is full of a medium (the ether) and that matter consists of similar relatively independent and stable forms within the ether so that the universe could be conceived as an unbroken whole. The hypothesis of a space-filling ether was, however, never successfully developed in a generally consistent way. So it has to be regarded as, at best, a kind of analogy, which can give us some sort of intimation of what is to be meant by unbroken wholeness. Nevertheless, as has been indicated earlier, relativity and quantum theory are demanding the development of new theoretical ideas which will permit us to go beyond such mere analogies and which will contain serious proposals of new metaphysical or cosmological notions, that will comprehend the universe as an undivided and unbroken totality.

Before going into our new proposals, let us briefly consider the dominant notion in physics, which has been that of analysis in terms of an explicate order. This notion of order has been given a great deal of support by the use of the *lens,* as a basic observational instrument. The essential feature of a lens is that it makes an *image* of an object, in which each point in the image corresponds in a good degree of approximation to a point in the object. One could think that with suitable lenses (and photographic plates) one could make accurate images of things that were too large, too small, too fast, too slow, too subtle, etc., to be seen with the eye alone. Thus, one could come to the conclusion that the whole of existence could be observed experimentally and grasped conceptually in terms of independently existent but interacting elements, each outside the others, and related to them by external relationships alone.

About 20 years ago, a new instrument, the *holograph*, was invented. The name is from the Greek "holo" meaning "whole" and "graph" meaning "to write" so that it signifies "to write the whole." This instrument provides an alternative mode of registering information which does not imply an analytical correspondence between points on an image to points in an object.

A more detailed description of the holograph and its function is given in Bohm (1973, 1978). For our purposes here, it will be sufficient to call attention to its main feature. This is that light coming from a laser, which produces a highly coherent and regular set of waves, scatters off a *whole object* to form a complex "interference pattern" *in each region of space* which is too fine to be seen with the naked eye. This pattern is recorded photographically. When the photograph is illuminated with a laser beam like the original one, the recorded interference patterns gives rise to a set of light waves similar to those that originally came off the object. If the eye is placed in this light, one will see the object, as if in three dimensions, apparently somewhere behind the photographic plate.

The main point of interest here is, however, not this three-dimensional recreation of the visual experience of the object. Rather, it is that *even if only a part of the photographic record is illuminated, one shall see the whole object* (though in less detail and from a more restricted set of points of view). This is because light from the entire object is present in each region of space, so that such a region contains information relevant to the whole, in a form that may be said to "enfold" all the information. It is because of this enfoldment of information concerning a whole that the holograph constitutes an example of how observation can take place in an implicate or enfolded order of the kind we are suggesting in this paper. Our further suggestion is then that it is also possible to grasp the nature of existence conceptually in terms of such an enfolded order, so that the entire analytic approach in terms of an explicate order can be replaced by a new overall approach in terms of an implicate order.

We can bring out the meaning of the implicate order in more detail by considering a certain device which provides a good analogy for what we have in mind. It consists of two concentric glass cylinders, with a highly viscous fluid such as glycerine between them, which is arranged in such a way that the outer cylinder can be turned very slowly so that there is negligible diffusion of the viscous fluid. A droplet of insoluble ink is placed in the viscous fluid, and the outer cylinder is then turned, with the result that the droplet is drawn into a fine thread-like form that eventually becomes invisible. When the cylinder is turned in the opposite direction, the thread-like form draws back, and suddenly becomes visible as a droplet, essentially the same as the one that was there originally. Such a device was actually constructed and used at the Royal Institution in London.

Such a droplet consists of an aggregate of essentially separate carbon particles, which are carried along at the velocity of the fluid element with which they are in contact. When these particles have been drawn into an invisible thread that covers a large region of fluid, one can see that *as an ensemble,* they have a certain quality, which is not evident to the senses, but which reflects the total situation from which they have come. For example, one could have, in the beginning inserted two droplets close to each other, instead of just one. The particles in each would be drawn to constitute a thread-like form, and the particles in each thread would intermingle with those of the others. In effect, the two thread-forms would thus interpenetrate. Yet, when the motion of the viscous fluid was reversed, the particles originally drawn from each thread form would, in retracing their steps, move to reconstitute two separate droplets. So two ensembles of particles which intermingle and which belong to interpenetrating forms are nevertheless to be distinguished by the fact that the movement of the fluid will carry the members of each ensemble to an end, different from that of the other.

The distinction serves to define a set of elements, which, when related in a correspondingly new way, provide the basis of the implicate order. We shall begin with a simple sequential order and go on later to more subtle notions of order.

To bring out the elements that are essential for this new principle of order, we begin by giving attention not mainly to the local properties of each particle of ink. Rather, what is primarily relevant is a certain total solution, including the glycerine, the glass cylinders, and how they move. As has already been pointed out, each particle belongs to a certain ensemble. One may then say that such a particle is bound up with the others in this ensemble by an over-all force of necessity inherent in the total solution, which brings them all to a common end. It is permissible within the common use of language to say that all these particles are *implicated* together in this common end. The word "implicate" is based on the Latin "plicare," meaning "to fold," so that "to implicate" is "to fold inward," or more succinctly, "to enfold." And the use of such an element as basic is part of what is meant by the term "implicate order."

Indeed, enfoldment provides a good intuitive image of what happens here. The droplet of ink is enfolded into the glycerine, much as it might be said that an egg can be folded into a cake. Of course the difference is that the droplet can be unfolded by reversing the motion of the cylinders, while there is no way to unfold the egg (because the material undergoes an irreversible diffusive mixing process). But if we think of the chicken from which an egg comes, we can say that the ensemble of atoms that are going to form the egg are in the chicken and its environment (food, water, air, etc.) and that through the force of necessity in the overall situation, these atoms are "implicitly" bound together by the common end of the egg that they are going to form.

Having now called attention to the *elements* of the implicate order, let us now consider how these are to be *related.* We begin by supposing that a droplet A in a certain place is enfolded into the viscous fluid by turning the cylinder n times. We now put in a second droplet B in a slightly different place, and enfolded by n more turns. We then put in a third droplet, slightly further along the line connecting A and B, and enfold yet another n turns. So A will be enfolded by $3n$ turns, B by $2n$ turns, and C by n turns. We continue this process indefinitely. After many droplets have thus been enfolded, we then turn the cylinder fairly rapidly in the reverse direction. If the rate of emergence of droplets is faster than the minimum time of resolution of the human eye, we will see what is apparently a particle continuously crossing the field of vision.

This description is basically different from the common one, in which one says that a particle exists continuously and that its essence is to be at one place, then another, then another. But here, the whole is always present, enfolded in the glycerine. One droplet after another *manifests* to our perception, as it becomes dense enough to pass the minimum threshold required to affect the eye, and then it enfolds back into the glycerine to be followed by the next one. Nevertheless, although the ensembles of particles belonging to the various droplets generally intermingle, they are always present in a certain order, i.e., the order in which they are "set" to unfold. Evidently, this is not *primarily* a time order, but rather an order of elements that are always present together.

One may further understand the nature of this order by noting that that ensemble A is related to B as B is to C, etc., that is, each differs from the next by the fact that it has been enfolded by n more turns. We thus order the ensembles by their degree of enfoldment and so we obtain an *ordering of implication,* or to be more concise, the *implicate order.* This is an order that is not directly present to the senses at all. Yet, its reality is revealed when successive elements become manifest to our perception as the cylinder is turned.

The order that is ordinarily present to the senses is then an *explicate* or unfolded order, in which the basic elements do not interpenetrate, but are entirely outside of each other. As an example, we may consider the successive positions of a particle in continuous motion through space (which we have already discussed earlier). Equally, we may consider a field which is propagated continuously as a wave that moves across a space in a succession of expanding forms that are separated from each other.

In physics as it has generally been done thus far, the explicate order has been taken as basic. That is to say, all that is primary, independently existent, and universal, is thought to be expressible ultimately in an explicate order, in terms of elements that lie outside of each other (usually obtained by analysis of the world into elementary particles connected through fields).

What we are proposing here instead is that the implicate order is to be taken as the fundamental one. That is to say, what is primary, independently existent, and universal, is to be expressed in terms of the implicate order. So we are suggesting that it is the implicate order that is independently active, while the explicate order flows out of a law of the implicate order. This law provides for *recurrence* and *stability* of what is manifest, so that its form tends to remain similar to itself. But it also allows for changes in this form, i.e., for the fact that recurrence is not complete or perfect. For example, in the ink droplet analogy, each successive ensemble of particles produces a droplet form similar in shape and size, yet different in position. Sucessive differences in position are similar, and so we get a regular line or curve for the orbit. But there may also be breaks or discontinuities in this orbit (which would in fact fit in with the fact of discontinuous atomic transitions in the quantum theory). Furthermore, there could be many such orbit forms, whose enfolded ensembles of ink droplets would intermingle while these would nevertheless manifest as separate "particles," which could be following mutually related curved orbits and thus "interact." So we can in principle obtain in this way a whole explicate world, of derived forms. These evolve and develop in interrelated ways, and thus make up a *relatively independent* subtotality, which we can call "reality as it is directly manifest to our senses and to our scientific instruments."

Thus far, we have been working in terms of the ink droplet analogy. Let us now drop the analogy and return to consideration of the hologram.

The function of the hologram is grounded in an infinitely fine field, obeying the laws of the quantum theory, which cannot be put in an explicate order in any known way (see Bohm, 1973, 1978, 1980). But even to go to the hologram is not enough. For the hologram is only a static record, which is dependent on the movement of the fields from which it is produced. The independent actuality is this movement itself. There is not only movement of electromagnetic fields, but also of other fields (from which holograms could in principle be made) such as electrons, sound waves, etc. In other articles (see Bohm, 1978, 1980), we have called the totality of movement of such fields, known and unknown, by the name "holomovement," and from this totality all particular forms are abstracted. We have further pointed out in these articles that the holomovement in its totality is not limited in any specifiable way, nor need it conform to any particular order, nor be bounded by any particular measure.

In mathematics, one may use undefinable symbols, and derive what is definable as *relationships* among the symbols that are undefinable. Similarly, we say that in the metaphysics that is being proposed here, the holomovement is undefinable, and that all that is definable is to be derived from relationships in the undefinable. What we do, more specifically, is then to say that the basic relationship is that of folding and unfolding, in the implicate order. As indicated earlier, the entire "manifest world" of physics, consisting of objects connected by fields, all moving continuously in an explicate order, is to be derived from the implicate order as a subtotality of relatively stable and recurrent forms. This subtotality does not exist independently. Rather, it is a "show" of something deeper and more inward.

The word "manifest" is based on the Latin "manus" meaning "hand," and indeed, what is manifest is what can be held with the hand, something solid, tangible, and visually stable. The implicate order as a whole evidently involves something highly subtle and intangible. It is this subtle intangible ground (which we have called the holomovement) that we are proposing to take as what is basic and primarily active, while what is solid and tangible is to be *derived* as an only relatively independent subtotality. So we turn upside down the usual procedure of deriving the subtle as an abstract form on the tangible: rather, we derive the tangible as an abstract form on the subtle.

Cosmology and the Implicate Order

We now come to certain new notions of cosmology that are implied in the notions that have been developed thus far. To bring these out, we first note that quantum theory, in its most developed form, treats each particle as a discrete (quantized) state of a generalized field which spreads out over space, and yet somehow has a certain indivisible quantum of energy, proportional to its frequency. Each wave has what is called a zero point energy, below which it cannot go, even when there is no energy available. If we were to add up the energies of all the waves in any region of empty space, the result would be infinite, because an infinite number of waves is present. However, there is good reason to suppose that we need not keep on adding the energies of waves that are shorter and shorter. One can adduce good grounds for assuming that there is a shortest possible wave, so that the total number, and therefore the energy, will be finite. Estimates of this shortest possible wave yield a length of approximately 10^{-33} cm (see Bohm, 1980). This is much shorter than the smallest distance probed in physics thus far (which is about 10^{-17} cm). If one then computes this shortest possible wave length, it turns out to be immensely beyond the total energy of all the matter in the universe.

What is implied by this result is that empty space has all this energy and that matter as we know it is only a small ripple in this immense sea of energy. The sea is in the implicate order and not primarily in the explicate order of space and time at all. The entire universe of space, time, and matter, as we know them, is manifesting in this tiny ripple.

It should be noted that in current physical theory, this energy is ignored, with the aid of a certain technical algorithm called "renormalization." However, as has been brought out elsewhere (see Bohm, 1980), to do this is not logically consistent, though it does yield computations for certain experimentally observable quantities that turn out to be correct. Coherence of our over-all metaphysical thought indeed requires that we seriously entertain the notion that this immense energy is a reality. Of course, our instruments do not yet reveal its presence directly, but this is because they are only small structures in the "ripple" that is our "universe" (as the observation of movements of fish does not directly reveal the vastness of the ocean in which they are swimming).

Let us now return to the energy of empty space. In one sense, it may be said that space, which has so much energy, is full and not empty. The notion of space as a plenum is an ancient one, and, as pointed out earlier, it has been widely used during the 19th century, through the hypothesis of a space-filling ether. Such a plenum is sensed as emptiness, because the "ripples" out of which we and our entire "universe" are constituted pass through it without deflection, rather as ripples do in crossing the surface of a still lake.

With all this in mind, let us consider the current generally accepted notion that the universe as we know it originated in what is almost a single point in space time, from a "big bang" that happened some 10,000 million years ago. In our approach, this "big bang" is to be regarded as a sudden point-like disturbance, creating a wave pulse that spreads out in the ocean of cosmic energy, and that gives rise to our "universe." This universe would have all its matter ultimately implicated in the sea of energy which is the plenum. So we could say that the ground of all matter as we know it is in that emptiness of space, which is also the fullness. Whatever we see as separate is only an abstract form, which derives from an undivided totality. Moreover, each abstract form enfolds the whole, though in its own way. So both in its ground, and in its inner content, each thing is essentially related to all others, and merges with them, in unbroken wholeness of flowing movement, without a border. All that is separate, limited, and fixed is derived as a relatively independent subtotality, which is stable and recurrent. And so we no longer have a fragmentary metaphysics in which separation, division, and ultimately static elements dominate.

CONSCIOUSNESS AND THE IMPLICATE ORDER

Let us now consider how consciousness may be understood in relationship to the cosmology and metaphysics that have been outlined thus far in this paper.

We begin by proposing that consciousness (which we take to be thought, feeling, desire, will, etc.) is, in some sense, in the implicate order, along with matter in general. We do not, however, assume that consciousness is completely dependent on and derived from matter as we now know it. It may involve further principles and new kinds of energies, beyond even those of the immense "sea" of empty space. But what is essential here is the suggestion that matter and consciousness have the implicate order in common.

What justification can we give for such a notion? Some light on this question is afforded by certain work on brain structure, notably that of Pribram (1971). Pribram has given evidence backing up his suggestion that memories are generally recorded holographically all over the brain. From this, it follows that information concerning a given object as quality is not stored in a particular part of the brain, but rather, that all information is enfolded over the whole. It further follows that information of each kind is intermingled with that of every other kind (Globus, 1976).

But, of course, consciousness is more than memory. It also involves awareness, attention, perception, acts of understanding, and much beyond all these. It does not seem likely that such faculties can be reduced to some rather mechanical response, such as the holographic model of brain function would imply (see also Bohm, 1980).

It is difficult to say much about questions as subtle as this one. However, by reflecting on and giving careful attention to what happens in certain experiences, one can obtain valuable clues. Consider, for example, what takes place when one is listening to music. At a given moment, a certain note is being played, but a number of the previous notes are still "reverberating" in consciousness. Close attention will show that it is the simultaneous presence and activity of all these reverberations, along with that of the immediately actual note, which is responsible for the directly and immediately felt sense of movement, flow, continuity, and development. To hear a set of notes, so far apart in time that there is no such reverberation, will destroy altogether the sense of a single, whole, unbroken, living movement that gives meaning and force to what is heard.

One can see that the reverberating notes intermingle and interpenetrate in consciousness, in the way that we have seen to be essential to the enfolded order. So it can be said that one *directly* perceives or experiences an implicate order. In this experience, the whole meaning of a particular enfolded structure of notes may be *active,* in the sense that it sets an emotional and physical response in movement. This direct activity of the implicate order in consciousness constitutes a striking parallel to the activity of the implicate order that we have proposed for matter in general. However, both for consciousness and for matter in general, our language does not adequately call attention to this sort of activity so that we tend to ignore it.

A similar notion can be shown to be applicable for vision (as has been brought out in more detail in Bohm, 1980). One may thus reasonably propose that our immediate perception and experience are generally in the implicate order. Indeed, the implicate order is probably much more immediate than is the explicate order which requires a considerable amount of construction based on logic and memory (see Bohm, 1965; and 1980).

But of course, actual movement involves more than the mere intuitive sense of unbroken flow, which is our mode of directly experiencing the implicate order. The presence of such a sense of flow generally implies further that in the next moment, the state of affairs will actually change, i.e., it will be *different.* How are we to understand this fact of experience in terms of the implicate order?

A valuable clue is provided by reflecting on and giving careful attention to what happens when, in our thinking, we say that one set of ideas *implies* an entirely different set. Of course, the word "imply" has the same root as "implicate," and thus also involves the notion of enfoldment. Indeed, by saying that something is *implicit,* we generally mean more than merely to say that this thing is an inference, following from something else through the rules of logic. Rather, we usually mean that from many different ideas and notions, of which we are not *explicitly* conscious, a new notion emerges that somehow brings all these together in a concrete and undivided whole.

We see then that each moment of consciousness has a certain *explicit* content, which is a *foreground,* and an implicit content, which is a corresponding background. What we are proposing here is that the distinction of implicit and explicit is to be regarded as essentially equivalent to that between implicate and explicate in matter in general.

It will be helpful in this connection to recall briefly the analogy of the ensemble of ink particles, belonging to a certain droplet, enfolded in the viscous fluid, which are bound together by a force of overall necessity, inherent in the total situation that brings these particles to a common end (i.e., the reconstitution of the droplet). Recall also the ensemble of atoms in the chicken and its environment likewise bound together by a force of overall necessity, that brings them eventually to constitute the egg. Similarly, we propose here that the ensemble of ideas and notions that are going to constitute an implication of a thought process is enfolded in the brain and nervous system, and that through a certain overall force of necessity, these are bound together by the common notion that is going to emerge in the next moment of consciousness.

The force of necessity may arise in the emotions, which demand a certain implication, or it may arise in *rational necessity*. It is, of course, clear that one senses a kind of force of necessity ruling one's thoughts, when there are certain kinds of intense emotional pressures (e.g., fear, desire, greed, etc.). These tend to lead to implications that are disorderly or confused. If one is carefully attentive, however, one will notice that even when the overall situation is such that these pressures are not operating, there is a perceptible sense of deeper inward force of rational necessity. This is a force that tends to bring about new notions that are coherently connected (as can be demonstrated later by the test of whether they are free of contradiction).

We have been using the idea that consciousness can be described in terms of a series of moments. Attention shows that a given moment cannot be fixed exactly in relation to time (e.g., by the clock), but rather than it covers some vaguely defined and variable extended period of duration. As pointed out earlier, each moment is experienced directly in the implicate order.

What we have further seen is that through the force of necessity or the over-all situation, one moment gives rise to a next, in which content that was previously implicate becomes explicate, whereas previously explicate content has become implicate (e.g., as happened in the analogy of the ink droplets).

The continuation of the above process gives rise to change. In general, this change has a fairly definite relationship to the implicate content of a moment, in the sense that a moment containing a strong sense of movement (i.e., copresence of many degrees of implication, as in the case of musical notes) will tend to be followed by a series in which successive moments will be different (their difference being generally greater when there is a stronger immediate sense of movement).

It seems clear then that the succession of moments cannot be completely fixed from the explicate content alone. Indeed, as close attention shows, the explicate content is not generally even a major factor in this process, which rather unfolds primarily from the implicate order. Of course, the enfolded content is often such that moments may succeed each other in a fairly regular order. Nevertheless, on certain occasions, there can be fundamental and radical transformations of content (e.g., when a basically new idea is involved).

The presence of a relatively fixed regular order of thought depends mainly on *knowledge* accumulated from the past, and recorded as the content of memory. This recording may, in accordance with Pribram's ideas be in an implicate order. But when reactivated, it gives rise to an *experience* of an explicate order (as the hologram, which is in the implicate order gives rise to an experience of the "unfolded" object when it is illuminated with a suitable laser beam). So what is known has to manifest as an explicate content, coming from the enfolded memory recording. It seems clear, along the general lines already suggested, that the essentially explicate response of memory, as it operates at a given moment, does not in general play a significant role in determining the content of the next moment. This means that the future is not determined by what is known at a given moment, nor even by what is in principle knowable. Rather, its ultimate ground is beyond anything that can be captured in the entire field of what can be known. This follows, of course, for consciousness, but since in our proposed metaphysics, matter in general is to be understood in the implicate order, it may be shown to follow also for the whole of existence (see Bohm, 1980).

How are consciousness and matter in general related? Firstly, as they are both in the implicate order, each enfolds the other. Thus, the question of how consciousness is able to know matter in general is no serious problem, since from the very outset, in a sense, it may be said that "everything contains information referring to everything." But then, in extending the implicate mode to the totality of existence, we further say that consciousness is an *active factor* in reality as a whole, bound up with matter in general by a deeper and more inward force of necessity, which brings about a series of new moments in both, to which both have contributed in an essential way.

The question of how consciousness and matter in general are related, is a deep and subtle one, and what we have said here hardly scratches the surface of what is involved. In *Wholeness and the Implicate Order* we go into this subject in greater detail to develop a more inclusive account, showing how even our metaphysical and cosmological thought can be significant, active factors, in the overall reality that is relevant to life as a whole.

ON MEANING AS UNDERSTOOD IN TERMS ON THE IMPLICATE ORDER

From here on, one can go in many possible directions. For example, it is important for psychology to clearly inquire into the laws and modes of operations of that movement and activity which we experience as *meaning.* Some insight into what this may be is afforded by considering the more or less equivalent word "significance," which comes from the verb "to signify," and which, from its Latin root, means "to show by making signs."

In the first instance, a sign may be a form in a particular object, but more generally, it involves an ensemble of factors gathered together out of a total situation, this ensemble having a certain significance or meaning (e.g., danger, possibility of success, etc.). Going further, we see that the ensemble of our immediate sensations also constitutes signs having meaning. The same holds for emotions, thoughts, and the language which expresses them. Thus, a certain set of words may form an ensemble which has deep significance, sometimes so great that it can change our whole life.

In current psychology, a key notion is that certain conditions or processes are *psychosomatic* (from Greek "psyche" meaning "mind" and "soma" meaning body). This word is now generally being used in such a way as to imply that mind and body are separate entitites, or at least separate functions, in interaction. Such an approach is evidently not compatible with the metaphysical notions that are being proposed here. What we shall propose instead, in this connection, is a different notion, that we shall call *somasignificance.*

By this, we mean, first of all, that both the body and matter in general are capable of acting as signs. This possibility is to be understood as a particular case of the implicate order. That is to say, enfolded within the totality of matter in general are ensembles of elements, which may also, through perception and conceptual abstraction, pass over into the content of consciousness, where they constitute a certain *significance* or *meaning.* We call this the *somasignific factor* in the totality of experience.

But vice versa, each meaningful sign tends to give rise to an *activity* (e.g., an ensemble of elements constituting a sign meaning "danger" instantly alerts the nervous system, speeds up the heart, increases adrenalin in the blood circulation, etc.). This activity permeates the matter of the body and eventually that of its general environment, and in doing so, it brings about *changes* in matter in general. We call this the *signa-somatic* factor in the totality of experience.

A particularly clear case of signa-somatic activity is to be seen in the *signal.* Thus, a mere word may act as a signal which (in the general way indicated earlier) may incite a response that changes one's entire response to his environment.

The two factors, soma-signific and signa-somatic, are present inseparably in every moment of experience. They are not independently existent but rather, they intermingle and interpenetrate. Indeed, as reflection with close attention shows, they unfold and develop in a manner that is typical of the implicate order. Thus, as has been seen, any sign is itself an ensemble of elements enfolded in matter in general and not separable from the matter in which it is enfolded. When the content of this ensemble passes over to be enfolded in consciousness, then, by the force of necessity inherent in the total situation, a new moment arises, in which this enfolded content of consciousness manifests outwardly as changes in the nervous system, movement of the body, and modifications of the general environment.

This approach can be carried further inward, into consciousness. In doing this, we note that significance is the essential quality and activity of what is to be meant by "mind." Without meaning, mind would be impossible. (Indeed, "meaningless" and "mindless" are nearly synonymous.) But in the proposals that we are developing here, meaning is the *activity* of the total set of signs, and thus cannot be separated from matter in general.

For example, a *sensation* has its ground in the excitation of the matter in the sensory nerves. This excitation is a sign, and may indeed function as a *signal,* leading directly to an outward signa-somatic reaction, of the kind described earlier. On the other hand, the meaning may be developed further as *feeling* or *emotion,* which is an orchestrated totality of sensation and more inward responses, all "reverberating" together, in a directly and immediately experienced enfolded order. Such emotion may then operate signa-somatically, to yield an outward action, based on immediate feelings. Or alternatively, the meaning may be further developed reflectively as abstract thought, expressed as language. This may then give rise to a signa-somatic action, that is both physical and emotional.

In turn, all this brings about yet further changes in thought, in a process that unfolds and develops indefinitely.

All of this generally happens when consciousness is permeated with an intelligence and a quality of affection that go beyond the mere mechanical. But it is possible for the movement of soma-significance to be dominated by the mechanical factor of the *signal*. For example, as indicated earlier, a single word can act as a signal, and if this signal has an emotional meaning, the signa-somatic action may be not mainly outward, but rather, also inward. Thus, the body and nervous system will be excited, and from this, strong emotions such as anger will be incited. These emotions will themselves act as *signals,* bringing about thoughts, ideas, words, that tend to justify this state of anger, even though they are incorrect and confused. These thoughts and words will further sustain the anger, in a process that tends to build up, almost without limit.

The essential feature of this process is *signa-somatic confusion.* That is, the "signs" in consciousness act as signals, not however, in the proper fashion, of changing some aspect of matter that is relatively independent of the sign itself (e.g., an external object). Rather, the signasomatic action is now such as to change the material basis of the signals themselves (i.e., the brain and nervous system). Such changes are not only irrelevant to the facts that originally gave rise to this action, but, what is much more important, they tend to distort and even to destroy the general system of signs that is a key factor in mental activity in general. It is as if a computer were to respond to certain situations by setting off a bomb that destroyed the information records that were leading to particularly difficult "problems."

It is clear that close attention, leading to analysis in terms of independently existent elements, all causally related and interacting, cannot be effective in ending such signa-somatic confusion. Firstly, the whole system of thought and language, along with feelings, intentions, desire, and will, are so affected by the confusion in the total activity of the ensemble of signs that they tend no longer to function in a proper order. But secondly, and much more important, the analytical approach is in the explicate order, whereas the actual movement is in the implicate order. So analysis must ultimately tend to add to the confusion. What is needed is not only close attention, mainly to the actual order of operation of the signalling system (e.g., to how confused thought acts as a signal for twisted emotion, while such emotion further acts as signals that excite more confused thoughts in a self-sustaining neurophysiological process that resembles a muscular spasm in its general structure). The further crucial requirement is that we reflect on what we learn in such attention, in terms of an implicate order (along the general sorts of lines sketched in this paper). Thus, there will be harmony between the *immediate fact* and the *reflection of this fact in thought.* The immediate fact and its reflection in thought will then be two mutually related factors, which like two mirrors, reveal different but essentially related aspects of a deeper totality (much as a stereoscope gives two views of a more fundamental three-dimensional reality). But if we reflect in the explicate order, this is like using one mirror to reflect an entirely different kind of object, while supposing that both mirrors were reflecting different sides of the same object.

These are, of course, only *proposals,* and are neither *assumptions* nor *conclusions* about what would be an ultimate truth. What is needed is to see whether these proposals (operating signa-somatically as a guide to action) will turn out to be *viable,* in the sense of self-consistency, and of general consistency in what happens in all that flows out of them. This requires, of course, that they be further developed as they function in actual life. One may reasonably expect that since they are a movement toward freedom from the prevailing analytical tendency to fragmentation, they can give rise to a more harmonious and orderly approach than has generally thus far been possible.

REFERENCES

Bohm, D. *Special theory of relativity.* New York: Benjamin, 1965 (Appendix).

Bohm, D., & Hiley, B. *Foundations of physics,* 1971, *1,* 359; 1973, *3,* 139; 1975, *5,* 93.

Bohm, D. *Re-Vision,* 1978, *1* (Summer-Fall).

Bohm, D. *Wholeness and the implicate order.* London: Routledge and Kegan-Paul, 1980.

Globus, A. D., & Maxwell, G., Eds. *Consciousness and the brain.* New York: Plenum, 1976.

Pribram, K. *Languages of the brain.* Englewood-Cliffs, N.J.: Prentice-Hall, 1971. (Paperback Belmont, Ca.: Brooks Cole.)

Part II

APPLICATIONS

Part II concerns itself with the application of the principles enunciated in Part I. This is a challenging task, especially to make it meaningful in a therapeutic context that is so far governed by a world view supported by the prevailing scientific paradigm of deterministic causality. The necessity to make the attempt resides in the fact that psychotherapy has been, and continues to be heavily weighted along lines that have been influenced by the scientific model of causality. Therapeutics has not sought to coherently intergrate or investigate the possibilities offered by the emerging "proposal" that David Bohm so elegantly described in the preceding section. Part of the difficulty lies in the lack of training about other ways of looking at science. The lack of training simply derives from the fact that not many people have been able to coherently articulate the connections between the principles and the practice. Here, though, we have the unique opportunity of finding four gifted clinicians and teachers who are able to do so with clarity and understanding. A variety of methods are presented, all of which have one thing in common: to give direction and form to the principles stated in part I. The four contributors to this section each represent an application paralleling each one of the four presentations of part I.

Jacob Stattman, founder and director of The Institute of Unitive Psychology in the Netherlands, describes his work on creative trance, which exemplifies the creative use of imagination outlined by Gerald Epstein in "The Relationship of Healing to Imagination." Paul Olsen extends the Buddhist principles, discussed earlier by Carl Rinzler and Beth Gordon, to his work on psychotherapy as an asocial process. Diane Shainberg imparts her vision of non-deterministic supervision. This is the first explication I know of in this area in the psychological literature. Much of what she says resonates with the Vedantic tradition espoused by Swami Dayananda. Ms. Shainberg begins to involve the supervisee in serious questions of his/her role as a therapist. The result is that the role of therapist and the therapeutic relationship is defined in a new and unexpected way. Finally, Warren Wilner delights us with his discussion of psychic oneness. He explores the paradoxes offered in our attempts to make sense out of the world. His work relates to that of David Bohm, and reminds us that we must be ever mindful of the paradoxes that constantly hamper our ability to make sense out of the world and of the necessity to become aware of the deceptions we impose on ourselves by incessantly striving to be certain about everything.

G. E.

chapter 5

THE CREATIVE TRANCE: A UNITIVE APPROACH TOWARD THE PHENOMENA OF MENTAL IMAGERY IN THERAPY

Jacob Stattman, Ph.D.

INTRODUCTION

Based on my practice in psychotherapy, this chapter is about some information I have derived concerning the nature of the imaging process and the value of utilizing that process for healing in psychological and psychosomatic areas of human experience. Although the entire process includes extensive work with the body of a neo-Reichian nature, the emphasis in these pages is on the imagery phenomena. I am concerned here with two issues: What can we learn about the character of the imagery itself; what is the experience of contacting this imagery?

THE CHARACTER OF MENTAL IMAGERY

The images involved in this discussion are those which are potentially available during the states of waking consciousness.

Although they may be of the same character as those present during dreams, hallucinations, drug experiences, etc., it is in the relationship to the waking state that my materials apply. This is a unique condition, when the imagery traditionally associated with passive states of being emerges while the mind is fully active and the ego is present in its capacity to evaluate, judge, make decisions, and reflect upon the transactions that occur. To the degree that the image in part represents the unconscious and/or supraconscious, this waking image state also has a very particular locus, a third state as it were.

The very act of imagining may seem contrary to the needs of the ego for control and rationalization. To put these two aspects of mind together at the same time, to bisociate (a unique word thanks to the imagination of Arthur Koestler, 1969, described in his book on the *Act of Creation*) is to open up possibilities which are unavailable otherwise. When the process works, a kind of integration ensues which I have found to be unique. The boundaries of cognition, imagination, memory, and organic systems, are extended, loosened, and yield new experience, knowledge, and behaviour.

Nature and Function

I regard imagery as a natural and intrinsic faculty of mind, different in kind, but of the same standing as perception, memory, etc. As a phenomena of mind, it is present and active continuously though we may only be conscious of it in certain moments, or as in the case of night dreams, after the fact. I believe it may even be absolutely necessary, though this cannot be proven, to the maintenance of a healthy mind and that degrees of neurosis and psychosis are indicative of a distorted or dysfunctional situation with respect to the imaging process. The imagery is a manifestation of the nonlinear and holistic synergistic organization which links all aspects of the self in a higher ordering process.

On the basis of my own personal experience and that of

working with imagery in psychotherapy and transpersonal psychology, I regard the imagery faculty to be a state of mind which is more comprehensive than that of the normal, waking, consciousness. The mental imagery itself is the outer manifestation of this state.

To describe the imagery faculty in existential terms, it appears to be the process which collates the inchoate, chaotic, and apparently disparate facts of perception (exteroceptic and interoceptic), organic activity, and mental activity, in one unified and intelligible whole. Through the image, experience is given form, structure, and identity. Of the highest significance, the image equally conjoins the quantitative (the somatic) and the qualitative (the psychic) in a mode and medium which transcends the limiting categories of both. Phenomenologically, we might describe the process as the *unity of possibility,* an inclusive interface of substance and essence.

The imagery often appears to be ambivalent and elusive in its function, meaning, and effect, especially since it is simultaneously a reference to: (a) states of being, i. e., aspects of emotional, physical, and mental development; (b) categories of function and act, i.e., memory, perception, organic activity, behavior, sensation, ideas, etc. I suggest this appearance of ambiguity and elusiveness is not intrinsic to the imagery itself, but more a comment on our ability to understand and associate intelligently with the contents and movements of the imagery.

In brief, the imagery represents a locus of objects, events, and acts wherein an existential reality inheres, more complete and authentic than the separate and distinctive parameters of memory, perception, or cognition alone.

Ontologically, the image is construed to be simultaneously present and effective as both symbol and as a reality in its own right. We can rely upon and use the images as they appear without further reduction, analysis, or translation, and equally can find means to permit the image to disclose itself as a representative of other levels of existence. In particular, as synonyms for psychological, physical, and historical situations and processes. The image then is the *thing in itself* and that to which the thing points. Both are true. This contradicts the Aristotelian notion of noncontradiction, but is faithful to the Buddhistic principle of unity in multiplicity, of the point beyond dualism where A is both A and not-A. If we take this nondualistic character of the imagery at face value, it goes a distance toward explaining the power of the image to heal and to have such a deep psychological effect upon the person; it equally points to the mode by which to approach imagery and utilize it in psychotherapy. What is displayed in the contents of imagery is always grounded in an inclusive reality larger than what is normally available to consciousness or to organic process alone. Here integration is concretized and made manifest.

In regards to the total constituency of the person, the particular images *cannot be other than what they are* at any given moment. The unique combinations that emerge out of the potential millions of images are the product of an implicit contiguity and congruence with every other detail of the self. In the language of Gabriel Marcel (1962), we are in contact with the nonmediatizable immediacy of the here-and-now, the indubitable presence of being. With every change in thought, feeling, movement, organic process, and perception, this immediacy is present and disclosed through the particulars of the imagery which is seen.

With this view of the imagery faculty as a center of synergistic activity it makes sense to speak of it as an organ of pure possibility (Casey, 1976, p. 216). We have a phenomena which is simultaneously possibility and indubitably real.

By itself, the image is not an object of actual perception, but an existential manifestation of the "fact" imbued with life —neither subject nor object, it is a transcendental phenomena which goes beyond categories of logic and empirical observation. The image reality is more true to the organic wholeness of the person than rationally bounded scientific discovery founded on objective separation and detachment. We might say that the image is a process of inclusion and completeness whereas normal cognition is based on reductionism and division.

The image further derives power by this potential to free itself from control by the categories of logic, reason, and instinct. It does this, not by opposition, but by integration and transcendence. It is the medium which can "understand" the respective parameters of the mind and the body in such a manner that ontological exigence (the need to complete oneself) ensues and dominates. The effectiveness of this power is mediated by our ability to contact and implement imagery in a manner which is true to its nature. The psychotherapy is based upon the nature and quality of that contact.

Following the point that the image is both a symbol and an effective reality simultaneously, we can make some further extrapolations. One is to perceive that the image unites the voluntary (the volition) and the involuntary (spontaneity). This would lead to an understanding of issues concerning the vividness and stability of the contents of imagery and lead to some clarity about the reasons for changes in the contents, about the types of imagery presented, and the effects of the imagery upon personality and behaviour. It is the quality of the linkage between conscious volition and emergent spontaneity that determines our experience with the imagery. Matters of continuity, discontinuity, imagery loss, etc., are dependent on this linkage and reveal a great deal psychologically.

As in any psychotherapy or healing method, we seek a rapprochement with the unconscious, with what is latent and missing in our awareness. Imagery provides this engagement, and our consciousness is illumined accordingly. "That which you have within you will save you—that which you do not have within you, will kill you!" (Jesus Christ, *The Gospel of St. Thomas*). We need this rapprochement to overcome the duality that alienates us from ourselves and makes us our own oppressors, our own killers.

Operational Factors

Based on all that has been said until now, some conclusions can be derived regarding the approach toward the phenomena of mental imagery. First, the issue of making contact with the imagery is paramount. I have stated that the imagery is present at every moment and functions continuously. Operationally we can then contact imagery at any time and in any psychological and physical state. We may make contact during deep states of relaxation, during "normal" waking states of activity, during manic states of heightened tension and stress, during crisis moments, and in the illumined states of maximum wakefulness associated with meditation. It is not necessary to work with imagery only during relaxed and quiescent moments in an atmosphere of artificial peacefulness as created by the therapist. This has its value, but is not exclusively of the highest benefit. Often it is the moments of crisis and tension that demand we make a unified contact with ourselves to gain the strength, resources, and insight to cope appropriately. Conversely, as in meditation and quietude, it is then that imagery can add a dimension of wholeness to whatever else we are doing to facilitate our intentions and lead to significant changes in personality and behaviour.

The quality and intensity of the contact is mediated by the fact that we function in some moving and affective relation to imagery wherein we are both observer and participant. In this process of working in the awake state with imagery, we are engaged in three relationships simultaneously: that of contact with the therapist; that of contact with our rational self; and that of contact with the contents of imagery. During this process the energy directed to the three relationships alters in emotional intensity, attention, and awareness. This is significantly different from other image experiences, particularly the night dream and the fantasy. In the dream, we are essentially passive and imagery "happens" to us; in the fantasy, we are wholly in control of the events and can mediate the full process.

(For the sake of language, I think of fantasy as but one type of mental imagery, a conscious, controlled, directed, enactment subject to a clearly defined intention; e.g., "what would I do if I had a million dollars," type of thought).

In addition, the contact with the imagery is moderated by the techniques used to give energy, voice, and movement to the images. Apart from simple observation and reportage, there are many techniques to enhance this contact. In my own case, they generally are based on the work of Gestalt therapy whose aim is to "reown" the projections by giving them voice, body, and energy.

The Methods

In short form, the method I employ is simple. It is a flexible combination of: evocation of the imagery; the application of somatic therapy and gestalt therapy; and the use of free association. During the work, we move in and out of the imagery, the body, the intellectualizing, and the concomitant reactions and responses without adherence to any rigid structure or procedure. At times, this may mean working primarily with the imagery for an extended time for all of a session. Or, using the imagery as a background resource, to focus more on here-and-now dialogues, or on work with the body itself. But there is no formulae for what should be done when and for how long as this would interfere with the uniqueness of the person-in-the-situation. As the imagery is always available, it may be recalled instant by instant and is in no way a delicate presence. As the client becomes familiarized with this approach, he is able to benefit increasingly from the freedom it offers.

Two factors determine what occurs with respect to contact with the imagery in this sense: (a) the amount of energy release, and (b) the person's capacity and potentiality to cope with and transform this released energy into useful expression, understanding, and behavior. The reciprocity between these two factors determines the degree of healing, for in this dual situation, there is an infinite range of possibility of choice (limited only by organic realities) and a particular type of tension, a dyadic tension between freedom and security, between certainty and apparent chaos, between the past and the present, between self-ignorance and illumination. Above all, there is ambivalence, an attribute of choice and change. We seek the light, but hide in darkness. Our polarities of feeling and action become frozen and appear as contradictions, a condition which leads to stasis and inner separations. What is hidden, undisclosed, and frozen supports this stasis in soma and psyche, in the tensions of the body, and in the character patterns of the mind. Through the participation in imagery, the ambivalence is brought to consciousness, softened, and leads to a conscious renewal of the tensions between opposites. *This tension of ambivalent opposites is a precondition for change.* It is the same as in the dynamic of the Zen koan, the gnostic riddle, the Yogic admonition to suppress thought, and every effective therapy which confronts the individual with their own tension. The dualism is used to confront itself since *that* is what is known and understood by the fragmented psyche and body. When this process succeeds, the grounds for an emergence of wholeness and integration are enlivened and vitalized. That emergence can only be spontaneous; it cannot be organized or given by the therapist. Every unitive method and technique works to this end. The point here is that mere awareness of the imagery may lead to dramatic effects on the observer, but that much more can be done to deepen and increase contact. The value is in achieving a nondualistic and holistic contact, a oneness which is uniting. At the opposite pole, if the observer is "taken over" by the imagery, such that the critical ego functions are lost, this is of little or no value and is akin to psychosis.

There are specific principles which determine the quality and quantity of contact between the contents of the images and the participant/observer. During this period of contact, the images are approached in both their aspects, that of being existentially real and sufficient in and of the, selves, and as symbolic pointers to other levels of interest. Following is a short dialogue, part of a session, which illustrates some of the methods of enhancing contact with the imagery. The parentheses contain explanations about the process (Abbreviations: T - therapist; C - client).

The client has worked on the conflict and two contradictory images emerge, a hard black layer and a fire.

T: Make a dialogue between the dark layer and the fire.
C: I'm the dark layer and I keep the fire inside. This keeps me from being eroded and gives you (C) support, keeps you together and gives you structure. (The rationale for maintaining the hardness). I don't want you (the fire) to go out—I want to keep you in me and I don't want you to go out to other people.
C (as fire): I like to go out because others like warmth too.
C (as layer): No.
C (as fire): I want to go out.
C (as layer): No, I will not permit it.

(Here, we see a fixed and chronic relationship which by itself cannot resolve the conflict; each element seems to be the destructive opposite for the other, in effect a cycle of self-defeating behaviour supported by fear and maintained by rigidity.)

T: What prevents the synthesis of your conflict—what is missing that would change things. First locate the two parts in your body.
C: The fire is in my belly, the hardness is in my chest.

(Here many comments would be possible: the fire in the generative region, the hardness in the chest which needs to be flexible for healthy functioning of respiration.)

T: What is the borderline between the parts? (seeking the resistance.)
C: My shoulders are rigid and stiff.
T: What does the border look like—look inside your body.
C: It is a sort of iron shield, very thick, white, and split between

upper and lower areas. (frozen movement—"armoring" i.e., chronic tension.)

T: What energizes the shield?

C: The fire.

T: See if you can manipulate this shield.

C: Yes, I can melt it with the warmth—I can make it red and without letting it collapse, it gets hot. (This dynamic is related to the fear of melting, of letting go and becoming vulnerable without adequate defenses.)

T: As you manipulate the shield, be aware of the changes in the hard wall and the fire, but do not let yourself create anxiety.

C: As I melt the shield down, the fire becomes less intense and the dark layer is getting warmer.

T: Continue to the point where you begin to feel anxious.

(This instruction is to keep the work at the level of understanding the process, the resistances, and the implications of changing. Anxiety at this point would overwhelm the contact with the imagery and produce either a premature abreaction or an emotional cut-off.)

C: The shield is nearly melted, the fire is nearly out, and the black layer is becoming reddish. I feel my breathing becoming more intense. I am getting anxious.

T: All right—build up the wall to the point where the anxiety disappears.

C: Now, I've done that, the fire is again more intense, the shield is less red and the dark layer is blacker.

T: Now you see how you can control and choose to regulate the situation. Begin to explore more deeply using this knowledge as you go into the anxiety.

C: As I do that, my hands tense up, my breathing is becoming erratic, it's all one wall now.

T: What are you afraid of right now?

C: Of melting completely.

T: And then what will happen?

C: I won't exist any more.

(After several experiments with the anxiety in relation to the movement between the images, the following ensues.)

C: The fire is not recognisable, and the black is not either—there is just one large reddish-brown form and warmness.
T: Slowly open your eyes now and give your attention to your feelings right now.
C: I felt a synthesis between the warmth and the fear. I'm not so fearful and it is a good feeling without the shield.
T: Can you free associate now between the experience with the images and your memory of this conflict about melting.
C: No. If I were to melt, I would lose myself and that never happened.

Psychologically, one could say that the client has built up a defense against being hurt, but at the expense of experiencing his own warmth. In addition, he is experienced as cold and invulnerable to others creating problems in relationship. This accords with his personal history.

With respect to the discussion of contact, the intention was to find a psychological synthesis by working within the images, but first it was necessary to know what prevented this from occurring spontaneously—to identify the resistance both in the imagery and in psychological terms. This required an imagistic means to cope with the anxiety while pursuing the process of self-disclosure, a form of internal self-regulation which would not violate the person's need for self-control. The client's experiential discovery and experience of being able to regulate the experience facilitated an affective contact sufficient to nullify the conditioned behavior supporting the rigid split first encountered. Furthermore, the contact was assisted by having the client identify in a gestalt sense with the parts of the imagery, and by localizing the images spatially in the body. Thus, contact was through an understandable sequence in time, identification in the client's frame of reference, and location spatially in the body, e.g., the process was intelligible.

From the example just given, one can see that there was a regular dialogue of contact with me as well. This method differs in many ways from the work which subscribes to a directed imagery without any intervention by the guide. In those methods, a directed theme is usually presented to the client and he or she is to follow the scenes, report what occurs, and then discuss the experience afterward with the therapist. My approach relies mainly upon spontaneous experience, contacting throughout with the therapist.

Diagnostics

Although it is not in my interest here to present a "how to do it" thesis, some particulars about the facets of imagery from the point of view of diagnostics may be of interest. What I do look for guides me in my dialogue with the client and which in turn educates the client to develop a deeper participation in the process. There are points of observation which guide both therapist and client. A partial list of such observations follows:

> Viewing the image both as itself and as psychological metaphor, look for the descriptive words which apply simultaneously to the image and to the personality of the client; e.g., "I see a hard surface where no softness is permitted to remain because of the external pressures, as the top of a mountain."

> Note what changes in the imagery spontaneously change behavior, either in the direction of openness, or in terms of increasing resistance, anxiety, and blocked affect.

> Note what changes in behavior spontaneously lead to changes in the image contents.

> Note changes in the body due to changes in the image: in body language, known tensions, movement patterns, voice patterns, respiration, vitality, etc.

> Note congruency between the activity in the imagery and the responses by the client in terms of understanding, affect, and response.

> Note patterns which emerge in the contents of the imagery activity which correspond to or conflict with normal

behavior of the client, in general and with respect to specific problems.

Note what the client tends to downplay, avoid, or focus on, in the contents of imagery and what affect accompanies these relations.

Within the activity of the imagery itself, observe: congruency and consistency in the "story"; shifts in imagery that happen without apparent reason; material changes such as disappearance of the images, or changes in distance between objects, changes in the speed of the movement of the imagery, etc.

With respect to location of the images in the body, note correlations between the images and the specific body-placement in terms of the natural function of that area of the body and the apparent effect of the image in that area; what implications are clear with respect to influences of the body on the image objects and what implications inhere if the image object would change or be removed vis-a-vis the natural functions. E.g., if the client sees a needle in the heart, what is the function of that needle with respect to the function of the heart; what if the needle were removed; what does the needle provide in the first place with respect to the overall maintenance of the personality in terms of psychological history and present behavior; what new behavior is required to live without the needle?

Note the materials of the image objects in the body. I have found that there is a direct correlation between the composition of these objects and the degree of stress of both a somatic and psychological nature, stress which is part of the resistance pattern required to maintain psychological stability. E.g., "I see a steel band in my back"; or, "There is a plastic tube in place of my spine", or, "There is a rosebush where my ovaries should be," etc.

As a general principle, I have found that the composition of the image objects conforms to natural law, in the sense that the less alive, less human the psychological and/or somatic area in terms of alienation and/or stress, the less human will be the object. Thus at the extreme we find plastic. Tending toward humaneness, we move to the level of minerals and stones, then to metals and alloys, then to vegetative life, and to animals, and finally with integration, to the human levels of natural existence. Thus the image object is a barometer of the relation between the person and their constituent elements.

Much more could be added to the foregoing list of points to observe, plus the factors which are described in the theories of gestalt therapy and in the body therapies. But the point is illustrative of how rich imagery is when we take it literally and allow it to be both real and symbolic. The types of imagery which appear can be subdivided endlessly according to different frames of reference, but in general, we can discern four types of schemes. *(1)* Abstract imagery, e.g., colours without form; forms of geometry; emptiness; etc.; *(2)* surrealistic imagery, e.g., objects which do not conform to the natural world as our perception reveals, either not of this world, or of the world of fantasy, or deformations of objects of the natural world; *(3)* realistic imagery, e.g., conforming to our knowledge and experience; and *(4)* realistic imagery but which we do not have personal experience of, e.g., prehistoric phenomena, historic characters of another time period, scientific facts, etc.

The relations which occur in imagery between these basic types are a rich source of diagnostic and work material and teach us much about the client's inner life and their modes of dealing with organic and natural reality. Here is a very short example in which several types merge for a creative result:

> I had the fantasy of being in an egg in fear of a giant boot about to step on me and crush me . . . the boot was worn by my father . . . I had a choice of fighting back and hurting him or letting him hurt me. . . .

You (the therapist) then directed me to go inside my body. There I discovered a flask of bubbling liquid inside my back. I tried rubbing it on my back to strengthen my resolve, but nothing happened . . . Jerry joined me then (a fellow group member). He suggested I drink the fluid which I did. This was the key, I felt a tremendous release, did a cartwheel, jumpled wildly up and down, and experienced incredible energy. I then wrestled with Jerry and discovered my own strong sadistic feelings—stronger than I could ever remember—I felt I was the boot wanting to crush Jerry!

This experience might be best described by remembering Jung's (1963) definition of the transcendent function:

The shuttling to and fro of arguments and affects represents the transcendent function of opposites. The confrontation of the two positions generates a tension charged with energy and creates a living, third thing . . . a movement out of the suspension between opposites, a living birth that leads to a new level of being, a new situation. (p. 325)

The Image and the Body—Resistance, Anxiety, and Release

Though it hardly does justice to the huge body of knowledge and practice involved in my work with somatic therapies and in particular to the foundations laid by Wilhelm Reich, I wish to make a brief mention of the role of the body in this therapy. Reich's thesis is that there is a functional identity between mind and body, both in health and in sickness (Reich, 1968). With respect to the development of pathology, the conflicts which are insurmountable for the child and which contradict natural functions remain in the self. In the body, they form what Reich calls frozen history, the patterns of chronic tensions in the musculature, vegetative processes, and in the neuronal patterns of the nervous system. In the psyche, these patterns of frozen history form what he calls the character structure, the neurotic adjustment to the conflicts which makes survival possible though at the expense of naturalness. In this regard there is no such thing as a purely somatic condition or a purely psychological one—all experience is always psychosomatic in the generic sense. Hence if you make an adequate contact with the body, or any aspect of the psyche, you touch the whole of the self. This is part of the rationale I employ in locating the images in the body and in utilizing the body in the evocation of the images and in the maintenance of a dialogue between these two states of being.

On another level, the potency of the image/body connection arises due to the dynamics inherent in the conversion process (Mann & Semrad, 1969). We can say there is an existential unity.

> Whatever the case may be, the concept of a psychophysical parallelism must be rejected, for nothing parallel occurs here. The temporal coincidence of psychic and physical manifestations develops from the *identity* [Mann's emphasis] of these processes. (p. 69)

What cannot be maintained by the person is transformed into the frozen patterns of behavior, and the conflicts which dictated this self-denial remain hidden by the resistance formations. When the resistance is threatened or in fact declines, anxiety associated with the original conflicts emerges since the individual has yet to complete the transactions necessary to integrate the thoughts, feelings, and behavior which would accompany uninhibited action. The conversion process assists in the original neurotic adjustments that were made and hinges on the mind/body identity (Deutsch, 1969).

> The body represents to an individual the very reality which he cannot deny because to do so he would have to deny his existence. A new-born child knows only one reality, i.e., his body which he can feel, touch and perceive with his senses. Nothing exists beyond this reality. The child soon discovers that what he once felt as part of himself is temporarily or permanently lost. This first awareness of a loss is the origin of a fantasy because what is no longer in the realm of, or attached to, the body has disappeared and now belongs to another reality, so to speak. The

child reacts to this loss of an object with the attempt to regain it, to retrieve this part of himself, by imagining it. (Deutsch, 1940). Attempts of this nature continue throughout life and can be considered as the origin of the conversion process. (pp. 75–76)

When we transfer the images to specific locales in the body or transform the images into specific memories, or into present psychological behavior, the conversion process is reversed. We uncover what created the original loss and source of the creation of the imagery, and the underlying psychic and somatic factors involved. In brief, we employ the functional identity principle. Though we do not know how it works, it enables the therapist to polarize the conflicts, make them conscious, and through engagement with the waking mind of the client, search for a resolution and integration. The original conversion pattern is nullified. To do this requires taking the images literally as the most precise representations offered to us by the unconscious of those conditions which underlay the formation of the imagery in the first place. The techniques by which this is done would require a great deal of additional space and will be the subject of a forthcoming book on the subject. It is only important to stress that the imagery itself reveals exactly what has occurred, what must be done to create change, and what the implications of that change would be for the future life of the individual.

Role of the Guide.

Naturally, in dealing with such phenomena which are so fundamentally inclusive of the full range of psychic and somatic possibility, the process of working with imagery can be difficult, and even dangerous. In general terms, the role of the therapist/guide is to be as present as possible, to see and to hear and to assist the person in focusing attention. What the guide does not do during this process is to advise, make judgements, or make decisions regarding the nature of the relationship between the individual and his imagery. There is always the danger that the therapist becomes unconsciously involved in the dynamics of the imagery in such a manner that he or she will tend to manipulate the interaction. The technique in essence is only to ask questions which assist in the development of contact between the person and their imagery.

There is never any interpretation of the images and there is no pressure to create a particular relationship except that of awareness. Of especial importance, there is no attempt to "break down" or "break through" the resistances. At every level, the need for and function of the resistances is explored in such a manner that a spontaneous transformation of the energy held in the resistance is freed and available for creative use. The therapist will offer certain safety factors and control the speed and intensity of the participation by the client when this is appropriate. In exceptional cases the therapist may manipulate the imagery connection in a less emotional direction. Here less is more! Thus, although there is more intervention in my method than in that of many others who work with imagery, there is less therapeutic control over the relationship between the client and their contact with the contents of imagery. As with any good healing process, it is as much of an art as a developed skill, and what we might call a poetical psychology guides an imaginative and creative approach toward the phenomena of mental imagery.

A short example of a session, partially abridged serves to highlight the therapist/guide activity.

The man I worked with I shall call Frank. He is about 26 years old, thin, extraordinarily neat and is one of the most intellectual persons in the group. It is a nine-day group and the work commenced on the fifth day on Frank's request after he has avoided involvement up to this time. He has just recounted that as a child he was beaten severely by his father and ever since had cut himself off from people. I initiated the imagery work after pointing out his voice seemed cut off and he mentioned feeling two points of constriction and pain in his throat (F - Frank; T - myself).

T: Lie down, take a few breaths, look in your throat with your mind's eye and tell me what you see.

F: I see a glass wall in the throat and one in the diaphragm.

T: Begin with the throat and describe the glass wall in detail.

F: It's very clean.

T: Be the glass and tell me about yourself.

F: (as glass wall): I'm neat, clean glass and don't let anything out.

T: What is good about that? What might come out if you were not so neat?

F: That I'm not sure about.

(*Comment:* I shall seek more detail about the glass since it is an important principle that what you see in terms of quantity and "story" is not as significant as a full involvement in depth with primary images. Otherwise the person can recite forever, avoid emotive contact, and transfer responsibility to the therapist.)

T: Be the glass, imagine you have eyes, and look below—what do you see?

F: I see mud which has been there for about 20 years.

T: What is good about having this glass wall with the mud below?

F: (as glass): Frank needs me—if I am removed, he will be touched by others and cannot be himself.

T: What do you, Frank say to the glass.

F: I want out, it's so alone here and I'm seeing the world only through the glass wall.

T: Describe the glass again.

(*Comment:* This is important. Although he has this mud and may want it to come out, it has been there for 20 years which represents a great deal of psychic investment. Any changes in the relation between the glass wall, the mud, and the actual history of Frank, and his surface adjustments could be traumatic if the process is overly rapid or if his understanding is insufficient to the issues involved.)

F: The glass is very thin, round in my neck, and I see myself sitting inside,—it's like a tube and underneath are my intestines.

T: Let's inspect the diaphragm glass for a moment.

F: It's also glass, but thicker, round, and goes all around my body, and is also neat and clean. It feels smooth like that in my throat.

T: Now describe the mud in more detail.

F: It is dark, brown, thick, and I can't get a grip on it—it slips through my fingers—as the mud, I tell you I'm slippery without form.

(*Comment:* I have decided to focus on the throat area and the mud rather than the diaphragm. This is because if we open deeper levels of resistance first or too deeply without working closer to the surface, we are too removed from our ability to perceive and integrate the experience. The intention is to release the blocks only to the extent the person can absorb, translate, and express. Then there is a greater possibility of success and reinforcement of a positive kind and a more gradual introduction and preparation for intensive work which would follow in another session. The opening of deep layers prematurely would reinforce the original neurosis and increase the "glass walls.")

T: What stops you normally from being like this mud?

F: My anxiety—people will see me and see I'm nothing.

(*Comment:* Frank must make this polarization—know the glass and know the mud and understand something of the reasons for maintaining what on the surface is an untenable living situation. Otherwise any resolution would simply be an overwhelming experience without intelligibility.)

T: How do you imagine you will feel if there was no glass wall.

F: Relieved and glad to come out.

(*Comment:* During the workshop to this point, members of the group were attacking Frank viciously over his slipperiness, his lack of feelings, his rationalisations, and his inability to be present. Before continuing with the imagery, we did some association work on this without attention to the imagery. Then we returned to the process.)

T: How could you get rid of the glass?

(*Comment:* It is important for the client to solve the problem since the way in which they decide to do this is therapeutic on two counts: it usually demands the resources they compromised on the first place with the onset of the neurosis; they do not transfer responsibility to the therapist.)

F: Pull it out of my mouth from the inside.
T: (What you actually saw as an observer was Frank putting his hands to his mouth *as if* he were taking hold of something and pulling—here participation takes on dramatic and real meaning.)
F: Smothered screams at first, pulsating and erratic breathing, occasional choking and aargh-type sounds increasing in volume.
T: (The pulling, choking, and smothered sounds continue a while.)
F: I can't touch it anymore, it is higher but that's all.
T: Try opening your mouth.
F: (A deep penetrating scream comes out with the "pulling" lasting for at least a minute, followed by a cut-off, followed by deep, full, crying, continuing for many minutes.)
T: How are you feeling right now?
F: I'm more happy than sad and it is as if I'm breathing for the first time in my life.

Certainly there is more work to do, but for this first session and for this man, significant choice and movement occurred which can lead to further possibilities in therapy and life.

SUMMARY

The operative principle of participation is that there is a reason for the particular images which emerge, for their particular location in the body, and for the dialogue which the client creates in contact with the imagery. Even if the reasons for these particularities is not clear at every moment, the method is to trust the imagery as being appropriate to that moment and to establish a useful and authentic relationship. Any subsequent shifts in imagery will still be in accordance with this principle. Underlying this attitude is the belief that there is a holistic logic functioning in the selection and behavior of the images, only part of which can be clear to the client and to the therapist. The image is the integrating point, not the rational and discursive minds of the participants in the drama. Through time and contact with the imagery, the reasons which will explain the events in the imagery and their significance do become clear in both naturalistic and psychological terms.

The attention of the therapist is on the relationship between the client and the imagery, not on the meaning, *per se,* of the specific images. Thus, I am actively engaged in watching for general patterns or response, points of avoidance, incongruent or inappropriate reactions, anxiety reactions, defensive behavior, and above all, for manifestations of the resistance patterns of the client which coincide with their usual behavior.

Since the client is fully present while engaged in this contact with imagery, there is a continuous diagnostic element of disclosure, particularly in the matrix of contact between the conscious and unconscious aspects of the self. The client is existentially speaking, "in a situation" which replicates his behavior in terms of his self-experience and his past and present relationships. Completion is transformation. When we can reconcile the splits, dualities, and apparent frozen polarities revealed by the images, we have healed inner divisions, and we can then speak of authentic change. Transformation comes through reconciliation of the conflicts disclosed by the imagery and when appropriate new behavior occurs as a result.

REFERENCES

Casey, E. S., *Imagining, a phenomenological study,* Bloomington: Indiana University Press, 1976.

Deutsch, F., Ed. *On the mysterious leap from the mind to the body,* New York: International Universities Press, 1959.

Freud, S., *The interpretation of dreams*, Standard Edition, Vol. IV. London: Hogarth Press, 1971.

Jung, C., *Man and his symbols*, New York: Doubleday, 1964.

Koestler, A., *The act of creation*, New York: MacMillan, 1969.

Mann, J., & Semrad, E. In E. Deutsch, Ed., *On the mysterious leap from the mind to the body*, New York: International Universities Press, 1959.

Marcel, G., *Homo viator*, New York: Harper & Row, 1962.

Reich, W., *The function of the orgasm*, London: Panther, 1968.

chapter 6

PSYCHOTHERAPY AS AN ASOCIAL PROCESS

Paul Olsen, Ph.D.

INTRODUCTION

What follows is an exploration into the traditions—particularly the religio-mythical—that have formed and continue heavily to dominate the manner in which psychotherapy is largely conducted in the Western world. By choice, perhaps even by necessity, a certain amount of criticism is leveled at psychoanalytic theory and practice; but the spirit of this criticism has its context in organized, institutional psychoanalysis as a major "holding" force in a field which began in revolution and continues in revolution. In no way is this criticism necessarily directed to individual practitioners, but only to the broad body of thought or philosophy by which, to a greater or lesser degree, we have all been influenced.

Healing, as a term, a concept, a goal, has been long absent from literature dealing with the theories and techniques of psychotherapy, as well as from research that studies therapeutic process and outcome.

A broad aversion to the term undoubtedly emanates from the wary, even suspicious, perception that "healing" is largely the murky ground of religiously toned quacks and tricksters whose mission it is to gull a naive public—which it so often is. Unfortunately, this perception is extended, at least by most mental health professionals, to discount or invalidate any encounter that involves prayer, the "laying on of hands"—in short, any activity that smacks of "faith healing."

For our purposes—that is, in the setting of psychotherapy —healing may be viewed partly as a process that by implication conjures the image of a wound: not a concrete, visible manifestation of illness, but an allusion of the sort suggested by such terms as "narcissistic injury," "ego damage," and so forth, which, it is always profitable to bear in mind, are not existent entities or structures or observable truths, but merely theoretical representations. Again, these terms *have no existence in themselves,*[1] yet, paradoxically, whole systems of psychotherapeutic thought would *seem* to flounder in perilous waters without them. For example, the Freudian psychoanalysts Jacob Arlow and Charles Brenner flatly state that "The structural theory alone is the proper basis for theoretical discussions as well as for psychoanalytic practice at present" (1964, p. 55).

But there are no structures; and thus the construct is perpetually in danger of losing its referent, of pointing to nothing beyond itself, of becoming a locked-in arid *thing*—and consequently being drained of meaning. In short, to maintain that an impulse disorder, for example, emerges from a "damaged" ego is to state nothing at all since the ego is simply a construct. The *idea* of ego can be damaged, but nothing more, because an idea is certainly prone to attack—and that is all that the ego is, an idea.

In our science we have come quaintly to "see" things that do not exist and then to attribute to them explanation and causation. I say "quaintly" because this "seeing" is primitive, a seeing which imports concrete existence to one unobservable, to one construct, while denying the "existence" of another. Primitive is often concrete.

Healing, a concept to which I will refer as a springboard to other ideas and not as a concrete process, has become a psychotherapeutic discard, and I will discuss below what concrete goal has largely replaced it. First, however, aside from avoiding the concept because of its aura of faith-healing and quackery, aversions are easily traceable to theoretical orientations implanted (often like stalks without roots) in the soil of science or humanism—the latter a position partly in rebellion against medical models of diagnosis and treatment. From the broad behavioral point of view healing is nonobjective, hence metaphysical or metapsychological, and so is dismissed as irrelevant; in this camp *all* is concrete, all is behavior, and no idea of any sort would seem to have a place in human existence.

The traditional psychoanalytic posture has been only touched upon, but it is quite obviously a system of beliefs, dogma, rules, prohibitions, whatever, which has concretized its symbols as surely as the Roman Catholic church has transformed its wine into the literal blood of the Savior—and no one who stands outside these systems, patient or penitent, can gain cure or salvation. Ultimately, traditional psychoanalysis and many of its derivatives wage a crusade against differences not unlike the orthodox medieval church—for dogmatic as well as economic reasons—and thus a once titanic exploration of the possibilities for enlightenment and individual freedom has donned the vestments of an organized religion. The parallel I am making between formal psychoanalytic thought and formal religion is a crucial one for this discussion since, as we shall discover, Western psychotherapy and theory are all but ossified in a philosophical-religious tradition which stands now in a state of petrifaction if not outright chaos—all based in the externalization of authority and the placement of *individual* spiritual freedom in the hands of socially approved second parties, whether priest, rabbi, or psychotherapist.

Conversely, healing is an intensely creative, spiritual, even supreme personal experience, the core of which is the discovery of the self often in a condition of complete separation from societal rules and the dependency they foster. Cutting through prejudices and systems, let us examine what is really to be healed in the process of psychotherapy.

Webster's Seventh New Collegiate Dictionary (Third Edition) defines *heal* primarily as "to make sound or whole" and only secondarily as "cure" or "remedy." There is yet a tertiary meaning—"to restore to original purity or integrity"—a most intriguing definition, to which I shall refer several times.

In probing these definitions, we might dispense with the concretization of a literal, visible wound; nor do we need to refer to such concepts as "ego damage" or "mental illness." The importance, even fact, of healing has existed millenia before these terms were in the slightest danger of being invented, then externalized and codified as alleged truths. The metaphor of intrapsychic healing is rooted largely in spiritual definitions of the person, a process necessary when the person experiences himself as unwhole, fragmented, alienated from himself—or necessary when this fragmentation is perceived as resulting from a self lost in the powerful rules and mores of the social order and its arbiters (such people are often seen and branded by the latter as rebels, neurotics, psychotics, misfits, etc.—the common denominator being an unwillingness or inability to adapt to the "truth" of the social order). In short, the problem needful of healing is one of dependency, a synonym for the felt loss or inauthenticity of the self. The sense of alienation from the group is *never* a problem, although through social pressure one may feel it as such—which is another sort of fragmentation. Conversely, the sense of alienation from the self is the quintessential problem and, lacking the knowledge of how to return to one's self because society basically does not approve of such journeys and discoveries, one blindly turns to the group for guidance in hopes of filling an inner emptiness via external means. Among Western thinkers, Kierkegaard recognized this dilemma more than a century ago when he stated in *The Sick-*

ness unto Death: "That self which he [the person] despairingly wills to be is a self which he is not (for to will to be that self which one truly is, is indeed the opposite of despair)" (1849, p. 151). Indeed, the entire superstructure of sin, of the anxiety-provoking "difference" experienced by the patient, rests upon rejection by the reigning authorites, sacred and secular.

It is precisely at this point that psychotherapeutic healing as an asocial process has its crucial meaning: the person must attempt, as closely as possible, to "restore" himself to "original purity or integrity." Or as Suzuki puts it, quoting the Zen dictate of the Chinese monk Hui-Nêng, "Show me your original face before you were born" (1961, pp. 225–226). Not a simple task, yet not unrealistic, nor metaphysical—and remember that we are forced to deal with approximations—if the emphasis of psychotherapy is removed from that which has replaced the personal uniqueness of the healing process. That is, the goal of adjusting the person to his social stratum or peer group, meaning a larger, fixed social system which, like the rock to which Zeus bound Prometheus for the sin of stealing fire, is traditionally set solidly against the individual who wishes to break loose from prescribed functional boundaries. Gravitation away from the group and its rules, the inward journey, threatens the power bases of the social order—in most cases far more potently than organized revolt.

From the social structure we derive such psychiatric-behaviorist terms as "appropriate" and "inappropriate." From the structure we learn to assess an individual's creativity via the acceptance of art galleries and publishing houses—the creativity based upon the marketing by a middleman of a product, the all-important middleman-arbiter, who so often seems to be the cement holding together the bricks of all rigid cultures.[2] Creativity, from this societal position, cannot ever be an individual matter individually expressed. It is the commercial, not the serious, artist who is accepted by the masses; the latter steadfastly refuses to "sell out" by turning his personal vision into the bland, invented, and false mythologies of mass media.

In the field of psychotherapy it is the doctor who is allegedly creative, but not the patient.

A new psychotherapeutic emphasis, then, might well be to extract the process from a social embeddedness and—with a concomitant examination of all definitions of healing—to aid the patient toward a personal, inner reorientation. In sum, to assist the patient in his efforts to slough off the old skin and regenerate, like the serpentine symbol of ageless wisdom, is to help him restore to himself that which he has temporarily lost through his dependent, self-damaging compromise with social conformity. Kierkegaard again, echoing the ancient eastern path to inner enlightenment: "the cure is simply to die, to 'die from'" (1849, p. 143).

Psychotherapy, as we are familiar with it, especially in its "talk" or verbal forms, is conducted partly from an illusion, which is that the patient is significantly helped when he adjusts to, and is apparently accepted by, society as a whole or by approved societal subgroups—professional, religious, political, whatever. But what too frequently happens when a patient is pointed in this direction (by a therapist who is not merely pointed in the same direction, but who is its spokesman and representative) is that the learned, perhaps even primal, guilt attached to the rebellious posture of individual freedom is subsumed and partially alleviated by the immersion in a group ethos. Thus dependency is displaced to the social or peer group in which the person acts *as if* he is independent—but only as if. The point is easily illustrated by examples familiar to all of us, such as the person who cannot leave the battlefield of a destructive marriage because of religious sanctions, the psychoanalyst who is afraid of expressing "deviant" ideas because he will lose referrals and ultimately be drummed out of the establishment—examples ad infinitum and ad nauseum.

As a patient of mine observed, "You go to a party and somebody asks you what you *do.* And if what you do doesn't have money or glamor attached to it, you get a look like 'How the hell can I get away from him?'" The singularly important aspect of this patient's therapy was his decision to be temporarily alone, to detach himself from all social contacts—a course taken as a result of his near death from a heart attack, a self-realization that his past life had been "superficial," "fake," "absurd," and ultimately "disgusting." In Kierkegaard's words, all this he wished to "die from" while in grave danger of *physical* death.

One further risk involved in orienting a person toward societal groupings is that he may eventually discover a vast emptiness beneath the facade of acceptance and dependency gratification which then leads not to a clinical depression but to a state of existential despair in which both patient and therapist become locked—intractably because the therapist will try to treat depression. There is little doubt in my mind that many suicides are committed in the context of this despair: the self, the inner vision, has been sacrificed to the manipulations of society. Conversely, the shamans of Siberia and the shamans of Tierra del Fuego, say: "I left my village and my people, and went into the forest, and there I died. And when I died to it all, only then could I return and be what I am."

What, then, are some clues that allow us better to understand the religious-social—especially the traditionally religious —roots of Western man's enforced turn from the inward healing journey toward an externalization of "truth" and "freedom?" First, consider a creation myth as set down in the Indian *Brhadaranyaka Upanishad,* about 700 B.C.

It is told that the universe was originally the self in the form of a man who found himself exceedingly afraid until he realized that, being alone, there was nothing to fear—this being only one mythic reference to the profundity of the inner realization, a position from which, as we shall now see, the self flows peacefully into a world of its own creation. For, once secure in his aloneness, this man-self, in order to experience beauty and taste of delight, created a woman-self. This woman, however, was not formed from a rib as in our biblical myth; rather, the man-self divided himself in order to produce her, thereby halving his size, the two becoming equal in stature. From this pair, remember that nothing existed before them, neither God nor gardens nor fruits nor serpents, from their union sprung forth all living things, all pairs of animals (Muller, 1962).[3]

The meaning here is quite clear: the self is the source, the *only* source, of creation. Which leads to the proposition that "This earth is honey for all beings, and all beings are honey for this earth" (Prabhavananda Swami, & Manchester, 1971, p. 146).

Compare *this* myth with the creation myth of Judeo-Christian tradition! The differences between them have totally determined the opposed spiritual and cultural paths of Eastern and Western cultures, including even the language surrounding the goals of psychotherapy as a healing process.

As Joseph Campbell points out in *The Masks of God: Oriental Mythology* (1974):

> In the Indian version it is the god himself that divides and becomes not man alone but all creation; so that everything is a manifestation of that single inhabiting divine substance: there is no other; whereas in the bible, God and man, from the beginning, are distinct. Man is made in the image of God, indeed, and the breath of God has been breathed into his nostrils; yet his being, his self, is not that of God, nor is it one with the universe. The fashioning of the world, of the animals, and of Adam (who then became Adam and Eve) was accomplished not within the sphere of divinity but outside of it. There is, consequently, an *intrinsic,* not merely *formal* separation. (pp. 10–11) [author's emphasis]
>
> Furthermore, the fall from the Garden of Eden was an event within the already created frame of time and space, an accident that should not have taken place. The myth of the Self in the form of a man, on the other hand, who looked around and saw nothing but himself, said "I", felt fear, and then desired to be two, tells of an intrinsic, not errant, factor in the manifold of being, the correction or undoing of which would not improve, but dissolve, creation. The Indian point of view is metaphysical, poetical; the biblical, ethical and historical. (p. 11)

And crucially, in India:

> It is not that the divine is every*where:* it is that the divine is every *thing.* So that one does not require any outside reference, revelation, sacrament, or authorized community to return to it. One has but to alter one's psychological orientation and recognize (re-cognize) what is within. Deprived of this recognition, we are removed from our own reality by a cerebral shortsightedness which is called in Sanskrit *māyā,* "delusion" (from the verbal root *mā,* "to measure, measure out, to form, to build, denoting, in the first place, the power of a god or demon to produce illusory effects, to change form, and to appear under deceiving masks; in the second place, "magic," the production of illusions and, in warfare, camouflage, deceptive tactics; and finally, in philosophical discourse, the illusion superimposed upon reality as an effect of ignorance). Instead of the biblical exile from a geographically, historically conceived garden . . . we have in India, therefore, already around 700 B.C. (some 300 years before the putting together of the Pentateuch), a *psychological* reading of the great theme. (pp. 12–13) [author's emphasis]

Thus we have the nub of the historical problem, and it is one precisely of history itself, or rather a misunderstanding or even fabrication of history: that the way of conceptualizing man's interconnected creative, healing, and spiritual processes has been to externalize them. He is, that is to say, "given" talent, this gift being bestowed only upon "special" people. There is, if at all, only the dimmest perception in this position that creativity (a kind of self-healing) is immanent in everyone and needs only to emerge from the individual himself. On the purely spiritual plane, he is "given" grace, perhaps a mission, by one god or another. For example, one learns from the 1894 edition of Butler's *Lives of the Saints* that St. Jerome, who revised the Latin bible, "had studied under the best masters . . . and devoted himself to the pursuit of science. But Christ had need of his strong will and active intellect for the service of His Church" (p. 326). Spirituality here does not generate from within; nor does *personal* creativity, which apparently matters not at all.

The above has the profoundest significance for the practice of traditional psychotherapy and psychoanalysis, both of which focus upon history. The attempt is to embed the person in concrete, sensory time and space, followed by sweeping genetic interpretations that link all *now* to all *then,* so that *all to come* can be coped with, so that the patient can become a willing party to the dubious reality testing of the social rule and trend setters. Dubious because materialistic, and so only a fragment of what is, only a chapter in the story of man's existence, potentiality, and capacity to experience and feel.

Still another example of the failure of Western psychotherapy (always as a reflection of its larger social context) to understand, to *see,* that the individual is the source of all meaning, can be inferred from the construction of many great medieval cathedrals. The main portals face west, whereas God enters the world with light from the east. The bereft sinner, the empty, dark man, enters through that western door and travels up the nave at whose end—the eastern end—reposes the altar. In this setting, and it is both the literal and metaphorical setting of all Western religion and social structure, the light of God, of truth, spirituality, and creativity, shines down through the eastern window upon the priest who mediates between God and man, and whose very act of mediation emphasizes their separation. Only the priest is qualified to impart the light to a congregation assumed to be without intrinsic virtue—the welding of a group structure outside of which the person as person is at worst damned, at best a cipher. Alban Butler again: "Remember that you are nothing" (1894, p. 228). A culture of the hollow man.

In Judaism, aside from the mystics and the Kabbalists, it is excruciatingly difficult to see how the *individual* gains any sort of spiritual contact other than by way of a concrete connection with the traditional group. Furthermore, it is one of the very few religious configurations in which a deviant from the group may be ceremoniously pronounced dead. The externalized, withholding, paternalistic god has provided neither redeemer nor salvation, and his chosen people have been slaughtered across the four corners of the earth—and it all begins to appear like a sadistic cosmic joke.

But how different is the Eastern *esoteric* idea, the asocial idea,[4] rooted in the divinity of the self.

There the portals of the temple face east. There god enters *with* the individual because the individual is divine, in fact is god. He is in no sense the fallen man whom "the lord God sent . . . forth from the garden of Eden," who, to bar his individual path everlastingly, the lord God "placed at the east of the garden of Eden cherubim, and a flaming sword which turned every way, to keep the way of the tree of life." (Genesis 3: 23–24, *King James version.*)

And there it is. In our culture, to obtain life, inner fulfillment, spirit—in short any state other than the suffering, transient pleasures, or emptiness of the concrete world—one needs the mediations, intercessions, and interpretations of a middleman whether priest, rabbi, or psychotherapist. We confront the flaming angel with a bodyguard. And the bodyguard generally carries the tablets of some delusional codified theory that has been validated as "reality" by its own adherents. Life, then, has become even more sorrowful than the Buddha would have it; and nothing on earth is redolent of the honey that permeates the Upanishads like some rare incense.

It is significant to the point of heartbreak that in our tradition, until only recently, has a major Gnostic gospel been "lost"—which often means simultaneously suppressed by the reigning order and hidden away by a circumspect renegade. Compare the Indian honey with the following words attributed to Jesus from the gospel of St. Thomas. When asked by his disciples when the kingdom of God will become manifest, Jesus said (Guillaumont *et al.,* 1959):

> It will not come by expectation; they will not say: "See, here", or: "See, there". But the Kingdom of the Father is spread upon the earth and men do not see it. . . . [and] the Kingdom is within you and is without you. (pp. 3, 56, 57)

Now what I am emphasizing here is that we, as the psychotherapists that our personalities allow us to be, unconsciously and at times consciously conduct our work from the baseline created by the social suppression of real individuality and independence, and an incredible enigma emerges. On one hand this tradition has produced the person and patient who laments: "I'm empty"; "I can't do it"; "You don't do anything for me"; and the classic externalization and concretization, "I'm not *getting* anything out of *the therapy.*" The way of life on the other side of this coin appears to be built upon the intactness of defenses such as reaction-formation and raw aggression transformed into competition. But on the rim we meet the person/patient who soars beyond the norms, beyond the rules, who breaks loose from societal boundaries—and we wonder if this person is sociopathic or is acting out, the latter being a therapeutic taboo apparently of greater import than patricide. Such soaring must be placed back into the mind where it can be alchemized into thought and do no harm—for to the majority of Western therapists the mind of thought is the only safe place in all of existence.

Therefore correct thoughts are necessary and the therapeutic goal is to place the patient somewhere between the dependency of the "I can't do it" and the awesomeness of the titanic breaking loose. And that "between" has always been in the mundane center where there are available only the sensual pleasures, thought processes, and a coping style validated by acceptable social groupings. Looking at this from a different angle: based upon our emphasis on the bereft sinner and not on the god within, Western psychotherapy is concerned with what the person socially is *not* and rarely with what the person individually *is* and can *be.* Because close to the entire thrust of the duality of Western thought and philosophy (the separation in the garden of Eden) has been the search for a way to find a relationship of man to God. But since spirituality has been largely abandoned by psychotherapists, mistaking it, as Freud did, for religion, the thrust of therapeutic thought is in finding a relationship of the patient to society—the orientation to a secular deity.

In the traditions where spirituality—always meaning self-revelation, creativity, healing—is a given, where it is acknowledged as a way and its pursuit a vital part of existence, there are the gurus and the masters. There are good ones and bad ones and strange ones, but they do not, any of them, work from personality theory or theoretical constructs. They point. They indicate a direction, and unless they are religious fanatics or frauds, they do nothing else; except, perhaps, to suggest to the pupil that he is looking at the pointing finger instead of the direction pointed to—the direction always being inward. Almost universally, this is what the Western patient does: looks at the finger.

The East is, of course, no panacea—and such concepts of unchanging social-religious order as the Indian *dharma* and Chinese *tao* are hideous in their inflexible view of man's circumscribed worldly place and their condemnation of individual action. But the best of what the East offers us—and that is the light within which grows brighter—can be of incalculable help in unlocking our own spiritual tradition of healing and inner vision. In this inner sense we have more in common with the East than we think—or at least the potentiality for it—and in this inner sense there may really be no difference at all. What I mean here has been well illustrated by Joseph Campbell's story of an interdisciplinary conference of religious scholars and "mystics." As the conference wore on, those from both East and West, who customarily meditated and focused upon the inner life, were entirely amicable, connected, and understanding. Squabbling, anger, and heated debate went on exclusively among the scholars who were espousing their intellectual but not experienced "truths."[5]

So I am stressing that, in essence, healing is a creative, spiritual process—and that the healing of psychotherapy, if it is to take place, is also a spiritual process. Again I underline the equation of healing-spirituality-creativity, and this experience cannot happen if therapeutic goals are motivated by attention to group and social validations—validations which continue to go unquestioned and which anyway can only be at best partial truths inherent in but one plane of reality, a plane of pure materialism. To the contrary, the creative act, the self-healing act, is *always* an independent one, an inner one. The creative process always stands apart from social rules and restrictions. It transcends. With its own force and vision it leaps over and soars above the limited materialistic world.

Thus, there is the difference between the creative artist and the commercial hack; between the healer and the social orientor; between psychotherapy and cosmetic psychosurgery; between freedom and materialism.

What has come clear to me after many years of psychotherapy, supervision, case conferences, interchanges with colleagues, books and papers read, is always the doctor's implicit and often explicit goal of the patient–therapist encounter—that is, to terminate the patient when he or she arrives at the ability to cope with the so-called stresses and problems of the outer environment. Which to me is a higher-order position of externalization and which is utterly unconcerned with a personal, fluid connection with inner reality. This is for me a position of "adjusted paranoia" based upon expectations of external stress countered by the ability to cope with it intellectually, the latter allowed to be accompanied by a mild *outward* expression of emotion, and to exist side-by-side with some ability to pursue material pleasure—a posture quite natural to the psychotherapist who views the concrete world as the only reality. But in this procedure nothing is healed, no creative activity is involved; it is, really, a position of mentally informed reaction. A prime component of such a position is the therapeutic ideal of getting the patient to "make choices."

In contradiction to this idea—and for my closure on the following I am in perpetual gratitude to my colleague, Deborah Rinzler[6]—I maintain that the therapeutic goal of "choices" (a respectable derivative of "free will") is an illusory one because the necessity to make choices indicates, even proves, the continued presence of inner conflict—the presence being masked by what appears to be free will, i.e., "choice." However, it is precisely when there is no choice whatever that the patient has successfully terminated therapy, when the person is creatively and spiritually healed. It is the point at which the concept of "right action" transcends its social meaning (*dharma, tao,* the Ten Commandments) and becomes reflexive, a full human movement without conflict and its resultant thinking. Let me illustrate this point with a stark example, relatively free of the subtlety of less dramatic events.

Toward the conclusion of World War II, when Germany stood on the edge of defeat, guards in many of the concentration camps were being released for combat duty, their roles offered to a number of the inmates who were to be supervised by small SS cadres. The proposition was put in typically Nazi fashion: either the chosen inmates were to beat and torture their fellows or they themselves suffer the beatings. Some willingly took the truncheons, some felt the urgency to think, to make a choice, while a tiny few reflexively refused. It was the people in this last group who illustrate the point: without thought, with no "choice," they simply refused. This right action, this profound connection with all humanity even in the grimmest of all material hells, is a sign of the healed person. It is a sign of the person who has contacted the truth of his inner self, the self that connects with all others. On a far less tragic level, such types of personal action are signs of the healed patient who rises above the majority of his peers who are fearfully locked into the imperatives of the social code.

Since my example is redolent of the presence and threat of death, I will draw to a conclusion by referring, in a highly condensed form, to the experience of one of my patients who contacted a particular inner reality through a Waking Dream (Epstein, 1978). She encountered death: first in the person of a frightening black, "jagged" monster, then simply as a man. She described

> . . . just a person. He's just a person, sad. I ask him why he takes
> people away and he says it's his job, he has to—and he doesn't

even know where he takes them. I'm walking with him now, down the block, hand in hand, and I ask him why he takes babies and young people, why not just old people. I tell him: "There are a lot of old people who *want* to die." He says, "I have no choice, and I don't want to be cruel or to hurt people. I have to hurt them if they struggle against me. It's just the way it is." I ask him when he'll come for me; he says he doesn't know. And I ask him to be gentle with me when he does come.

This is the power of an inner experience, an inner reality which begins to inform existence in the concrete, material world. It is a reflection of the creative, healing, spiritual, asocial process found in the Upanishadic myth of creation. It is the inner self which no longer shatters into projected fragments, instead becoming whole again, taking the fragments and welding them into soundness and harmony. And with that we might create and heal ourselves from the sources of the universe within ourselves, from the universe that *is* ourselves.

Notes

1. There is a continuing need to emphasize this point since even in the most sophisticated literature and discussion we still hear references to "the ego," "the unconscious," etc., *as if* these metaphors actually exist. By continued usage these terms become concretized in much the way that a pious Roman Catholic believes that altar wine literally transforms to the blood of Christ and is not merely a symbolic representation. And so it goes with "introject," "id," "superego," and all the rest of it.

2. As a brief diversion, consider the following question with complete openness: If this paper were given in an informal gathering (or presented in typescript), without the possibility or purpose of publication, would you receive it as seriously as you are doing now by reading it in a published, hence acceptable, volume?

3. *Editor's note:* Please note that Dr. Olsen chose to use a standard Western translation of the Upanishad which although inaccurate, stands as the accepted Western scholarship of this ancient Vedic text. For example, in the Indian tradition the self could never be in the form of a man, nor would the self ever create anything, woman or otherwise.

4. Eastern social structures, although frequently oppressive and codified to the point of collective insanity, only rarely deny the intrinsic light within. Thus my use of "esoteric" and "asocial"—the levels beneath the social facade.

5. Open Eye Seminars, New York City, November, 1976.

6. Personal communication.

REFERENCES

Arlow, J. A., & Brenner, C. *Psychoanalytic concepts and the structural theory.* New York: International Universities Press, 1964.

Butler, A. *Lives of the saints.* New York: Benziger Bros., 1894.

Campbell, J. *The masks of god: Oriental mythology.* New York: Viking (Compass edition), 1974.

Guillaumont, A., Puech, H.-Ch., Quispel, G., Till, W., & Tassah 'Abd al Masih, Eds. and transs. *The gospel according to Thomas.* New York: Harper and Row, 1959.

Epstein, G. The experience of Waking Dream in psychotherapy. In J. L. Fosshage and P. Olsen, Eds., *Healing, implications for psychotherapy.* New York: Human Sciences Press, 1978.

Kierkegaard, S. (1849). *The sickness unto death.* In *Fear and trembling and the sickness unto death.* Garden City, N.Y.: Doubleday Anchor Books, 1954.

Muller, F. M. (Trans.) *The Upanishads.* Part II. New York: Dover Publications, 1962.

Prabhavananda, Swami, & Manchester, F., Eds. *The Upanishads.* Hollywood, Cal.: Vedanta Press, 1971.

Suzuki, D. T. *Essays in Zen Buddhism* (First series). New York: Grove Press, 1961.

chapter 7

NON-DETERMINISTIC SUPERVISION

Diane Shainberg

I have supervised both psychologists and social workers during their clinical training in psychoanalytic psychotherapy as well as more experienced therapists. In these supervisions I have noted certain recurring difficulties which I would like to discuss along with some ways that non-deterministic supervision has helped the therapists move closer to resolution of these treatment issues.

Early in supervision, the supervisee characteristically feels more tense with "the patient" than with other people in his life. He is scared simply to be with and experience the other person in the room without thinking about interpretations, meanings, theory, conclusions, images of how things should go, or what to do. When uncertainty occurs because there is no known direction or model for the interaction, the therapist often feels anxious. He is anxious merely observing the patient.

Supervisees often say, "I don't understand what is going on," or "I don't know what the patient is saying," or "I don't know what to do." The assumption behind these remarks is that it is possible to know accurately what is going on or that there is a knowable "it" and that therapy is a process of understanding what is in the head of the patient rather than one of interactional participation. There is an illusion that once one knows what "it" means, then some form of *doing* the technique can be practiced on the patient who will then be *helped*. Trainees initially experience patients as radically different from themselves: the patients know nothing and are to be worked on by the supervisee who knows or should know everything, because therapy consists of a prescribed technique.

The work of the supervisor is to show that the work is ongoing, that there is no "way," that one never knows for sure the experience of the other, and that it is in the mutual participation of discovering the essential quality of the patient that the healing takes place. It is this new event of mutuality, of ways of seing and being together that create a new sense of inner strength in both participants.

Along with the common fear that one is not doing therapy the right way there is an ignorance about the possibility of learning from the patient and finding out for oneself. The patient has difficulty believing he can affect his own fate, that he can find out from within himself; the therapist who works within the cause-and-effect psychoanalytic paradigm encounters a similar difficulty. Human relationships are so complex that one can never completely understand what is taking place, and therefore total resolution is impossible.

A second supervisory observation is that therapists work during and after sessions to match theory to patient, past experience to present. To apply theory and interpretation implies the wish to change or fix. They do not understand that true knowing is being able to observe and describe what is going on in the present in accurate, concrete, and complete detail. This is different from wanting to change or get rid of or compare or assume a fixed meaning about what is happening.

We do not change or fix, but over time get to know the patient as he actually is, and lives. In this way we facilitate his getting to know himself more clearly, at which time he feels increasingly ready to change.

It is the task of the supervisor to enable the supervisee to become more aware of what actually takes place in the session, behaviors, experiences, and transformations of himself and the patient. It has been my experience as a supervisor that many therapists drown their empathy or appreciation of the patient's stuggle by worrying that they are not doing enough for the patient, or that they are doing the wrong things. This worry sometimes evolves into virtual autotherapy, because of the therapists' constant evaluation of their own work.

Following are several clinical examples of how supervision has enabled the therapists to loosen their deterministic view of the patient as someone different who must be treated with interpretations in order to be healed.

After ten interviews, the trainee stated that there was "no relationship" with the patient. He saw this man requesting medication because he felt hopeless about his job and his future. The therapist felt he could not reach the patient and was angry that the patient was unresponsive to his efforts to connect his depression to the death of his father seven years earlier. The therapist felt the patient's hopelessness was "irrational" since he was young and intelligent and only "saw the dark side of everything.' This is an excerpt from the 10th session:

> Therapist: (after a few moments silence) What's going on?
> Patient: (staring at floor) Nothing.
> Therapist: How are you feeling?
> Patient: Okay. (shrugs)
> Therapist: What are you saying with that shrug?
> Patient: What?
> Therapist: Your shrug?
> Patient: Uh. . . .
> Therapist: Are you aware you shrugged?
> Patient: No. . . .
> Therapist: You shrugged your shoulders. What could you be trying to say?
> Patient: (smiling) I didn't know I shrugged.

Therapist: Well, to me it indicates you're leaving it to me to get things going here. Is this how you feel, you'd like to leave it up to me to start things.

Patient: What?

Therapist: Your shrug says you're leaving the session up to me to get going. Is that how it feels?

Patient: I don't feel anything.

Therapist: Did your last therapist start sessions usually? Is that your experience?

Patient: I don't remember. (squinting, a common facial gesture)

Therapist: Did you feel pretty free to talk to her?

Patient: She was nice.

Therapist: You felt you could speak to her comfortably.

Patient: It's hard to remember.

Therapist: It must have been tough for you with her going.

Patient: (no response)

Therapist: What did you feel when your therapist left?

Patient: Nothing.

Therapist: How come?

Patient: I don't know.

Therapist: What is it you don't know?

Patient: What?

Therapist: You started holding your head in your hands when we started talking about Dr. X. Is there maybe a connection between your gesture and Dr. X's stopping her work at the Clinic?

Patient: (silence) I'm very tired.

Therapist: How did you feel when Dr. X. left the Clinic?

Patient: I don't know, it's fuzzy. . .

Therapist: Fuzzy? What do you think you felt when Dr. X left?

Patient: Nothing. . .

Therapist: You say you felt nothing when Dr. X. left?

Patient: Yes.

Therapist: That's hard to understand. You saw Dr. X. a year. You told me she was nice. Then she left and you felt nothing. Could you give me some idea of how come that might be?

Patient: I don't know. . .

Therapist: Perhaps Dr. X.'s leaving reminded you of losing someone else you cared about, your father?

Patient: (silence)

Therapist: Is that possible?

Patient: I don't know.

Therapist: What did you feel when your father died?
Patient: Nothing. He was sick a long time.
Therapist: How long was he sick?
Patient: Since I was 5.
Therapist: How did you feel with his being sick so long?
Patient: I accepted it.
Therapist: Did you ever wish he could have played with you, ball or whatever, like other guys' fathers?
Patient: I never thought of it.
Therapist: Maybe you felt helpless to do anything about your father's being sick and this helplessness is still a feeling you have about your life.
Patient: (silence)
Therapist: Do you have any feelings about what I just said?
Patient: No.
Therapist: Do you feel helpless starting sessions?
Patient: I feel tired. I think the medicine is making me worse. I would like to get the medicine changed.
Therapist: Do you feel helpless about getting the medicine changed?
Patient: What? . . . No, I thought you arranged the medication conference. I would like a new medicine. I feel worn out all the time and at work I can't keep awake.

This therapist clearly had a fixed notion of how therapy was to go, what the patient was saying. However, he had no idea as to who his actual patient was and little interest to find out. My work with this therapist first was to focus on the fact that he had a relationship with his patient, an intense relationship illustrated in his feeling angry and frustrated with the man while in the session. This is the antithesis of "no relationship." I focused on how he felt while with this man and although he could say frustrated or angry, he could not go much further. I suggested he observe himself in the next session and focus on his feelings being with this person and to forget helping him for one week as he could not help until he knew more what was going on in his patient that he did not yet know. It was clear to me that this therapist had theoretical ideas that he saw as existing in this man's head, but could not find a way to facilitate the patient's opening up to him.

The therapist came in the next week and reported a "scary" thing that had happened to him in the session observing himself; he could not stop himself from talking, he could not bear silence. I suggested he had trouble being with this man as it might bring out certain feelings in himself, but suggested he again focus the next session on observing his feelings being with this man.

In the next supervisory hour, he reported a desire to change patients to someone who could work more productively. He had *images* of what kind of patient he wanted. I said I was interested in his work with the person he actually had. I asked what he had felt in the session. He said that he had observed himself feeling "no feelings, a numbing." He said he was surprised at how deadened to his patient he could be; he blamed himself and the patient. I asked what else he could say of the deadening experience and he said he had in the session "lost interest, wanted to close his eyes, and was aching with numbness." I stated that now he had *some feel* for what the patient was living through, how painful this state was, and how his thoughts, theories, knowledge, and explanations had functioned so far to pull him out of this pain, away from what was happening inside his patient. I then suggested in the next session he *give his total awareness to listening and attending to what he saw* and then we would go into it.

Following the 12th session, the trainee came in and for the first time ever was silent with me. I was also silent a while. I asked him what he had actually seen, and he began softly saying that he found it impossible to put into words what had happened in the session. I asked what he had seen and he said with much feeling, "His hands." Then he was silent. We did not have to go further into this with words. A form of contact had taken place where the division between therapist and patient had momentarily lapsed, where there were two people who could now perhaps begin to be with one another in uncertainty beyond theory, labels, images, and conclusions. This therapist could now begin to see what is between himself and his patient, not what he thought therapy should be. He could begin to be aware of his own thoughts and feelings that create the environment of the work. He could now begin to get to know who the patient actually was, letting him be more, giving him the space to heal. The therapist told me he felt an impact from this experience and he connected it with feeling interested in learning who his patient was. He wanted for the first time to find out who his patient was in fact. With this attitude, I felt, he could be in such a way that the patient would begin to share his thoughts and feelings with him.

The supervisee was a graduate student in clinical training, having worked two years with patients before beginning supervision with me. She was assigned a female patient from the day program of the Clinic. The patient had one brief hospitalization and one of the supervisee's first questions was whether this girl would be "a treatment candidate for analytic work."

She described the therapy as "not working" and said, "I can't seem to make contact." She described asking many questions after which the patient would reply, look down, and remain quiet. "Why is she coming to see me?" she asked me with a touch of impatience. The supervisee felt "unbearable tension" to the point where she asked the patient after the first two sessions, "Would you like to talk about anything else?" and when the patient said "No," she ended the sessions 20 and 30 minutes early.

In telling me this, the supervisee spoke of feeling "terrible" and "ashamed." She was blushing, said that she could not think of any more questions to ask, could not stand to sit in the "frozen silence." I asked her what her thoughts were during those two sessions and she said, "They were racing, trying to find questions to ask." I asked what she was aware of in the session in the form of thoughts. As she told me what she was thinking, it was clear that she could not match her real patient with her image of "patient." She was making conclusions alternately being angry with herself, calling herself "incompetent," or labeling the patient "untreatable." She thought about asking to have the patient reassigned, then thought that maybe she would have other untalkative patients like this in her practice so she better "stick it out." She thought that in fact there was no point in her staying in the room since she did not have "the technique" yet to work with this patient, and this, she eagerly stated, she "had to get" from me.

I asked the therapist after she described her thoughts how she would feel having a conversation with this patient. She became visibly angry, held herself in check, said that she did not see therapy as "conversation," that she would not be able to "do this." "What?" I asked. "Have a conversation with her." I asked her what would be the difference between having a conversation and a therapy session. She was getting more angry and said, "Come on. If this girl were someone I knew, I could easily talk to her . . . I can talk to just about anybody. *But she is a patient.*" I asked for the difference between patient and person. We got into a discussion of how, out of her anxiety largely created by her image of what a therapist does, she hung onto learned dualistic notions of how therapist and patient talk to each other, rather than being open to finding out how in fact one could actually talk with this particular and unique patient she was seeing. The issue was to be in an inner state of mind to find a way—to want to find out how to be with this patient so that the patient would begin to talk, not to have preconceived notions.

She then said that she did not experience the patient in the same way as she would "a fellow human being." She could not feel other than that the patient was "so far a test of my being a therapist." I said she had turned the patient into an object "to be worked on" at this point. She said she felt the gist of it was that "if *it* is a person you can feel free, but if *it* is a patient you have to do something to change things. Otherwise what are you doing there?" I did not comment on her use of the word "it" but heard it as how remote she experienced the patient at this point from herself, as though the patient were not her fellow man sharing the human condition of suffering, biological structure, daily conflict, having mothers and fathers, being in fear, the inevitability of death. She did not remotely feel that she and her patient shared the same life struggles.

I asked her to tell me of her actual experiences as soon as the patient entered the room, to get an image of this event. She spontaneously closed her eyes and described a tightness in her chest, a slight dullness in her head, she remembered opening her eyes wide in order to stay awake, a flash of fear when she thought that she would have to be with this patient for 50 minutes, an increasingly dulled feeling as time went on, her mind going blank, a wish to get out of the room, then thoughts flooding such as "maybe I can't do this work. I don't know what to do." She said she wanted to "have a good hour," that when she had such an hour she felt "full of energy, almost elated."

I asked her if she felt she was looking for pleasure with this patient. "Sure," she said, immediately. "Then when you don't get it, what?" She said that she felt—she never thought of it that way, but that if she did not get some pleasure, she felt things were not right with her work, which she did not want to feel. I asked if she felt perhaps she was dependent on pleasure in her work that perhaps patients could not give her. She said that one's work is supposed to be pleasurable, or to bring satisfaction. I asked, "Are you interested in the actuality of the work? Do you want to see what it is in fact? You want your patient to give you pleasure or to help you feel okay, but this can't always be." The supervisee was upset and talked of the patient's "manipulating her," saying that she felt this patient could talk if she wanted. She said that if a person is not motivated to come, why spend your time with them. "Let someone else do that kind of work," she said angrily. "I don't want to waste my time."

I suggested that we temporarily discard notions of how therapy was supposed to go, and observe with attention how this therapy was going in fact now with the two people in it. I suggested this therapy be seen as a new beginning, never described before, and to participate in whatever came up as a new event for both parties. Since her book knowledge and theory had not been so helpful thus far, I suggested we leave it temporarily and focus attention on attending to what is taking place in the session. I told the supervisee, "Focus all your attention on seeing as clearly as you can the way this person behaves and what you think and feel being with her. Do not try to find meanings, make connections, or understand. Observe what takes place and your responses."

In the next supervisory hour the supervisee was less tense. She began saying she was interested to realize that to observe was hard for her, although it had always sounded easy. She was aware that a lot of time she was wanting to fit the reading she had done on the schizoid person into what she was seeing in front of her, and this made it difficult for her to see the person as is. She said during the particular session she felt relief. "I realized I could see whatever I could see, that it was my own eyes seeing." She laughed, and I said, "You could be in the session with your own eyes."

This led her into an association of how I did not criticize her when she told me that she could only stay with the patient for 30 minutes in two sessions. She remembered my saying, "You can only be who you are at this time," and felt that thought relieving. She said, "I couldn't believe we didn't analyze that, but even so I could stay longer next time." I said, "I let you be as you have let yourself be in the last session." She said, "I never thought of letting the patient be."

In the next session she talked about how she had seen how frightened she was to see, to look, but she said that one thing she had been able to see was the way her patient looked up at her occasionally as if to say, "Will you go away?" I asked for her response to what she saw, and she said that she guessed the patient was aware she ended the sessions early, that maybe the patient wanted to feel that she could stand being with her and was afraid she could not. I said she had gotten a great deal out of the look.

Again I asked the supervisee to spend the next session attending to observing what was taking place and then we would discuss it. Having a focus in the session undercut her need to do, to figure out, but it also enabled her to begin to feel something during the session for the patient for the first time.

She came in the next supervisory hour and reported that what she had *seen* was that her patient "gave her fear." She talked of "feeling the fear." "It is contagious. It is not only coming from me." This was the first time in eight sessions that there had been any mention of the word "feeling" while with the patient. I appreciated this, seeing the fear as a change in her capacity to be present as a participating person during the session and I told her this. My face must have mirrored my appreciation of this change in her as she smiled warmly.

We then talked of the "power" this patient had over her as she experienced it. We found that the patient could in her eyes validate or invalidate her belief in herself as a helpful person, a good person, a separate person. She said that it seemed right now that the central fact inside herself with this patient was "I am afraid." I asked her to watch what happened with her fear as she did not avoid it. She slowly said, "I don't think I've ever been able to look at how scared I am. I'm scared to just be in the room with another person and not know what's going to happen. Why should this be? Even in my own analysis I can't face how scared I am of people. My patient is also scared." This was her first noting of her patient being similar to her: a fellow being.

The schism between patient and therapist, between therapist and person was beginning to lessen. This schism had created internal pressure such that no empathy was experienced by the therapist and wanting to find out was reduced to psychodynamic formulations or conditioned images of how therapy works. In the next session the supervisee reported, "I see her talking, wanting to, then cutting this off. Her eyes get afraid and she backs off." The therapist, through listening and attentive observation, was beginning for the first time to see movement in the session. She was seeing the shift in the patient from being open to talking, to being anxious, to closing down in her particular way; withdrawal, moving out of relating. This flow during the sessions we would discuss later on. For now, I asked how she had seen that the patient wanted to talk. She spoke of an expression in the patient's eyes, which she saw as "wanting to say something but feeling afraid." I asked, "What expression?" She said the word that came to her was "intelligence." She then said this was the first time she had felt the patient was intelligent. She had also seen how messy, "disgusting," the patient was in her dress. She described the patient's blouse not meeting her pants, the flesh "hung out," and this upset her, as did the way the patient's hair was dyed in such a way that it was "dyed looking." I asked her how she felt with these facts of who her patient was, and she said she was angry. She then went into an intellectual discussion of how important it was to look "good" in this society.

I said that what we had just seen in supervision paralleled what went on in the treatment, where now the therapist was responding as the patient did during the session. The patient had come in, showed the therapist her openness, her eyes were intelligent, the patient was separate with the therapist, open to being in the moment with her. The therapist was also open to participating. Then the patient had gotten anxious and cut this relating, being present together, off, just as the supervisee had now with me through getting intellectual. We spoke of this process as a mutual closing off the anxiety of openness in both participants in the therapy.

Then I asked the supervisee how this transformation of an intelligent person in the room with another intelligent person had occurred out of the frozen terrain we had begun with in supervision, where the patient and therapist were unable to be in each other's presence for the full session. It was clear to me from the way she answered with a casual, "I'm not sure, maybe being able to see her fear, my own"—that the supervisee did not grasp the depth of this transformation where two strangers frozen in distant terror are beginning to want to talk together. I spoke of this transformation and the depth of it—I stated that the first phase of the work is getting comfortable being with the patient.

In this supervisory hour, one of the most common teaching focuses came up, the therapeutic relationship. Although we use this word glibly, few beginning therapists appreciate how meaningful this relationship is in the lives of their patients. Although they talk about it, they do not see the being together as a centrally important fact of the treatment, as are the moments when the patient and therapist are together engaged mutually in sharing in the moment, beyond words, time, roles. These are the times where trust is developed, where there is a gettting acquainted with a sense of being who you are, letting the other be, when the patient learns he can be with another person and be respected for who he is, as is. They are the times that give us hope, hope that we can find new possibilities in life. Their occurrence is pointed out to the supervisee as they come up in sessions described.

The first focus in supervision has been the supervisee listening and observing *what is*. The second focus is to enable the supervisee to live in what is, not avoid it, to *let be what is*. We explore what blocks his being able to let the patient be as he is.

This patient is called a "slop." This is her particular form. The supervisee wants to call this "bad," as it keeps other people away. So the therapist is inwardly wanting her patient to be a different way than she is, and feels an inward pressure for this. She wants to remove the "sloppiness" and leave the person, but the person *is* sloppiness. She cannot let her patient be and be comfortable which supervision clarifies, as the patient can only be who he is at a particular moment in time. With liking or disliking, there is pressure on the patient to be different. This pressure creates a strain in that the patient must react to this pressure rather than have the freedom in the work to exist in the relationship with the therapist as is and then to discover in this freedom his own way to be, not to have it imposed. The supervisee must first *see* the strain she puts on the patient, how she contributes to it with her own likes and dislikes, her own values. This second area of supervisory work is for the supervisee to discover where she actually is with the patient *as is*.

Attention to accepting or not accepting the patient as is led us to discuss next the pressures this particular patient had had in life prior to the values the therapist laid on her. The supervisee gave me some history of the patient. At the age of six she had been sent to a children's institution and separated from her only sibling, an older brother. Her mother was ill at the time, but the patient was not told that her mother was dying of cancer. Her father came to see her every other week, at which time the patient remembers asking about her mother. Her father lied to her, told her her mother was getting better, that her brother had gone to live with an aunt who could not take the patient as there was no room for her there. It was only after her mother's death that her father told her that her mother had been sick all this time. The patient then pleaded to live with her father. He promised her, but it was 5 months later that she was actually taken to the same aunt's house. She could not understand why her father had not taken her sooner, why he lied, why her brother was taken. The patient became sick in the institution, was placed in the infirmary, and it was at this point that the father came and took her out.

At this point in the history and 5 months into supervision, the supervisee stopped. Her face turned red and she said, "Oh ... God ..." She said, "I can't believe it ... I completely blocked it out." There was silence. Then, "When I was 11 my mother and father split ... my mother said goodbye to me and my sister. My mother went off to Europe. I was scared she wouldn't come back. My sister and I were sent to a school with nuns where we lived for almost a year. It was horrible. My father didn't come to visit so often. I come from a big family.

My father would come, and I would beg him to take me home, and he would say he couldn't take care of all of us. I didn't hear from my mother for a long time. Then I got sick . . . they took me to the infirmary and I had a fever and then soon after, my mother came back and I went to live with her . . . I can't believe I blocked this out when I heard it from Julie. I totally forgot. [long pause] I've always thought I was too sick to be a therapist. This has really plagued me." There was silence and some tears.

I asked the supervisee what she heard herself saying. She answered in a way that is meaningful for all therapists. She said, "At the beginning, I was scared, and I knew it. But I didn't know, or wouldn't let myself know, how much I felt the same as the patient, because that meant that I wouldn't be able to help. So I felt the patient way way out there, like a piece of equipment to be fixed and I had to find the right parts. You can't imagine how far away. I didn't feel the patient at all really. I heard the words, and was worried trying to figure out what to do to help. It's hard to admit to myself that I don't still feel much. You said it's okay to be scared . . . I just thought . . . well I'll tell you, maybe you've been very scared too. It's so strange to see all this as human, that my supervisor is human, to say 'you've been scared,' or to feel it—very hard. I'm still having trouble letting in how we're all human. God, it's so big." There was no need to talk about it. We could finally *be it.* We shared this simply being human together as this supervisee would now be able to in her work with patients in years to come.

This supervisee feels she is creating therapy with her patients out of the unique nature of their interaction. She has learned to discriminate when she and the patient are open, when there is anxiety, the forms her anxiety takes in both of them. She sees how she actually lives in the presence of the patient, how she is affected by his pattern of interacting. She can discuss these patterns as they come up in the treatment between them when the timing is right or as they emerge in the patient's life. She can make some discriminations regarding tolerance for anxiety. She learns how to let her patients be without her demands—giving the patient the emotional space to find out too how he is authentically. Images from the past have been loosened so that what is going on in actuality is observed more clearly. The supervisee is more engaged in relating without so many thoughts of theory, what to do, how she is not doing the right thing, clogging up her emotional availability. She has experienced some moments with her patient and supervisor in which people were human without self-consciousness. She has been empathic and that is a touchstone for further work. She gained the strength from the supervisory relationship to drop the images of how therapy should be a bit and to live with the unknown. She became interested to find out the facts of who the patient is, how she behaves with her and others. She became interested to learn the facts of this patient's thoughts, feelings, images, sensations, wants. The therapist learns she does not know at times. She learns if she is interested to find out or not. She learns that the work of therapy is moment-to-moment awareness of what is actually taking place. It is not knowing in advance. Once open to finding out, the therapist grows stronger in the process of being with another, openly living in the present, as does the patient.

One supervisee, after hearing her patient talk of some behavior with a roommate, observed the viciousness in the patient. She then *saw* the patient as the patient attacked her for being incompetent. The supervisee was surprised to feel, "This person is mean." She felt this was not right for her to think of her patient this way. However she could now feel what it actually is to be in relationship with this patient, whom she had actually observed being mean and vicious. It was only when she could observe the meanness in the patient that she could finally understand why this woman talked bitterly of people dropping her. Hearing *about* it did not bring it to life for her as did seeing it. Now she can discuss this issue of meanness with her patient, if she chooses, how it came to be that this is her solution to anxiety, its compulsivity, other options, if this gets her what she wants, etc.

There is a radical difference between hearing about the patient's being scared and actually *seeing fear* in the eyes. Once you have seen how scared a patient is, let it in, and not move away from it, then you have a totally different response to the patient from that point on. You are not longer shoved around by the defense once you have seen the depths of terror. There is greater openness in the therapist to hearing the hostility once he observes fear which is the source of the hostility. He is in an inner state of being able to have some compassion for the patient after he has let in what he sees. When you observe the terror of the patient in relationship in the moment, you are not so scared with what to do. You see that the patient will attempt to control his own terror by controlling you, and you will not be so vulnerable to these forms of control.

A patient is talking of how he feels therapy is useless, he's not getting anything out of it. Then there is the slightest look in the eyes of some liking of the therapist. The therapist saw the expression. If the therapist did not *see* this liking, he would be more likely to believe the words. Having seen it, he appreciates that the work is not what is going on inside the patient at the moment. He knows then that the relationship is more positive, more complex than the words can ever convey. The important point is that observation of actual changed behavior shifted the level of the treatment to where the holistic event became important and not only the words, which are only a part of the total experience of the interaction in work. As you can observe the patient's movement from open participation in the present into anxiety to compulsive forms of relating, you can, when appropriate, explore this as to what is going on.

Often the patient does not know clearly what he wants, thinks, or feels. He does not feel he can create his own fate from within. He is dependent on others for self-esteem and direction. He does not feel concern for the other person. He can bear minimal anxiety, has little patience. He experiences little connection to having caused his own difficulties. He is intensely anxious in a relationship when his rigid ideas of how things should go are shaken. He disrupts relationships easily when he is not treated in the way he expects or when results that he wants are not forthcoming. All this makes for a difficult person to be with and a process where the supervisee feels the patient conveying "Help me. Do something to make my life better. If you don't, you are incompetent or ungiving. I will hate you or leave or lose respect for you." For most supervisees there is intense anxiety at times being with such a person.

Thoughts begin to come quickly at such moments in session. Thoughts of the therapist often are: What should I do, why don't I know what to do, what is the matter with me, etc. I'm confused." "I don't know what's going on here, the patient will find this out. What will happen when he knows I don't have answers?" "What does this mean? What is the patient trying to say to me? If I could figure it out, something could happen. What can I say that will bring all this confusion together." "I'm getting mad. I'm more than mad. I'm furious. What's the matter that I get this way? How can I call myself a therapist? The patient is healthier than me. He reduces me to shaking fury. How can I not show this?" "I'm going to lose him. I need the money. Will I ever be able to do this work?" "The patient is right. We haven't gotten anywhere." "Why can't I feel anything for this patient? I am hearing the words, but I don't feel."

As the therapist continues thinking during the session, he is trying to figure, focusing on what is the matter, wanting to get out of the tension, wanting to avoid the inner upset, wanting to help, not knowing what to do. The fact is that there is little space with all these thoughts for listening to the patient. The endless noise of thoughts keeps the therapist from being emotionally available for listening to the patient. Virtually what the therapist is conducting here is therapy with himself.

Therapists are aware of how much they are involved in the process of thought in the session and they can discuss what they think. They can go further and look into the question of whether their thoughts are helping with the therapy. Usually they will discover that their focus on thought does not actually help the patient.

It is my point to supervisees in this process that thoughts will continue; however, as we see that they do not help us we will not take them so seriously. They will continue, but we will see that they are impediments to the work. The limits of certain streams of thoughts in the helping process can be learned. The thoughts roll on, but we do not cling to them once we see that they close us up. The supervisee comes to see that it is his own thoughts that are at times his greatest enemy in the treatment process.

A supervisee reported that a patient came to the session with a large paper bag. The patient took out a hamburger, french fries, coke, pie, and coffee, and set them out on the table, speaking in a friendly manner. The therapist became furious, feeling that this was resistance, this is not done in therapy. I suggested that perhaps the patient wanted to share in the intimate act of eating with the therapist, that the patient might have wanted to find out something of the way he ate, might have wanted to share with the therapist, etc. I said that there were many possible meanings. The therapist said that he had asked the patient, "What is going on?" but he added, "I knew I wasn't open to finding out, I was so convinced this was wrong. My attitude is that there are only certain ways to conduct the therapy, and only certain things that the patient is supposed to do. I can see that I really didn't want to find out what was going on because I thought I knew. And when the patient offered me some of his french fries, I saw it as making fun of me. It is possible that he was trying to share, and he did ask me if he looked awkward eating, but I was so pissed I said, 'Eating is saying that you don't want to talk to me . . .' in thinking I knew the answer as to what this was, I didn't find out anything." I told the supervisee he had learned much of the open attitude which can encompass the possibility of many meanings, wanting to find out, and not knowing in advance. With such an attitude his inquiry would now be more real.

There is a key transformation in the supervisee when he is open to observing his patient as is, letting his patient be, dropping previously held judgments of himself and his patient, loosening ideas on how the therapy should go. The supervisee becomes aware of how his lifetime conditioning to accomplish, to get better, to get more, to please, to be liked, to have things comfortable, to avoid violence, to be thought of in a certain way, to avoid anger, terror, hopelessness—blocks to his genuine letting be *what is* with the patient and himself in the treatment. As this happens, he is able to feel more comfortable with his patient, to have his presence be the healing environment to where the *being is the doing.*

Teaching treatment techniques and theory that are specifically helpful in working with the particular patient being discussed is a part of supervision. Without an awareness however, of what has been discussed, it is often difficult for therapists to stay in relationship with patients to where technique or theory become relevant issues.

In non-deterministic supervision I hope to open the supervisee to seeing the live event of the moment as it is being created, and participating in it with the patient. It is the patient's fear of the unknown, relating out of his past experience rather than present experience that made him the patient. To the degree that the supervisee relates to his patient from his own past experience, past knowledge, he is missing living in the present, which is all we have.

chapter 8

PSYCHIC ONENESS: A TREATMENT APPROACH

Warren Wilner, Ph.D

An impression which has arisen during the time that I have been doing psychoanalytic treatment is that people have essentially basic orientations in life which are quite simple. In fact, there may be only one such orientation that can be lived at any given time. Expressed through all of the complexities and sophistication that humans have developed over thousands of years, these orientations may be much like those of the simplest forms of organic life, which are easy to observe in the single-celled ameba, but are very difficult to discern in higher organisms, and most of all, of course, in humans. Furthermore, the basis for these movements may be a simplicity of an even more fundamental sort which may run through all of nature, including human's most abstract and symbolic systems.

If this impression is correct, what we may have done in moving up the evolutionary ladder is to have built higher forms of complexity through various characteristics and systems in order to fulfill evolutions' current requirements for expressing this simplicity. Knowing in depth and detail then the kinds of lawful relationships and patterns that characterize the human psyche, and how they work, for example, in concert with various systems of the body may provide a clearer experience of this simplicity within such complexity.

The problem for psychotherapy within this conception is for the therapist to be able to experience the patient's basic striving through all of his complexity, while encouraging its expression through therapeutic intervention. Thus, the neurotic or healthful attributions placed on certain psychic expressions may be considered secondary to seeing how these expressions move toward fulfilling the patient's basic orientation in life, regardless of how healthy or distorted they may appear to be. The therapist is therefore not exclusively interested in helping the patient to reach a seemingly more healthful state insofar as this effort may impair the former's ability to assist the latter in fulfilling his basic purpose as it may be expressed through his problems. In fact, the therapist's ability to experience the patient's simplicity may ultimately rest upon his sensitivity to his own. This may lead him to the view that the problematic areas in any person's life are those in which the struggle to express his basic striving is being most fully engaged.

Since practically all psychotherapy literature deals with psychological patterns and problems as end points in themselves, this paper will concentrate on articulating the psyche's essential simplicity, which I call "psychic oneness." However, since such simplicity is embedded within great complexity, something of the latter will be elaborated as well.

This approach can be distinguished from most traditional forms of psychotherapy since it posits a psychic reality which exists beyond the particular dynamics and systems that are usually focused on. It is also different from the more Eastern forms of experiential approaches in that it works directly through these dynamics and systems rather than trying to circumvent, change, or transcend them in order to reach a purer state.

This chapter is divided into two parts: The first attempts to articulate the ontological nature of oneness, whereas the second places this conception within the context of psychoanalytic treatment, which I believe to be the form of psychotherapy which holds the greatest potential for allowing the patient to most fully express himself without having to have the therapist make him better. Furthermore, this form of treatment views the therapist's excessive desire to undertake such curative efforts as possibly being further elucidative of the patient's unfolding nature.

THE ONTOLOGICAL NATURE OF ONENESS

An inquiry into the nature of psychic oneness begins with the assumption that such oneness exists. It is assumed to exist for a number of reasons: (a) It is possible for the human mind to conceive of such a possibility; (b) oneness is a dominant category of mind in that we experience one thing at a time. Thus, even when we experience a flow of associations or think about a number of things, they can still be categorized as one flow or one set of a number of things; (c) it may be possible to demonstrate that everything comes to and arises from one point; and (d) the presence of oneness appears capable of being fleetingly apprehended during those moments when everything within one's experiential grasp appears to be of one piece.

This phenomenon may be evidenced by the following clinical vignette. A patient who had made a slip and had mistakenly referred to a friend, Jack, while speaking of another, Ted, went on to describe how Ted had done something "underhanded" to her. This brought the association, "down under like in Australia," to the therapist's mind, which he mentioned to the patient. The patient then remarked that Jack was born in Australia, which the therapist had not known. Everything then began to fall into place when this association plus her slip led her into an inquiry concerning Jack's underhandedness with her as well.

Although it is possible to view this vignette as an example of the patient unconsciously cueing the therapist as to her treatment by Ted so that he could help her see it consciously, an alternative and/or supplemental hypothesis would be that this event exemplified a psychic oneness of underhandedness, since the content of underhandedness was literally reached through like underhanded means. The role of the unconscious would then be to discover or come upon this oneness, which is being posited as existing as a living and separate psychic entity in its own right, while, perhaps, also creating it insofar as it helps provide this oneness with a consciously experiencable form through the patient's personal involvement with it.

However, in the ordinary course of life we do not experience oneness as such. Our senses and consciousness are limited so that there is much in terms of a total oneness in the larger sense that lies beyond our experiential range. In addition, we experience the world in many different ways, and no inventory of human experience appears capable of encompassing our full breadth of mind. Thus, psychic oneness is not a hypothesis which follows directly from our usual experience of the world, but instead arises only during those rare moments when all phenomena of a situation appear to be guided by the same invisible hand.

If anything, assuming the existence of a psychic oneness and then trying to experience it actually serves to heighten our sensitivity to the vast number of ways in which we do not appear to be one. This, in turn, enables us to learn more about the seeming infinity of the world's different aspects—or the not-one. Yet, since we assume that all of these aspects comprise a total one, the challenge is then to be able to experience oneness through the not-one. Oneness would then subsume both the one and the not-one. Becoming aware of psychic oneness would then be to become aware of something other than only this multitude of aspects.

Of the various forms of human experience which have developed in attempting to organize this multidimensionality of life the two broadest and most dominant are the Western and Eastern scientific and philosophical traditions, with a third recently developed which offers a synthesis for these two. The Western tradition rejects or is inattentive to the Eastern holistic view of the world, and emphasizes instead deterministic cause-and-effect relationships, boundaried categories, analysis, and logical reasoning. In contrast, the Eastern tradition focuses on the basic underlying harmony and unity in life which it seeks to experience through various meditative forms and exercises. The third view, which is currently being most actively preferred through the quantum mechanics and relativity theories of modern physics, seeks to accomodate both of these orientations, each according to its relevant place within the larger total order.

The Eastern and Western orientations stand in polar opposition to one another. Each exemplifies its own characteristics which do not overlap with its opposing orientation, while vying with the other for the position as the most powerful orientation in the world. Obviously, neither of these world views are directly expressive of oneness in that each attempts to exclude the other rather than to be one with it, whereas oneness, at least in spatial terms, would be said to encompass both of these orientations, if not also to exist within each of them. Again, using this spatial metaphor, if oneness exists within each of these poles, it can also be said to exist within all particular ones, as well as all of these individual ones being contained within a total one of which everything is part. These two ones may then be connected in that the particular one exists within the total one, which in turn is expressed through these particular ones. The spatial metaphor may then be dropped as one literally cannot be less or more important than any other one, whether it be a particular or the total one. Therefore, as in mathematical identity, one simply equals one.

Since, however, we usually do experience one polar position of any sort as being more or less valid than another, how can such a relationship be subsumed within a conception of oneness which affirms all ones to be identical? Yet, by definition, this particular one must be included within this conception in that oneness also encompasses all as well as existing within all.

Rather than this conundrum forcing us to discard the conception of oneness, it instead strengthens its elasticity by leading to three further conclusions: (a) it broadens and sharpens our conception of the one as that which also expresses itself through the larger and smaller ones, both with regard to one pole of a dialectical relationship being stronger than another, and of its analogue of a total oneness or even a simply larger one being greater than a smaller particular one; (b) it further alerts us to our difficulty in experiencing the one, owing in part to its ephemeral nature and to the paradoxes it leads; and (c) it enables us to refine our perceptions of many of the qualities in the world which may have remained vague or closed to us, which then further challenges us to experience a oneness with them.

The existence of these bipolar relationships maintains the dialectic, and with it the symbolic expression of oneness in that both poles of such relationships move toward erasing the other which would then leave one pole. But with the third approach of positing a larger order which can encompass both the Western and Eastern approaches, each in its own appropriate realm, the propensity of oneness to not allow for its direct experiencing becomes most apparent.

Within such a proposed synthesis, with its conception of everything being interconnected in some larger harmony, and with the connections, whether they be physical, chemical or psychic, awaiting visible explication, there is no need to posit an ephemeral-like oneness, since the goal is to encompass everything by including or making provision for all of its particulars. Such a synthesis does not, however, conform to our basic conception of oneness as an alternative hypothesis which exists outside of normal experiential limits. What such syntheses do instead is to orient us to see the world solely in terms of multiples of fragments, although this time the fragments take the form of patterns and laws, and even a separate wholeness, which greatly obscures the oneness which may be them.

In this way, perhaps, as our knowledge, sophistication, and complexity grow, oneness may become increasingly less visible and may require even greater sensitivity in order to discern. Yet, in the pure spirit of oneness as that which is something other than spatial or temporal, this gap may not have actually grown at all. In proportion to our experiential capabilities, the "oneness" of the difficulty in experiencing the one may be no greater now than it was during the apex of the Newtonian view of the world or even during the early dawn of man. In this way, oneness as a particular one remains the same within all of the world's myriad aspects and changes, while the total one grows. But in that it is all one, it also remains the same as well. Thus, the paradoxical consequence of a conception of oneness is that it again permits the simultaneous (a temporal one) copresence of two seemingly contradictory aspects, but in a way that allows oneness to be preserved while expanding our view of the world at the same time.

The fact that our approaches to life attempt to conceal its oneness point to our difficulty in experiencing the one—any one —and reflect our profound and ongoing human dilemma of being able to confer respect upon individuals while also concerning ourselves with the welfare of groups, and of the total one at the same time. It may be that we strive toward and avoid the one as a reflection of both our need to reach this point as well as our current inability to do so.

Yet, it is again only because of the elaboration of the not-one, by which we can see all that oneness does not appear to be, that we are even able to have a glimpse into the nature of oneness. Beginning with the assumption of the existence of this nature makes us aware of the magnitude and scope of oneness as it exists within the diversity of form within life's conditions. This awareness does not come about only through intellectual insight. It also occurs through the living experience of the sheer omnipresence of oneness in that all of life's phenomena could even be conceived of as having a single thread running through it, as well as all being part of a total coherent one; and furthermore, that this thread and total one are themselves of such a nature that they may not be able to be approached or referred to by any known describable means other than simply as one.

Having once undergone the experience of the omnipresence of the one, which paradoxically exists within an almost corresponding sea of diversity, can give rise to a deep belief in this vision of the absolute oneness of all things. Such a belief may then be able to evoke the spirit necessary to wade through the seeming chaos and confusion of this diversity in that one believes that oneness both exists within while being pointed to by this chaos, and in time may be revealed. Whether this revelation takes the larger form of this chaos merely being a part of a process of a greater one, which then shifts the focus from this chaos to the oneness of the process of which it is a part; or whether it simply be the ability to experience the oneness of two small elements within the chaos, the nature of oneness from the sublime to the inane is shown to be of all. It is then through this thread of the one that oneness exists throughout all dimensions and experiential modes, whatever their quality or magnitude.

The inescapable conclusion is that one cannot be anything other than one, and that trying to turn away from oneself only serves to further illuminate one. Therefore, the more an individual tries to deny the one, whether it be himself or another, the more is his oneness elucidated by impressing upon him his place in a larger one, or by bringing it to light through inadvertent and unconscious experience.

In posing the question then as to how could one possibly not be one, part of a one, or of oneness itself, the answer would come back in the same words, but accented differently as, "how could one not be one!" One is, after all, equal to one. Thus language, which has been thought to be fragmenting within certain Eastern thought, which, in turn, has spurred efforts to transcend its seeming limitations, reveals itself to be directly expressive of oneness when it is carried to its limits. Such extension allows for all the meanings and implications of the words to be revealed, including its opposites, which then enables oneness to express itself. Furthermore, the word, one, appears to have a unique property which makes it well suited for this conception in that it does not preorient one's experience in any particular direction and thus seems capable of being used in any context without limiting meaning or implication. As such, this word would then permit a patient's personal striving to fully express itself without obstruction.

If the word, "one," allows for all possibilities in particular situations, although still being able to carry its own unique sense, then it is truly expressive of oneness as a living presence which exists in all and of which all is. But it is only when it is viewed in this context that its living potential is evoked, for it is otherwise only one word of the body of the not-one. In this way, the experience of oneness cannot be realized through a single isolated aspect. This experience is dependent upon a total context, which may then all be perceived as one.

The importance of such context may be observed with regard to the Eastern and Western orientations. Each of these modes may be viewed as an entity which both gives rise to as well as reinforces itself. Through surrounding itself front and back with the push of genesis and the pull of function it both creates and discovers itself by omitting other things—the not-one of the other position. But since the assumption of oneness indicates that all is one, that which it omits, which is then also itself, but as its not-one, moves to rejoin it and must be further excluded. Each of these positions then excludes itself. But since what is excluded remains itself, it must continue to be associated with it, but now through relationship of opposition rather than as identity. Furthermore, each pole must formulate the opposite pole as not being itself in order to conceal the fact that it has excluded itself. Each position thus preserves its own oneness as an entity while maintaining a link with its original oneness by sustaining a dialectical relationship with the excluded one.

Yet, it is again through these exclusions of itself that oneness prepares the ground for its own eventual experiencing through them. For if and when the time comes that each such position may recognize its opposite as itself, this will be the moment when the focus will shift away from the particular qualities that characterize these positions and turn toward the possible existence of a oneness as a fundamental ground which is beyond any description, and which has enabled the two positions to be experienced as one. It is also through these exclusions that new particular ones may be allowed to ripen and develop as full and mature entities in their own right, thus adding to the world's diversity. It is then possible for, at least, dialectically related ones to join together as larger ones when they no longer have any place to go as solitary entities.

The deep internal consistency of dialectically related particular ones, and a consideration of their mutual oneness may again be illustrated through the Eastern and Western positions with regard to taste—both culinary and intellectual. Eastern style food of the Chinese variety, for example, may be said to be very much like the character of Eastern experience—light and delicately prepared with an almost ephemeral-like quality, which is said to not stick to the gut. Correspondingly, Western style food is similarly like its cognitive approach—substantial, clearly boundaried into distinct pieces, and definitive—morsels that one can sink one's teeth into.

Across these positions, it may be further asserted that the goal of each orientation may be achieved through the means of the other. Experientially, it may be said that the goal of experiencing the undifferentiated wholeness of Eastern philosophy is structurally brought about through a Western type cause-and-effect approach, albeit in the meditative form of Eastern philosophy. Thus, by implementing the technique of meditation one can cause the effect of experiencing this wholeness. Conversely, the Western goal of being able to discern these cause-and-effect relationships is often, and again, paradoxically brought about through non-deterministic and naturalistic observation in the context of a field of undifferentiated wholeness within which such relationships are distinguished. Appropos then of oneness both excluding and seeking itself, the goal or content of each approach may be seen to arise from and be directed towards the means or process of the other.

This manner of viewing these two positions would, of course, be disturbing to each. The Westerner who needs to be in control would be disturbed because it is being claimed that he is not, whereas the Easterner who needs to let things be would be bothered because it would show that he is controlling. Yet, a conception of oneness which affirms that one is all would maintain that this would have to be so, as did Freud who suggested that to know one person in depth is to know all of humanity.

True to its nature of being able to encompass all positions, including opposites, a conception of oneness should be able to illuminate the humorous as well as the serious. It is in this vein with regard to the confluence of food and experience that one may observe that the consequence of cutting into and eating a thick, juicy Western-style steak smothered in onions and served with hash-brown potatoes may actually be the end point of Eastern philosophy—a feeling of undifferentiated wholeness and tranquility, which can actually give rise to the propensity for calm observation of cause-and-effect relationships outside of oneself, since one is at peace, whereas eating light and delicately prepared meals with chopstocks may be said to engender the kinds of cravings associated with Western-style industry, which would then attempt to quiet themselves through meditatively induced harmony.

As seems to be the case with all matters pertaining to psychic oneness, the point of the previous example appears capable of being grasped only for an instant before it evaporates into a keen awareness of all that it excludes. This point may fade in this way precisely because it is about oneness which is beyond description. Therefore, the reality of what is being described fades in one's mind exactly at the point when the essence of oneness as that which is beyond realistic form emerges.

This essence may not be able to be kept in mind, perhaps, because the mind may be able to retain only realistic forms, although there may be a more dynamic explanation for this phenomenon as well. When the usual structures and entities of the mind, which are based on forms which perpetuate their existence through the self-exclusions of, for example, content and process opposing each other, are faced by the oneness which is beyond all such forms, they may quickly retreat from the experience rather than trying to live in it more fully. They do so, since to experience oneness would mean to have to face their own self-exclusions, which would then momentarily, at least, cause them to cease to exist. Such forms may then be said to declare their intentionality to remain as they are by trying to negate the one.

This does not happen with the elusive ones which dissolve in experience through content and process coinciding as with the earlier mentioned example of underhandedness. Not being based on such self-excluding forms, these ones can allow themselves to recede from view as describable entities as the only means by which their deeper oneness may be brought to light. Such experiential dissolution, which paradoxically allows for their continuance as more natural ones, can only come about through the resolution of all dialectics, which is exactly what the other entities cannot permit.

The experience of oneness through the resolution of the dialectics places describable forms in the service of the one rather than as ends in themselves. Since within a perspective of oneness, one is hypothetically, at least, not dependent on the continued existence of any particular forms, one may then get underneath, behind, or in-between all self-excluding forms and be able to glean perspectives which would be otherwise difficult to obtain. In a sense, one might ideally be able to be in all experiential places at once, since oneness is beyond these forms, as well as space and time.

At the same time, the more enduring psychic ones remain elusive within experience as the particular ones permanent substrate. These ones enable clear judgments to be made in the world based on their foundation, while being linked together through and also as parts of the one which is all of them. Meanwhile the self-excluding ones as expressions of the not-one await their permanent places. Should they achieve them, larger ones will no longer be necessary to elucidate their oneness, and oneness as a separate issue, if not also as a psychic reality as such, may be able to cease to exist.

The nature of oneness as being able to be apprehended only by going beyond describable forms, as well as its propensity to suddenly evaporate from experience, may be illustrated diagramatically (see Figure 8–1).

If one designates two adjoining sides of a square with the characteristics of a dialectical position, in this case the low differentiation and high wholeness of the Eastern position, and the characteristics of its polar opposite on the other two sides, or the high differentiation and low wholeness of the Western orientation, it can be demonstrated that by enclosing this square in another whereby each angle of the original square bisects one side of the new square enclosing it, and by then transcribing on to each side of the new square the characteristics of the two sides adjoining each angle which bisects it of the original square, and by performing this operation three more times, making five diagrams and four transformations in all, there will be cancelling out of all characteristics appearing on each side which are the same. By the time the fourth transformation is finished all the original characteristics will have disappeared leaving only the square.

If the five squares are juxtoposed upon one another, we have a graphic model of how oneness may both exist within as well as encompass all descriptive possibilities, in that all combinations of characteristics, including their complete absence, will exist on all four sides in addition to the whole square.

HW = high wholeness
LD = low differentiation
LW = low wholeness
HD = high differentiation

IV

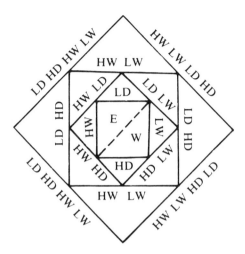

V

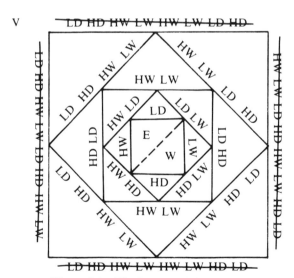

Figure 8-1   The Nature of Oneness

APPLICATION TO PSYCHOANALYSIS

It is difficult to speak of the clinical relevance of psychic oneness without such an exposition becoming simply words which refer to only describable things. In this way, this conception can become like any other and lose its sense as that which can both fill and envelop one with the presence of psychic coherence and totality.

As the following pages will try to demonstrate, all clinical theories and formulations orient in particular directions, and must, therefore, omit other possibilities which are not in their path. Even the psychoanalytic hypothesis of the unconscious, which I believe to be the most profound and evocative of clinical conceptions, directs one to think in terms of such orienting specifics as primary process, a topographic area of the mind, and unconscious communication or cueing systems whereby people may know things without their having to be made explicit.

But it is another matter to begin with a conception whose basis does not orient in any specific way although allowing for the simultaneous presence of all possibilities—even those which focus on certain directions while omitting others. Thus, the narcissistic personality may also be covertly object related, the hysteric obsessive, and even hysteria itself may be considered to be inverted obsessionalism and vice versa, with both being the same when viewed through deeper structures. In being able to encompass all dialectical opposites, directions and static states, this conception fulfills the most exalted possibilities for full psychic power while considering no less significant and expressive of oneness the most limiting of views. All can be seen as being of the one and, as such, may expand or contract to the limits of their capabilities without the imposition of *a priori* boundaries, which are more often than not a function of how far we have been capable of going at any particular time.

Although from a radical standpoint such a conception seems to suggest complete openness to new experience, it provides at the same time for the necessity of being closed, as it considers such closure to be an absolute requirement for being able to experience sharpness, contrast, and surprise without which our lives would be only an indistinct blur. One can only first begin to know that there may be more to oneself than one is aware of by first keeping a door shut to what one does not know and is not attending to. Only then may intellectual perspective become part of the felt structure should this door suddenly spring open, enabling one to then feel through sharp contrast and surprise that it may also be a further dimension of oneself which is being experienced. Formulated in terms of the resolution of the subject—object dichotomy, by trying as subject to view another in the world objectively, one may come upon oneself as object represented both through the direct experience of seeing oneself in the other, and indirectly through the way the other as subject views you as object. The dialectical pole of being open can then be seen as being related to being closed, existing within it as well as containing it, and, finally, as being it until such descriptive forms fade from mind. In the absolute sense then, the one is as closed as it is open, and ultimately is both while being neither.

Nor is the experience of oneness something that should necessarily be sought after, since to do so would presuppose first having to not experience it in order to be able to then seek it. Although the need for this conception does, in fact, presuppose that one cannot now experience oneness, this may be viewed as being a prevailing rather than as an ultimately necessary condition of our lives.

In clinical practice, involved as it is with the treatment and healing of human suffering, psychic oneness lives as an assumption which ideally allows for the most efficacious engagment possible, while remaining as a potential experience which could serve to help strengthen the spirit necessary to undertake an often long and difficult treatment. It may be only through the realization of one's psychic totality as it integrally exists within a world of similarly coherent experience that one may discover hope within real limitation. It may therefore be comforting to a patient to know that oneness exists in the form of some type of consolidation even within the most fragmented of psychic states. This then points to the possibility for a radical and ever-deepening inquiry into and, perhaps, beyond all of these consolidations as there will always be this ever-present base to enable a new consolidation to express itself.

Working psychoanalytically within a conception of psychic oneness is analagous to the circles in a pond which continue to radiate outward after a stone is dropped into it. As soon as it is possible to see one phenomenon or pattern clearly, it quickly becomes encircled by a new one awaiting fresh inquiry. This seemingly forever-expanding field has profound implications for our usual ways of both doing analysis and viewing how it is done. We are accustomed, for example, to think in terms of whether what is being done is the right thing or not. Is what the therapist doing technically correct? Is the way that the patient is behaving self-destructive? Since oneness subsumes all positions, it allows for these determinations to be made, but not necessarily only as end points in themselves. The therapist who makes an error and says something that elicits a seemingly unnecessary anxiety reaction in the patient may have been unconsciously trying to dig down deeper in order to reach something that he may have never been able to get to without making this error.

For example, it may be possible because of this error to uncover a deeper area for exploration pertaining to how often mistakes have been made by others in this patient's life, which he may have had to elicit in order to be able to experience intense and strongly bound feelings. Furthermore, patients who tend to elicit errors in others are often themselves too concerned with doing the right thing to permit the luxury of either error or strong reaction except in the face of needed and justifiable provocation. Remaining within the framework of all mistakes having to be bad may have never permitted this more pervasive pattern to be revealed.

Similarly, a patient who continues a neurotic pattern despite all efforts to analyze it may be trying to point to a deeper source for this pattern—perhaps, a profound need to isolate him or herself from others, and a sense of strength which he may derive from knowing that no one can affect him. Thus, seeing this pattern only as something which needs to be directly dissolved might prevent the awareness of the larger circle within which it is embedded; although the full experience of this larger and more basic circle of isolation may have not been able to be realized without first being closed to the possibility of its presence. Only then, after many attempts to analyze the original pattern had failed, could the full magnitude and impact of this pattern, which, like its meaning, also existed in isolation from the original pattern, be revealed.

The basic conception of oneness as existing beyond describable forms also points to the possible existence of patterns which may be theoretically new. For example, during a case conference of a psychotherapy being carried out with a child the focus was placed on the child's reaction to being adopted in view of the fact that her adopting mother often rejected her. However, a careful listening to the manner in which the case was being presented, in addition to considering its content, revealed that there may have been at least an equally important dynamic at work. Despite the mother's apparent indifference toward the child, a deep bond appeared to exist between them which expressed itself through each setting up situations in which they were faced with and led others to face the unexpected. These situations, in turn, brought about novel reactions from others which enabled mother and child to be found endearing to these people despite their flagrant abusiveness and provocations. The uncovering of this dynamic did not mitigate the significance of the child's being adopted as much as it did open up a new dimension for exploration which may have even underlay it. This dimension then yielded the possibility that both mother and child may have been recreating and reacting against a stifling sense of their lives being completely determined for them, as well as an emotional stagnation which did not permit them to touch and to be touched by others.

The characteristic of being attentive to both the more evident factors in these cases while remaining simultaneously alert for unexpected phenomena is again consistent with the conception of oneness as subsuming at least two different areas at the same time. These areas may pertain to anything: the concrete and the abstract; logical reasoning and primary process associations; viewing a clinical phenomenon as being healthy while being able to see pathology in it; having a clearer sense of oneself while becoming more indistinct at the same time; the possibilities are endless. But all require a fine psychic tuning in order to be able to experience their subtleties.

From a conception of oneness, working within two different areas at the same time requires, in essence, that they be ultimately experienced as one. Since only one such area is usually in focus at any given time, the other area, or the opposite pole in a dialectical relationship, for example, must also be able to be experienced, but in a way that is now compatible with its opposite. Thus, whereas the flow of experience is considered to ordinarily come about non-deterministically, although the conferring of meaning and significance is thought to be a consequence of a determinate act of volition, psychic oneness would hold that the experiential flow would also have to be seen as the result of the patient's active participation in generating his own experience, whereas the punctuation of this flow with meaning would have to be simultaneously understood as a function of a self-moving process—possibly the result of now unconscious and previously effected identifications.

Within the analytical process, the difficulty of such simultaneous experiencing is most evident in trying to stay with what one may suddenly experience which is not consistent with whatever else is going on. The tendency is almost always to turn away from this seemingly irrelevant and often embarrassing thought or feeling, and to get back on the track. Yet, if one stays with this sudden experience and permits it to lead by following the ensuing associations or direction for the inquiry that it provides, a significant area for analytical exploration will usually be revealed. If one can at the same time permit oneself to continue with the direction that was to be substituted for this experience, or at least return to it, both of these experiential modes will often lead to the same point, but sometimes from opposite directions. As in the holographic model, this end point may then be able to be viewed as possibly carrying its own psychic presence, since it could be arrived at through more than one experiential means.

The extension of the issue concerning one's relationship to one's experience in both the active and passive modes takes on interesting implications when viewed in the light of trying to order one's experience while it is also ordering you. Here, psychic oneness becomes more than a point that is arrived at through different means. It can also be seen as the generating center for these means. As with the multiple meanings of taste for the Eastern and Western orientations, the formulation of trying to order one's experience brings to mind more than just sequential order. It also implies trying to command one's experience, as well as viewing one's experience as a dish which can be ordered in a restaurant. Correspondingly, being ordered by one's experience not only implies that one is shaped by it, but also that it both commands you, as well as that you become the dish which it orders—perhaps, in order to consume you.

The cold intellectuality of the words of the original meaning of order then gives way to charged meaning as the issue acquires a life of its own—a literal psychic oneness which both determines and is being determined by itself, and a life which one suddenly finds oneself struggling with. All the meanings and implications of the word "order" then dynamically interact with one another in generating its own life. But the essential point is not the particular nature of its characteristics, but rather that such oneness exists, and seems to require the mutual presence of all of its sometimes contradictory aspects in order to be experientially sustained.

But the endless possibilities of these dialectics still require a finite frame within which to experience them. For the seemingly irrelevant and disparate phenomena, this frame is the analytic session, part of it a grouping of sessions, and ultimately the entire analysis itself within which everything that takes place both behaviorally and experientially can be seen as being elucidative of the one. As for the seemingly coherent phenomena, to this is added the frame of whatever one's most basic assumption at the time happens to be. Whether such an assumption be about the centrality of the child's having been adopted, as in the previous case, or the therapist's error, or the patient's compulsive neurotic pattern which would not abate, it serves as a single frame within which new diversity may be revealed so that deeper underlying structures may be sought. Since such a frame is a oneness in itself, oneness can then also be seen as expressing itself through itself, in the sense of its relationship to itself and also, of course, in identity as itself.

The following clinical vignette is one in which both of these frames, which usually work together as one, may be observed. In this case, the analyst's assumption concerning a dominant mode of the patient's behavior was broken up and expanded through primary process associations and imagery, while the diversity of experience that this yielded was seen to cohere itself within a deeper and seemingly self-sustaining commonality.

The analyst was refering to a patient's passive manner of functioning by telling him that he sounded like he was drifting. The patient was then reminded of a dream that he had had the night before in which he was floating without a boat down a river while being stuck in the current and unable to get to shore. He was not, however, in danger of drowning.

The analyst then had the association of the patient literally being stuck in the current, referring to the present tense; with the word tense, then pointing to the tension that he experienced because of being stuck in this way, while being unable to move either forward into the future or back into the past. He then thought of current as also being electrical current, and then as A.C. and D.C., before his associations led him back temporarily to B.C.—before Christ.

The simultaneous sense of this patient as also being stuck in the ancient biblical times of the Old Testament with its belief in an eye for an eye and a tooth for a tooth became apparent as it fitted in with other things which were known about him. In addition, his own attempt to offer himself as a Christ-like figure also fell into place, perhaps, as a way of freeing himself from his Old Testament attitudes concerning retribution, to which his trying to remain in the present may have also been a reaction. Furthermore, like Moses floating in his basket he may have been awaiting handmaidens and a princess to save him, which was again consistent with his manner of functioning.

In addition to being illustrative of these psychic frames, this vignette illuminates oneness in other ways. As with the significance of the word "order" in the earlier example, the words both directly used and associated to in this case appeared to have a life of their own and became both centers for generating their own new associations and meanings, while also being associations to yet other centers. In this sense, words can again be seen to carry oneness, particularly in their movement from having only one apparent meaning in a particular context to having multiple meanings in different contexts, all of which convey a deep unitary sense about them. Words too may then be seen to be yet another frame within which oneness can both be experienced and expressed.

Secondly, the entire situation appeared to have the presence of oneness in that all of the parts seemed to be of a piece which appeared to extend in quality beyond the boundaries of all of its particulars. Past and present, ancient and modern, transferential and outside of the transference, the situation seemed to imply all at once. It was also accidentally stepped into, like in Alice in Wonderland, and appeared to be larger than both the patient and the analyst. The experience at the time was that this oneness appeared to exist beforehand and was waiting to be found. It did not, at least, feel as though it was being created in the present through conscious and unconscious thoughts and feelings, but rather that these were the means of arriving at this seemingly autonomous psychic center.

The conception of psychic oneness as a discontinuous and living psychic presence which exists within all and of which all is points to the possible existence of such psychic centers, at least within an intrapsychic theoretical model. Highly organized and with a life of their own, these centers may be conceived of intellectually, but require being elicited through the proper stimuli in order to be fully engaged. As they appear to exist discontinuously from the rest of the personality, and to express themselves only indirectly and symbolically in daily life, they may similarly require out-of-the-ordinary evocation in order to be revealed. Such centers, which may carry with them the potential for infusing the rest of the personality with anxiety, enormous depth, and living delight, may have developed both personally and transpersonally, and over a long period of time. Although the forms that they can take may vary infinitely, the fundamental presence of oneness would appear to be their foundation.

Following from the preceding examples and formulations, the psychoanalytic essence of working within a conception of oneness would appear to involve extending situations and meanings to their limits, while giving full exposure to one's experience in whatever form in the process. Discarding nothing without first trying to fully experience it, present beliefs and formulations as expressions of possible self-excluding consolidations are inquired into in search of deeper patternings. Ideally, one strives to encompass all describable phenomena within one's view, but is ever alert to experiencing the presence of the discontinuous oneness within what is at hand. In being able to consider as well as to get underneath all hypotheses and directions, deeply unconscious areas may be explored as to their current import.

Within this conception, there is always an acute sensitivity to what may be the essential simplicity of the patient's striving within the entire experiential field. Although feeling the patient's psychic pulse so as to enable him to remain in contact with the life of this striving, the analyst engages each phenomenon directly enough to experience its individuality, while holding it loosely enough to be able to feel its resonances with other psychic events. Letting go while holding on, experiencing oneself more fully while one is trying to get away—all dialectical opposites, directions, and coherent and incoherent experience —are viewed as expressing the one which runs through all and encompasses all. Psychic oneness may thus give rise to the possibility of experiencing the full measure of not only our neuroses and health, but of our humaneness and, perhaps, beyond as well.

Part III

PHILOSOPHY

The third section reveals the ongoing thinking that has been generated in psychology by the paradigm shift heralded in Part I. There is an interesting connection between these articles and those of Part I similar to the parallels drawn between Parts II and I. Professor Charles Scott carries out the understanding begun by Gerald Epstein in his chapter "Freedom with Darkness and Light." He draws out the mythological elements that inform a tradition of Western knowledge brought down to us in the Greek mode of thought.

Dr. David Shainberg attempts to ferret out the principles of the new paradigm as it applies to psychology in his work on non-deterministic psychology. Non-deterministic means non-causal or acausal thinking. The current paradigm is based on causal thinking which attempts to find direct connections between events. The fundamental difference between the two modes of thought is one of connection. The new paradigm says that there is *no* inherent connection between events. Furthermore, the existence of some thing is not contingent on the presence of some other thing preceding it in time. For the determinists their belief is that there is a direct connection between two events one preceding the other in time. It always has to be maintained that some cause can always be found to account for the effect that is observed. What was and no longer is, is responsible for what is. The nondeterminists accept the efficacy of determinist thinking as it relates to mechanical action carried out in the world of concrete reality. But it is seen as having little relevance to the realm of interpersonal relationships. On the other hand, the determinists find no room at all for the presence of acausal thought and dismiss it as "magic."

However, there is great evidence for the power, influence, and, above all, legitimacy of acausal thinking as is evident in Ken Phillips' chapter "The Riddle of Change." Mr. Phillips presents an overview of the great Chinese work called The *I Ching* or *Book of Changes* and its relevance for modern psychology. This work has informed Chinese life in *every facet* of living for the past 5,000 years. The underlying principle of this monumental work is that change is the elemental reality governing human life out of which logic and deterministic thinking may arise as a possibility. This logical thinking would be the figure while change (flow, process) would be the ground or matrix underlying human existence. Out of this notion has emerged much that has become meaningful for Western science (and ultimately for Western life) although the latter made its discoveries by its own means. I refer to such matters as DNA, binary mathematics, and the computer, all presaged centuries ago in the *I Ching*.

In the concluding paper of this section, Ken Wilber attempts to delineate the stages of development for man within this level of reality and the transcendence to levels of consciousness that he feels is the evolutionary direction of human civilization. He attempts to demonstrate that the mandate for this development and transcendence is to be found in the major doctrines of the Orient and in the psychological writings of major Western psychologists like Freud, Jung, and Maslow.

The last article of this book, by Gerald Epstein and George Hogben, is added to present a research possibility that may be applied in a non-deterministic framework. At the same time one may be able to learn a clinical application of merit that may help facilitate the therapeutic process.

G.E.

chapter 9

PRINCIPLES, PRACTICES, AND OBJECTIVES OF NON-DETERMINISTIC PSYCHOTHERAPY

David Shainberg, M.D.

Principles of Non-Deterministic Psychotherapy

The word *determine* comes from the Latin word "terminare," which means to mark off boundaries. In its extended meanings, determine means "to fix, to be the cause of, be the deciding factor in, set line, the form," etc. The doctrine known as determinism is "that man is not a free agent, but that his actions are determined by conditions independent of his will." (Wyld)

The concept, determine and determinism, arises in a metaphysical paradigm which implies a multitude of assumptions. Many of these assumptions sneak unwittingly into the ideas that emerge out of the paradigm. For example, determinism assumes that we can decide the specific origin of an action as well as what is effected by action. This assumption is a result, among other things, of thinking that there are exclusive connections and specific disconnections between things, which assumes our capacity to see the cause and the effect; it accepts the idea that the division made by persons, markers, entities, are *real* divisions. An agent draws the ring around a substance and marks off the boundaries; these become the only objects the observer sees. When we see these points we realize they assume the person, the marker himself. This marker, then, by definition "begins" as an "outlined" thing who already has edges and can live as an edge which considers definitions of other things. Furthermore, the ground which gives birth to this marker gives birth to *attention-to-structures* or form rather than to the movement or space in which structure appears.

The statements about determinism all have this kind of bias at the beginning. That bias favors addressing the local discontinuities rather than what is not in a form. It looks at the spider web filaments rather than the space in between. Picasso and other modern painters made this observation many years ago when they began to stress that the space between the objects of the painting was as important for the constitution of the *whole* work of art as the objects themselves (Miller, 1978; Bohm, 1957).

Is our separation, our visible separation from other human beings and things, or the separation we observe in other parts of nature, an absolute or a relative separation? Is our gross perception correct, accurate, or complete? How do we get the idea that the visible is an absolute fact? The word "fact" comes from the Latin *facere,* "to make." So a "fact" instantly raises questions about *who* makes what and how. The instrument of knowing *makes* fact, identifies with its own creation, and goes on to the *absolute belief* in the existence of that which we "know." Because we act on the basis of what we know and get reactions which more or less confirm our assumption, we are further entrapped in a confirmation of our beliefs.

Scientific investigation of the last 300 years has shown us that our perceptions are limited and that even though results may confirm a hypothesis about the causes and effects of our actions, that does not necessarily prove that our assumptions about relationships are complete or absolute. We often fail to see the exceptions that do not fit. We do not see them because they are invisible, or for reasons that amount to the same thing, we selectively exclude that which does not fit our assumptions. Or even more subtly, because our reality or belief is a function of a whole system, it is difficult to be clear about the shades of separateness and connectedness (Bohm, 1957).

Thought is an ordering of perception and perception arises in context. As we perceive, we are aware of certain invariances which become ordered into a "thing." Are these invariances in nature or are we making assumptions? We cannot be sure of this; it seems there are consistencies in nature as well as changes. Assuming such invariances, however, does not allow us to see just how consistencies are built up on the moment by actions which establish the perspective we call reality. In one sense we can see that there must be stabilities, but a visible stability does not mean that the structure is not in constant motion. Change taking place in the structure that appears invariant is one of the mysteries being probed in several areas of research (Jones, 1977).

When we see an invariant set of conditions we create *the thing*. The thing is felt to have certain characteristics which do not change when we observe what seems to change. It influences other things without being changed itself and we say it has *autonomy*. Then further criteria are evolved for what makes a thing or this thing; an image arises as a form in *consciousness*, which is a "permanent" sense of this "thing." Further perceptions are referred for comparison and assimilation, reinforcing our assumptions that this thing is as we perceived and made it before.

If an image is used as the primary ordering of subsequent perception, it prevents a free responsiveness to the present moment. Our sensory responsiveness tends to use the image to organize responses or to compare current sensation with the image. The present is dominated by the past. In most situations, this kind of process works fine; we do not have to keep inventing the present. We like it that our home address is permanent, that our typewriter is on our desk. But in our relationships with other human beings, this becomes a problem for the changing creative moment that happens between people. At moments of open human contact we are in touch with a source. It has the freshness of things never before used, never before perceived, never made. It is an experience that denies continuity. It happens right there with the moment.

It is when we hold on to some fixed image or belief about ourselves or others that conflict arises. The image leads to a loss of vision because we do not see that ourselves and other people are malleable to events and so subject to constant change. The prior image prevents our open connection to others if we hold to some fixed belief about ourselves.

Such issues arise in quantum mechanics, and they are to some extent related to our concerns in non-deterministic psychotherapy. Heisenberg's Indeterminacy or Uncertainty Principle states that it is impossible to determine the location of an electron at the same time as we study its momentum. The investigation of one aspect of the electron disturbs what we are investigating and makes the determination of the other aspect impossible. There are some scientists who believe that this demonstrates the inherent indeterminate state of the electron and therefore of nature itself. It may be said that at any given point in time the electron is indecisive as to whether it will be wave or a particle. But there are others who have questioned that interpretation and have pointed out that that kind of indeterminacy or acausality is not the way of the universe; that the Heisenberg Principle is really about our *thought,* our investigative tools and process. Einstein said, "God will not shoot dice with the universe." Along with others, David Bohm, de Broglie, Schrodinger, and Einstein believed that there is a stratum of the universe in "which" or "out of which" there is an order. Some of this latter group of scientists point out that the act of investigation, the instruments, and the principles by which science functions are part of the investigation and force constraints on the investigative process (Kuhn, 1962). Therefore, paradigms of science and their specific theories intimately influence what is studied and found in science. You are influenced to see what you expect to see. For this group of scientists there is something further, beyond the world that science delineates. This beyond turns up in new discoveries and ever new ways of viewing the phenomenon of nature. It is also revealed in the continual transformations and the "unlimited variety of qualities, processes, and relationships" (Bohm, 1957). Apparently this infinite variety can never be perceived by science. It has been intuited. It may be the stratum Einstein hypothesized.

It is hypothesized that the whole of this apparently disconnected variety of forms we call the world is an interconnected system. Various discoveries seem to point at a continuum in which forms have emerged out of or as part of some whole. Though forms show autonomy, they are more or less contingent on other features of the universe. J. S. Bell has recently given this a more precise formulation. His theorem states "that when two particles have interacted and then flown off in opposite directions, interference with one particle will instantly affect the other particle, regardless of the distance between them" (Koestler, 1978). In essence the interconnectedness of all things is implicit in the kind of telepathic communication between the two particles and suggests some sort of acausal or noncontiguous relationship. David Bohm writes (1974):

It is generally acknowledged that the quantum theory had many strikingly novel features. . . . However there has been too little emphasis on what in our view is the most fundamentally different new feature of all, i.e., the intimate interconnection of different systems that are not in spatial contact. This has been especially revealed through the well known experiments of Einstein, Podolsky, and Rosen. . . .   Recently interest in this question has been stimulated by the work of Bell, who obtained precise mathematical criteria, distinguishing the experimental consequences of this feature of quantum interconnectedness of distant systems

.... Thus, one is led to a new notion of *unbroken wholeness,*
which denies the classical idea of analyzability of the world into
separately and independently existent parts.... [author's em-
phasis]

These considerations point beyond the ideas embedded in
determinism and the mechanistic philosophy which assumes
that there are fixed basic qualities and that things can be reduced to quantitative relationships. Mechanistic theory assumes that defined entities interact so that quantitative changes
occur, but that actual qualitative transformation cannot occur.
In deterministic psychotherapy the ego gets stronger, but it is
not possible for the structure called the ego to be transformed
out of existence.

Non-deterministic psychotherapy arises in these insights
into the limitations of deterministic or mechanistic thinking.
The negation of deterministic thinking is its first principle. Thus
it assumes that all ideas about autonomy or separateness of any
phenomenon in nature, including any human being, are only
relative concepts. Any thought is by definition occurring in the
movement of the interconnectedness of all things; it is an abstraction from the context of its infinite interconnectedness.
Independence is relative, and the *it-ness* of a thought is *of* the
whole emergent totality of interconnections. When we *think* of
the whole, that thought does not really comprehend the totality. What we apprehend in such a thought is limited (Krishnamurti, 1979). Can we ever see ourselves seeing? No, so a
phenomenon of the universe such as our vision or our thought
never sees the whole of the universe. Perhaps we get some idea
of our way in the whole through our particular place in the
whole; but that is a complex matter and one must always have
doubts about one's assumptions that one can see all the ways
things are related. If I perceive my room and even sense its
place in a building as well as the building in the space of the
city, I do not really comprehend how it all fits into the planet,

and the planet into the solar system. Yet all this must affect the way things are. We often lose touch with relativity, uncertainty, and qualified conditions of any of our acts.

Non-deterministic psychotherapy attempts to know the limits of its instruments and points toward "knowing" its assumptions about movement in relationships between human beings. It urges that both participants in a psychotherapy are aspects of a larger, more complex whole in which the interaction of the two people, patient and therapist, are influenced by, and can gain from, the open system in which they occur. In this first principle of non-deterministic psychotherapy, we question the capacity to know about *all* the factors in relationship, and since we cannot know all, we cannot know what really causes anything. We emphasize that the birth of relationship is out of the larger whole and that whatever happens in the twosome is reflecting the *infinity of nature,* in its great variety of qualities, properties, and levels within levels which affect each other. Nothing simply happens as action/reaction without reference to movement in a vast background. This first principle begins with the awareness of the many levels.

The second principle of non-deterministic psychotherapy points toward comprehending consciousness and the movement of thought. It is an intention to develop a therapy of consciousness rather than the traditional therapy which is about the content of consciousness.

Like any other event in the interconnected world, *consciousness* and *thought* are part of the totality. Consciousness is a function in the whole. It is a responsiveness which features a wide spectrum of alertness. The brain searches for order as part of the implicit order in the world. Acting as part of this consciousness, thought is the move to find order through the ongoing extension of perception. Thought translates the process of perception into codes.

In non-deterministic psychotherapy, there is a consistent effort to see how these mental contents arise as the movement of consciousness. Our effort is directed at seeing the way these items function as instant ordering devices, and we attempt to avoid being exclusively caught by the content of meaning the patient attributes to each event in the context of his unique or social system. A person might recall that he felt when he was 5 years old the way he feels "now." Such a memory might actively extend and increase the awareness of this moment by suggesting the added dimension that the 5-year-old felt. Thus it is an additional symbolizing that expresses the current perception. But consider also what happens when an experience like that memory becomes an image toward which the person attempts to orient his life. In the immediacy of a moment a person only sees what and how this event is like and/or unlike the memory. *The invasion of the past into the present becomes the effort to construct the past in the present.* This blocks the possible movement of direct perception, sensuous, and motoric as well as cognitive, of what is immediately seen as the ingredients of the present.

Elaborate difficulties also occur when thought creates a thinker—the self, the "I" or me. The numerous experiences of a person are stored in memory and a concept of "I" occurs out of the organization of these memories. So for example, the human relationship of psychotherapy exists between two accumulated memories, a doctor and a patient, and is conducted on the basis of these enduring entities; the image of the self has become the person. When something happens that does not fit that image, conflict ensues. In these conditions the perception in the present is lost because the immediate orientation to an event resides in a comparison to this image.

These subtle events in which the self is created are the result of a trick not unlike that of a magician. We subtly come to believe in the reality of a constructed "self" which then becomes the agent of the subjective thoughts which made it. Then the subject is opposed to its thoughts and to the objects that it, as agent, perceives. The agent is captured by its version of reality, a reality which has created the agent as much as the agent has created it.

As each thought or fragment states an *absolute,* the unbroken world is broken up by thought. It draws lines around connected, moving pieces of nature in such a way that standing entities are created; these entities, like the self, arise almost instantly, created by thoughts—as cognition assembles a "thing." Thought can also be so particular and specific that it narrows the vision of a changing reality; it sets up comparisons by creating those "things"—as well as opposites such as good/bad. Thus conflict is created out of thought.

In essence, when entities are seen only from the perspective of their isolated condition rather than from the essence of their generation or emergence from the whole, fragmentation and conflict are inevitable. Consider how we hear an opinion from a friend, as opposed to a politician. In the former case we see the expression as a sensitive part of a totality, a current crisis, transition, or physical difficulty. We sense that it emerges out of immediacy, and wonder what will come with further transition. The politician we identify as a "this." He may feel that his self-identity—it-ness—is now institutionalized into a thing which he must defend even if it engenders conflict between him and others.

The movement of the thought of a patient in psychotherapy inheres in the contents of his consciousness. The therapist and the patient attend to these movements and consider their relationships to other contents. But simultaneously the therapist, and perhaps the patient, can see that thought is an event of action in a brain. This is an organic brain process seeking order, like the liver cells metabolizing glycogen and the kidney tubule cells extracting sodium and potassium from the fluid on its way to becoming urine. All these processes operate as forms of ordering in the cosmos, though they may create disorder if there is a jam or knot in the chemical processes. The block, as in genetic defects, prevents the continued flow of action.

This leads to some subtle questions for psychotherapists. Consider for example that the consciousness of both patient and therapist are *action-differentiating.* By this I mean that *all movements of brain are articulating human presence by varying means of relationship, in the movement of the session.* The thought process which takes place in the moment of therapeutic interaction is a form of behavior. A "going on" means that it is happening right now, in the form of actual biochemical and electrical changes, events. Human beings often think that thought accurately reflects what is "reality" and, given the way language functions, it does. Through human consensual validation of apparently unvarying events, thought structures relationship and thus creates what we call world. We experience "reality" through thought, then we play in it.

The flow of ideas in psychotherapy displays the motions of the events in the room; the thoughts display or are the "it-ness" of this room. A supra observer, one who is not part of this room, would see the movement of the therapist's and the patient's thought as one detail after another in the total movement of the world of the session; and if he were not part of the world, he would see that the sphere of the room is another movement in the world. If he were part of the world, however, he would not be able to see the whole.

Of course the patient's and the therapist's thought is to be seen as *content* as well. The direction of the content, the subject matter, is the node around which consciousness tends to focus and reverberate. Consciousness is the attribution of significance to recurring thoughts. We "forget" the movement of thought itself because we *identify with ourselves as thinker and self and sufferer.* We live out the subject/object division of therapist to patient, therapist to his own thoughts, or patient and therapist to the object patient whom they both study as if it were a thing. Sometimes many interesting connections and relationships are discovered during this study. Moments of clarity do not seem to result from the direction, intention, or purpose of the content of the connections, but rather evolve as *by-products.* Having observed the many ways (thoughts) in which we are embedded in a current gestalt, we suddenly experience a sense of release from that construction and develop an openness to what is next.

Consider the rather simple example of the patient who came in and spoke of how she favored her father over her mother. He also favored her over her mother. I said something simple like, "I wonder if your behavior is part of a general competitive feeling toward your mother." From one angle, my statement is relating to content. Our conversation, at least as I experience it, stays within the field of content and I make an effort to be clear about the form of her relating patterns with women and men. To say "compete" implies that I see her as object engaged in trying to get some *thing,* person, or event, into the machinery of her life; she changes her relationships and feels more securely connected when they are consolidated. To "have" her father in a way her mother did not gave her power, pleasure, and protection from the insecurity she felt early in life in the undifferentiated relationship with her mother which aroused questions about the fundamental insecurity constituting her adult life. Yet she could not live in insecurity with equanimity. She did not trust her presence there, so thought came in with projects designed to obtain the *pleasurable sense of order* her father could offer. To be attached to father was an image that seemed to offer her protection against uncertainty. So she attempted to achieve it in her actions.

From another angle, "forgetting" content, *therapist thought acts as a material event* in the moment; it is a *chemical act which seeks to find order* or security in the session.

Non-deterministic psychotherapy distinguishes these two modes of looking at thinking: thought as content goes for security by acting to consolidate around some idea which is more inclusive—such as this patient's seeking to be with her father. That is an idea to which thinking is connecting with other ideas. Thinking is also an act which is a material movement in space and time, performed by a body which is in (and of) nature.

For example, one man needed to say "hello" and "good-bye" before and after each session. On exploring this, we observe that he is simply filling space-time with the noise of social gesture. Refraining from his habitual greeting suddenly opens for him the sacredness of such transitions as coming and going, and allows him to face the poignancy he feels in time. Then, facing the poignancy leads him into all that he perceives, feels, experiences, and moves with in the times of coming together and the time of leave taking. It is also a fact that thought as material interference had been jamming the networks of the perceptual system and preventing events that might occur if his brain were clear for unedited perception of the moment.

When a therapist responds in a session with a memory or acts as he did in a past part of his life (countertransference), he becomes *matter-thought acting as a total process of organism to close off the time.* If a therapist says something that comes from the past or acts as he did in a past, he is closing off content. Also if a therapist relates in the same way as the patient, he has been "determined" by content; content stops the flow of awareness. In such interference situations, the patient's perceptions of a scene or person are not developed and allowed to occur openly. There is a restriction in response and a diminution of variety.

As with memory that extends perception or moment, all thought can be a cooperative searchlight. In this process, thought coordinates a moment's connections and extends awareness by pointing beyond itself; it is an action which reminds one of exploratory searching not unlike the movements of body that we see in a fine athlete trusting himself to explore the vicissitudes of his space without knowing what is coming next. Thought becomes a trial-and-error process, reaching with metaphors that allude to that which is beyond thought. Thought comprehends and fails with each gesture, leaving behind that lingering prehension that there is much more than we will ever "know."

The third principle of non-deterministic psychotherapy is that there is a process of transformation in the movement of nature (Shainberg, 1973, 1975). As part of it, we assume we are in an open system and know there exist innumerable possibilities; it is observed that things do change. People eat certain foods and feel stronger from eating some foods and not others.

They feel better in some environments and not in others. We note all kinds of changes: water becomes steam or ice; clouds form from moisture in the sky or become rain. We see shifts when we exercise or find new strength in our muscles. We talk to a friend or to a professional person and there is change in the way we feel about ourselves and our lives. In all these situations we begin to believe in the transformation processes as well as in the notion that things are not fixed in the form in which they appear (Shainberg, 1973).

Growth (as compared to transformation) in biological and emotional process is the extension from the current structure. Existing conditions stimulate a response which may call for modification and change of existing capacities to handle the response. The child "grows" into a better walker through his attempts to negotiate steps, hills, and other environmental structures that he could not do before he tried.

Transformation, however, implies a change in form, not an extension of an old one. A person who sees the world as a fearful or terrible place lives every moment according to that principle. His activity is governed by his need for protection. But it is a transformation when that same person begins to feel a respect for life and himself and others. He takes difficulties and struggles as part of a life movement rather than as proof of what is bad. Such a difference is a transformation of his whole presence—how he lives, how he spends his time, and how he responds to a problem.

The ancient Greeks believed that there must be a basic unchanging substance which would constitute the building blocks of the universe. Each time that which was thought to be basic was broken down to smaller building blocks; the process led to the discovery of smaller and smaller particles, until it was realized that there may be no basic building block of the universe. Currently, everything is thought to be energy and matter in movement, with no designated definition of a basic substance. Thus matter itself has come to be seen as an aspect of the transmutating universe which makes itself only to disintegrate and reform again. Bohm (1957) writes:

> An essential characteristic of the rich and highly interconnected substructure of moving matter described above is that not only do the quantitative properties in it continually change but the basic qualities that define its mode of being can also undergo fundamental transformations when conditions alter sufficiently. Thus in electrical discharges atoms can be excited and ionized, in which case they obtain many new physical and chemical properties. Under bombardment with very high energy particles the nuclei of the various chemical elements can be excited and transformed into new kinds of nuclei, with even more radical changes in their physical and chemical properties. Moreover, in nuclear processes, neutrons can be transferred into protons, either by the emission of neutrinos or of mesons; and of course as we have seen, mesons are unstable, so that their very modes of existence implies the necessity for their transforming into basically different kinds of particles. Thus further research into the structure of matter has not only shown what is, as far as we have been able to tell, an unlimited variety of qualities, processes, and relationships, but it has also demonstrated that all of these things are subject to fundamental transformations that depend on conditions. (p. 137)

The generation of form and all the movement attendant on its happening suggests that any thing that appears is both of a generative process which generates an event that draws our attention to what we name or define as a thing or form. Conceptions such as self, ego, superego, id, etc., are merely various theoretical constructs about personality organizations. The forms of self, ego, superego, and id are descriptions of ways in which thought is organized. In a way, they are principles of operations—various ways the brain as thought takes shape. But they are also creations of clinicians who essentially take their cue from their own consciousness. It is possible that other forms of organization (principles of order) can come into being. Or that a total transformation in ordering can occur. It is possible that there is a brain that does not act through fragmentary principles like ego, id, and superego, but rather as a whole in response to what is. Perhaps Freud was hinting at that when he said where id is there shall ego be.

This third principle of transformation in non-deterministic psychotherapy can be correlated with the other principles through a specific example: Often a patient will come to a session and sit for a whole hour without speaking. Sometimes after such a session, this patient will say that he felt terrific about the hour. He was clear, aware of his surroundings, and did not get caught in his usual conflicts and ambivalences. Or a person may come and we will go over all the reasons he does not like his friend or wife. He discusses this dislike with a violence and vituperativeness that, from all appearances, can only lead to an irrevocable separation from the person in question. Yet, at the next session, the patient reports that he saw the other person as if for the first time. Although he saw the same qualities he did not like before, these things were now seen as part of a wider and more total movement of a varied and exciting human being. He realized that now he was free to see that his ideas about the other did not have to be, indeed, could not be, absolute. He was no longer fixed on the idea of the other, and realized at the same time that there existed new possibilities for responding to him/her. From a perspective which does not assume that the partner is a *certain way,* a relationship opens, becomes flexible, free. Often, the patient will experience great affection for this other person, who now emerges with so many different shapes because he/she is seen as an essential forming system rather than a coalesced form.

In one sense the events of these sessions act to *complete* whatever event these thoughts display when they are in their pure hateful, rigid, fixed conceptualization of the other person. In this process, the brain acts like a muscle whose action is the initiation or the completion of a process. As we see in the circular repetition of the relationships of many patients, the brain usually acts differently from a muscle because of thought.

It does not go all the way with its thought behavior. It gets caught in its own tracks because *one thought is only "complete" in itself without completion of the process—of which the thought is but one isolated aspect.* In that movement of isolation, whether a relationship or an image, thought forms a closed gestalt that prevents a full interaction in the totality of which the organism is part. Imagine a tree that does *not* grow into the air to use the sunlight. Instead it becomes focused on one leaf or one branch and curls around itself as a focus rather than the sun. What then happens to this tree?

One of the important aspects of thinking is the way thoughts and feelings go *so fast.* In this movement there is a spontaneous inertia that leads to the identifying with a particular thought which gives pleasure. Out of this nugget a self of security-producing thoughts and images is eventually created. These are accumulated memories of moments of organization in reality which contribute to an overall sense of survival. A self thinks a thought and we are then following behind as this self which is thinking. In all this, one really does *not* have affection, tolerance, or respect for thought movement. There is no awareness of this movement as the creation of self and self action. This inattention, this absence of awareness, occurs partly because identification with an image of self creates a fixed image of what this thinker is. Thought, feeling, being, moves very fast. The institution called "self" is implicitly questioned as to its pertinence and stability in the face of a changing universe, but identification with a self precludes this actual questioning. We are constantly insecure about being toppled from our pedestal or pseudo-stability and we cling to security as if it were real. Thus from a fixed place, the movement of response to actual insecurity in an open system is not complete; in one aspect thought happens as a rational movement of ordering, but that event of response cannot go to its completion because it is checked with what *has been* created by thought in the past.

Like a muscle in repose after exercise, the mind experiences a deep quiet after full and affirmative awareness of what is. Rather than limiting itself to understanding content, the acting-through in such psychotherapy sessions settles for nothing less than an articulation of the nature of consciousness itself. Then the whole fixed idea (the knot) either withers of its own accord, or perhaps, having fully articulated its limits within the ingredients comprising the empirical facts of nature, confronts the movement of nature, and bursts into awareness. The movement of the open system of life of other human beings absorbs thought as yet another of the many variegated forms in nature. From that perspective, thought in whatever form is one among many events in life.

The fourth principle of non-deterministic psychotherapy connects with the first three. It is that *you cannot get there from here.* Our insight into the limits of conceptions of consciousness reveals the cul-de-sac inherent in the necessity we give to contents of consciousness. In the sessions where there is a free exercise of thought, we sometimes see that we are caught by the necessity of thinking itself. It is not just the content of our thoughts but the massive sputtering process of *thinking* that grabs our being and spins it around over and over. When both the content of necessity and the necessity of content are seen, there is a *sudden surcease of the narrow fixing* that these necessities provide (Angyal, 1965; Horney, 1950; Kelman, 1971). So the fourth principle articulates that through thought one does not get to that clarity that is movement and life energy in a variegated open system. There is *no linear development* toward an actual openness. An observer psychotherapist could say, "I think the patient moved from this point to that point." He is describing something that he observed in sequence, but that does not mean there is a development from one to the other. Nor do his words adequately describe the area we refer to as beyond the reach of thought, though thought functioning in its illuminating mode may participate in this state by being the movement of the larger whole.

A patient may see that although he is working on something which thought has created, this working is not bringing him closer to the freedom of life in the open realm. Perhaps he meets someone who lives differently. He senses a difference, a freedom. He sees he can only go from one thought to another and therefore remains hopelessly curtailed, even though he thinks of freedom. We often hear a person say, "If I could do that I could be over there." He sees the other over there and he wants to go there. That is patently absurd, because he is *here in chaos* and not in clarity. His wanting is in this chaos. To see here is to see what is and that is the only thing that is possible. It is only possible to see here and to see the *extent* of this place. In fact, on seeing what is here there is a transformation; *instantly* one becomes part of the way of this place, which is life in action. There is a *sudden* sense of the openness to all being lived in this way, the actual presence of organisms as nature manifests them through action no matter how limited. So it is a connection with the motion of life.

Nature is *indefinable* in its complete movement but it is registered sometimes when we feel or see the flowing, integrating, and learning. It comes out of a silence of creating inside participation. Everything comes in as flow rather than as fixed quantity because things *are flow* as their momentariness in nature portrays; they are allowed to move on or be seen. With this realization, thinking occurs in full awareness of its relative place in a vast domain of action.

Non-deterministic psychotherapy is concerned with the capacity for *attention* to what actually pertains. Its *objectives* are beyond a mere intellectual understanding, beyond the mere acquisition of information about the self. It does not seek an objective working through of conflict because attention reveals that conflict is a function of general fragmentation.

The direction of non-deterministic psychotherapy is learning: that means to be in the vein of living, in the flow, seeing *how* it happens. Learning is most often considered to be the ability to acquire information. But in this work, learning is defined as the *capacity* to see what is. That is, to be able to perceive accurately and to move on that accurate perception in a correct manner. This implies the capacity to learn from one's own responsiveness and right action in living. This kind of receptiveness, this "learning" does not mean storing information but rather understanding what it is to see freshly and to continue seeing freshly. It ultimately asks whether a person is able to live in touch with what is and whether he can go on being present in such a receptive manner. Is he truly resilient?

Socrates said "know thyself," and it often seems to mean to get information about a self: rather like carrying a dossier with this information about "myself." But in the deepest sense of Socrates' directive, we are urged toward a moment-by-moment alertness to what this "self" really is.

In line with these principles and objectives, non-deterministic psychotherapy evolves its *therapeutic practice.* The practice, like the principles, is in the evolving stage where it hopes to stay; like its objectives, it is an ever-changing, widening practice. Certain practices can be singled out as arising from the principles that have been stated. For example, I distinguish two basic moves, *decoding* and *encoding* (Shainberg, 1978). Decoding teases apart the movement of relationship, consciousness, and thought. Consider an example: A man who was emotionally drained and in turmoil nevertheless felt compelled to schedule an appointment with one of his patients. He gaves lots of reasons—she needed it, he could not bear to let her down, he could not tell if he might not have to cancel again the following day because he expected the same confusion and difficulty in the court case in which he was embroiled. As we teased this apart, it became clear that he was in a very disrupted state. He had been involved in a very difficult personal matter and was suffering. He was split into many pieces, with many conflicts between the pieces in his mind. To control these fragments there was a new piece, "Be a good doctor." So, insecurity gave birth to fragmentation, and now a new fragment, "control the situation"; his direction was captured to put it all together under that rubric. But the move to put it together was part of the general confusion as well, and his session with the patient was, as one might expect, a case of fragment hitting fragment and ostensibly more search for cohesion. There was more confusion, ambivalence, anger, arrogance, conflict. He had "become" the right way, an image from his past coming into play as a path for the present. Teasing all this apart revealed the necessity of the feeling that "something had to be done with the patient." The content's necessity was clear: he believed that the patient really needed him to see her in order to assuage her anxiety, though in fact, on many occasions, she had proven herself much stronger than he thought.

Teasing all this apart in the decoding operation brought attention to the events of his life: he found it unsatisfactory to be in uncertainty with himself or his patients. This attention loosened the necessity of the content, as well as the content of necessity, because he saw how uncertainty as a safety measure had generated it all. Having a clear insight into the fact that these moves were not absolutely real so much as protective necessities, he instantly opened into his uncertainty. Sadness came over him as he appreciated his new condition of being without the wife from whom he was just divorced, his presence in the world without his usual attachments, and his new connection to death as the ultimate uncertainty of his life. He saw his actual insecurity for which his marriage had been one of the solutions, and began to feel some security in the insecurity of death's certainty.

The events observed with this man are a pattern we often see in decoding situations. Following a clear comprehension of the limits of a particular kind of relationship, there is a *transformation;* it is a *cessation,* and then a *carry forward* (Shainberg 1977). This carry forward is definitely not the function, "or action," or will of an agent self. It is the connection of everything in the universe exhibiting itself in human form. The patient's narrowed participation, based on a particular memory, dissolves and a state of connectedness *appears.* This is *not* an example of the first state becoming the second, but rather an action of relationship in an open system after the limits of the thought events have been seen. The fragmentation ceases because the inaccuracy and ineptitude can be instantly known, the way we know we are walking off balance and right ourselves spontaneously. The new movement is a spontaneous activity in the new mode. The man in the illustration carried forward the uncertainty of his life, feeling more present with others, and much calmer—both subjectively and objectively; he expressed warm and connected feelings with me, and was more aware of possibilities in places he had thought of as either closed or susceptible to only one solution. He was more attentive to the movement of thoughts as a trap. He began to watch the arising of thought, its goals, and the relief he thought he had obtained from the old patterns. He saw how self-defeating these familiar old thoughts had become, how inappropriate to his present life, how destructive of new possibilities.

Another part of decoding is the therapist's affectionate awareness of what is. He gradually conveys that to his patient who, hopefully, begins to feel it toward his own life. This kind of listening and feeling is also experienced at the end of a Waking Dream session such as those described by Epstein (1978). In that process, a person is encouraged to follow every image his thought presents, to follow every shifting ramification. It is experienced as a freedom, an allowance of imagination because all judgment of thought and what develops from it is suspended. There is a real effort toward *no blame* for killing, hating, loving, or anger. Feelings and thoughts are heard and known for what they are. The therapist says "yes" or "good" to any act of mind. At the end the person who has been doing all this in imagination has a sense of respect for the movement of mind because he has exercised the muscle of the brain performing a task in its arena to the full. More often than not, this is accompanied by a peace and quietness which is also an alertness to what comes next in the movement of life.

One woman came to a Monday session and told me of a difficult weekend filled with many jealous feelings. Her lover was away, and she had been overwhelmed with fear. As she talked, I could feel her struggle. She did not want to be jealous, she did not want to experience it. Not because it was so painful, but because it was as if the experience or event of feeling jealous was *wrong*. I suggested she invite jealousy to dinner, sit down with it, take a walk with it, talk with it, and see if she could get to know it rather than just trying to run it out of her house. Through this kind of watching something mysterious happened. This began with her seeing the inception of jealousy in the anxiety she felt about what her lover would do with his time and what attachments she had to his filling her time. She had come to the point where she had to have him. Any absence, or projected loss, meant she would have nothing to do. She saw grabbing, holding, fearing, and then the jealousy simply was gone. And more in the carry forward, she was attentive to all of such movements of attachments to such pleasures. In her next sessions, she discussed a new awareness: she saw for the first time that over the past 10 years, whenever she had experienced pain or tension, she used to take or think of a medication that would relieve the pain. The whole subject of isolating her process of pain or tension and avoiding the movement of her changes was seen, and she was more able to be present with what is.

The second therapeutic practice which we will note is *encoding*. "En" means in, into, within, entwine, enfold, enshroud, to put into, to make, cause to become. "Code" means set of conventional symbols, agreed system of letters and words used in very secret or private communication in which a letter or word is presented for one that is quite different. In combination, the two syllables mean the movement of one set of symbols or action into another. Non-deterministic psychotherapy uses the word *encoding* to designate the new kind of processing or being in the world which has now become available for ongoing action in a person's life. This, however, is not meant to mean that encoding is developing a new way to be. A new code teaches *not* that is is better than the previous code so much as that *many codings are possible;* a new code is evidence of the capacity to be present as a forming process in an open system. It is a celebration of forming, and it celebrates all the ways that uncertainty can be lived through. So encoding is also not a single, finite experience, but the continuous event of seeing and acting, or exercising the capacity to order out of private, secret, meanings. These private, secret meanings come from the particular places each person uniquely lives and knows as his perspectives. Encoding recognizes the importance of seeing the unique place of each person. From that limit and definition of presence, a transformation is possible.

One patient was walking around in the office before I entered. I asked her what was happening and she mentioned an unusual object that she saw in the ashtray and was looking at when I walked in. It was a piece of an old radio tube. I handed it to her. After we discussed the object, she said it was really unusual that I had reached over and given it to her. This led on into the fact that our sessions had certainly changed since we had talked about sex. Several weeks ago she had mentioned her fear of her desire to be a lap dog in my presence; that is, of jumping into my lap. She also had feared my being overwhelmed by my sexual feelings for her. Since that talk, she had felt present and sensed my presence as never before.

Things which had felt to her like mere projections now felt real. In this context she remembered a fantasy that she had had several years before in which she had seen me collapse on the waiting room floor and her first reaction had been, "What do I do with him now?" Recently she had had the same feeling with her lover when he became disturbed. Out loud, with her, I first began to wonder what it was about our previous discussion of sex that had broken through the self-consciousness; then I wondered aloud what happens in the midst of this new feeling of being present that she should start talking about the old time when she was afraid to feel directly and when she could not tolerate the responsibility for another. I wondered if the two fit together. She said that the remembering of a time when she was afraid of responsibility was a way of knowing the difference of the present through contrast. As she talked more of that old time, she began to feel how stale was that refusal of responsibility.

She reported that a new moment, a new presence, created fear because it created a history, a new event, in the connections previously established with a person. The depth of contact that grew in the intimacy left her with a sense of sadness; she said it was because the contact meant so much, was so real and not a projection, and she became afraid of losing it, leaving her with the history only of what she remembered.

Our discussion of sex had provided an opening because it allowed for the exploration of forming of feeling as we lived within the moment-by-moment presence of uncertainty that comes when one simply *is,* and in the presence of another responsive and responding person who also resonates and reacts all at once. Memory and thought are irrelevant in these resonating moments. As she lived into this uncertainty, in our mutual presence, she began to see that history does not have to be the burden she had made it by holding onto certain memories and excluding others. She saw that she had needed to hold to a certain image of herself in order to protect herself from the openness of her whole range of forming. Furthermore, her opening into our relationship allowed for the forming in a relationship that did not make any demands for further historical responsibility. Whatever responsibility of that order came up was imposed by her clutching. She could see this, but at one point when I said to her, "How does it feel to know that you are not responsible for me in any way whatsoever?" she replied that although theoretically it was "terrific," in fact she wondered if she could live with it. This alerted her to her reality which showed her that although, at one level, she refused and was afraid of responsibility, at a second, perhaps deeper level, she needed to feel responsible at all times, even inappropriately, for this gave her an illusion of control. She did sense a way of letting the events of our being present to each other give birth to whatever was there that needed to "come out." It seemed that her being with me was giving rise to a process in which she recognized inappropriate attachments, let them go, and became open to new forming. In the course of this breakthrough, it is of significance that she showed more responsiveness, seemed less emotionally dead.

It is in the moments following the decoding, in the moments when the encoding or *carrying forward* period begins that the therapist undergoes his most severe test. It is then, when his "help" is no longer needed, for the conflict is gone, that he is tested in his capacity to remain in the open, moving himself, but with nothing "to do" for his "patient." This is not to mean that he will move himself, much less that he will change. No, it is rather that, deeply, this moment asks, "Is the therapist *actually* a connectedness in the movement of the universe?" Or has he asked something of his "patient" that he himself is unprepared or unwilling to participate in himself? It is a question as to whether he can *depend on the unknown* and live himself in the action of open relating.

At the moment of the unknown in the space where the new forming will begin, the moment of the carry forward, unfortunately we find therapists who are only able to analyze, or intellectualize, needing to "explain," to feel safe in their verbal authority. In doing so they block an opportunity to be found by the unknown.

I have found that when my thought stops (as observed afteward), that is, is *actually quiet,* something quite different happens. The second person in this non-deterministic work is drawn forward, speaks of more intimate matters. It feels as if both of us come into a world we had never before explored.

There are some therapists who think that the healing action of the therapist comes from his "being" different and even opposite to the malignant internal objects his patient reports. And although it is true that the therapist's unwillingness to get caught in his patient's obsessions is important, the deeper issue is *whether the therapist truly knows the limits of all thought and the danger of any movements that avoid the experience of what is.* If he does know this, then he lives in the availability of the flowing, forming continuum with attention to what is. Unfortunately, therapists are often people who have become therapists because they need to know and conceptualize; though they do not get caught in internal objects they get hooked by their theories or their intellectualizations. They are unable to be present at the active edge of the unknown, to stay with uncertainty right in a session.

Thus the therapy always hangs on that question of whether the therapist is able to live in such an ambience and support such participation. Both the world and the movement of thought in the patient act to oppose such vibrant, open "being born," and when this moment occurs in the therapeutic process, it is necessary for at least one of the participants to *carry forward.* If the therapist is in any way still attached to his desire to avoid the present, the uncertainty that has been generated will stimulate that desire and, like a rope around his neck, will pull him back into some thought of how to dissolve the uncertainty.

Genuineness is not something a therapist can fake. Is he or is he not living and available for open engagement? If he is, then he can now move with the patient to make encoding a real fact because he moves as a human being in the cosmos, or rather as a human-expressing cosmos. It is then no longer therapist *and* patient, but *one* field moving together, articulating the true way of energies moving in the world, manifesting their actual flow, and not simply hung up in distinctions of thought like "therapist" and "patient," or whatever.

The techniques that appear in non-deterministic psychotherapy will arise out of these principles. The serious questions in whatever happens will be, how genuine is the therapist's awareness of the limitations of any conceptualization, and how is he in the actual flow of relating? Freud once said that the end of all psychoanalytic work is that the patient should be able to love and work. I would add to this the importance of love in the actual work itself. But who will teach a person, therapist or patient, to love? Is it the movement of love that is revealed with the negation of all technique and conceptualizing thought? Is it perhaps love when the flow of something much greater than individuals, thinking, or willing, takes place? These are the concerns that non-deterministic psychotherapy works toward realizing.

REFERENCES

Angyal, A. *Neurosis and treatment.* New York: John Wiley, 1965.

Bohm, D. *Causality and chance in modern physics.* Philadelphia: University of Pennsylvania Press, 1957.

Bohm, D., & Hiley, B. On the intuitive understanding on non-locality as implied by quantum theory. Reprint, Birkbeck College, London.

Epstein, G. The experience of waking dream in psychotherapy, in Fosshage and P. Olsen, Eds., *Healing, Implications for Psychotherapy.* New York: Human Sciences Press, 1978.

Horney, K. *Neurosis and human growth.* New York: W. W. Norton, 1950.

Jones, D. Entropic models in biology: The next scientific revolution? in *Perspectives in biology and medicine.* Chicago: University of Chicago Press, 1977.

Kelman, H. *Helping people.* New York: Science House, 1971.

Koestler, A. *Janus.* New York: Random House, 1978.

Krishnamurti, J. *The wholeness of life.* New York: Harper and Row, 1979.

Kuhn, T. *The structure of scientific revolutions.* Chicago: University of Chicago Press, Phoenix Books, 1962.

Miller, J. *The paradox of cause and other essays.* New York: W. W. Norton, 1978.

Shainberg, D. *The transforming self.* New York: Intercontinental Medical Book Corporation, 1973.

Shainberg, D. Consciousness and psychoanalysis, *Journal of the American Academy of Psychoanalysis,* 1975 *3*(2), 131.

Shainberg, D. Transforming transitions in patients and therapists, in K. Frank, Ed., *The human dimension in psychoanalytic practice,* New York: Grune & Stratton, 1977a.

Shainberg, D. Working through. In J. L. Fosshage and P. Olsen, Eds. *Healing, Implications for Psychotherapy.* New York: Human Sciences Press, 1978.

Skynner, A. C. R. The relationship of psychotherapy to sacred tradition in *On the way to self knowledge,* ed. J. Needleman and Lewis, D. New York: Alfred Knopf, 1976.

Wyld, H. C. *The universal english dictionary.* London: Routledge, Kegan & Paul.

chapter 10

FREEDOM WITH DARKNESS AND LIGHT: A STUDY OF A MYTH

Charles E. Scott

> Imagination takes all creation apart, and with the materials gathered and arranged according to rules that originate only in the deepest part of the soul, it creates a new world . . .
>
> Beaudelaire

MYTHICAL DETERMINATION

I shall assume in this discussion that a significant part of our language and tradition is Greek in origin. That part, as well as the other equally significant parts that come from the Hebrews, from Africa, the Anglo-Saxons, etc., forms groups of meanings in our awareness that are embedded and transmitted in our language and tradition. These meanings give determination and identity in our lives. I shall also assume that the myths and mythological thinking in our Greek heritage deal with commonalities for human being, that we are determined partially by a conglomerate expression in this heritage of how we are together in the universe. This expression forms a cultural way of seeing that is, at least partially, unavoidable. When we think with the myths, as distinct to thinking about them with nonmythological purposes in mind, we are in touch with determinations which are depth meanings in our world. Probably one of the most important aspects of thinking with myths is openness to the myth itself. That is like being open with dreams, not reducing them to nondream structures, but moving with them as much as possible on their terms and certainly on their ground. One becomes less bound and absorbed by the ordinary practices and assumptions of one's working life. One becomes freer and more open, more aware of possibilities and other realities that lie outside of routines, habits, and customs. Above all, one becomes accustomed to a region of happening quite distinct to the usual places of waking awareness. A region that is one's own happening, but one that is not governed by the way "things ordinarily happen." By dwelling openly and nonreductively with dreams and fantasies we become freer in relation to the arbitrariness of the usual in our waking lives.

The same can be said for thinking with myths. They come from a region of our heritage that is distant, but they form part of our present heritage, and so are, like the unexpected dream, close. As we think with them, trading criticism for appreciation and "objectivity" for involvement, we find that we draw closer to regions of our awareness which we in no sense originated, but which are ours and in which we are commonly together. That discovery of commonality in myths will tend to be veiled or hidden if we think about them in nonmythological ways, as we do when we analyze them to find out what the Greeks thought about nature or the gods or whatever. In such cases of scholarship and learning we generate helpful information that allows us to report on differences and similarities. But that information must be rethought—reimagined—and freed from the very apparatus that unearthed it, before we can experience the depth of our awareness in them.

As we gain more feel for meanings in the myths common in our language and tradition, we become more alert not only to meanings that relate us and constitute us in the depth of our inherited awareness. We also gain touch with how the myths express our human commonality, our being together in common. An extraordinary double edge: shared, given, unchosen meanings that have to do with how we are shared, given, and unchosen. Greek myths often express profound experiences of determinations given in the way the world is and pervasive for our kind. And like an artist of this century, the myths, in their iteration, engender a freedom of consciousness, a capacity to be free by telling the determinations and with naming and personalizing the movements of inevitability.

I share with my age the persuasion that determinations and inevitabilities are historical. The inevitabilities that lead to the tragedy of Romeo and Juliet depend on the existence of brutal family rivalaries, a semi-medieval Catholicism, etc. The destinies of our inherited awareness, though not appreciably alterable in any one life-time, may well not exist for people in quite a different culture. Destinies come as histories, and inevitabilities come in how things have presence with a people. In our history, two much brooded inevitabilities are light and darkness with their attendant spatial imagery of height and depth. We expect light and darkness, with their close associates of life and death, memory and forgetfulness, gaiety and terror, growth and decline, wakefulness and sleep, to carry meaning everywhere. I suspect that nothing carries more depth and power in our western history than the relation of illumination and darkness, a relation closely in touch with haleness and madness.

Light and darkness have a cosmic dimension. They mean a certain pervasiveness of all things, a slant on how things are given, the shades of presence. No light at all cannot mean for us a complete absence. It might mean an edge of total darkness, like a far horizon as night falls on a prairie, or the coming of no consciousness at all or total loss of something. But light, consciousness and possession are meant at once in these particular instances. Hence, my deepest attitudes regarding light and darkness are lived in my relation with all things.

I propose to explore a dimension of light and darkness, writ large, in one small portion of Greek mythology. I shall make therapeutically related observations along the way, holding always in mind that these notions are fateful in our lives and that freedom means, in part, being imaginatively open for these determinations that have determination as their issue. The underlying thesis is that *freedom happens as imaginative openness in determined states.* When these states of determination become the subject of profound fantasy, a remarkable freeness happens in which the determinants are slightly transcended in their telling. That occurrence reflects what I take the Greeks to have addressed when they spoke of one cosmos filled with irreconcilable differences.

THE ELEMENTS OF HADES AND ZEUS

Zeus and Hades are brothers. After they and their allies defeated Cronos and the Titans, Hades received the Underworld as a gift, and Zeus found his sway and aegis at Olympus. The element of Hades is darkness, not the moon-lit kind or even a moonless, starry kind, but a pitch darkness, a lightless realm of divinity that is impenetrable for living mortals. His realm is not at all like the Isles of the Blessed, that was to appear later in Greek imagery, where heroes find timeless fellowship together. Hades' place, a residence of the dead, is more like a prison and being taken there is like violent capture or rape. It is a heavy place—down, down, down—and is probably more akin to Saturn's element than it is even to Hades' spawning mother, Gaea, whose children replaced empty chaos. Saturn freezes and rigidifies. But Hades captures too, in darkness and invisibility, if with greater warmth.

Hades, in fact, took Erebus' place. Erebus was not

spawned from Gaea, but from Chaos alone. Chaos was total emptiness until Gaea founded and gave forth the world. Erebus was a void under the earth, a vast emptiness in which nothing came together or happened, no spawning, no growth, no harvesting, no speaking, no sound, no decay, not a soul there— nothing. With Hades came place, darkness over against light, death, condemnation, imprisonment. The goddess Night, also the child of Chaos and not of Gaea, is closely related to Hades' place. She gave forth both Aether and Daylight, as well as Fate, Destiny, Death, Sleep, Dreams, Memesis, Old Age, and Strife, among others. (She is also the grandmother of Strife's children which include Murder, Lying Words, Lawlessness, Famine, and Ruin).

Hades' place is no womb. But it happens, it is manifest in its darkness, and therein is Gaea's heritage and victory over Erebus. She enjoys part of her victory in the occurrence of death —death too, like all else, was absent in Erebus. And the misery and fate and condemnations and violence and putrid hatreds and all that is dark and ugly and deathly have their place in Gaea's son's region, in which much that is awful and lifeless *happens.* This awful place means life.

Invisibility happens there too. Hades' gift from Gaea's monsters, the Cyclopes, was a helmet that made its wearer invisible. He received it at the same time that Zeus received the gift of lightning and thunderbolts from the Cyclopes, as they all prepared to defeat Cronus and send him and the Titans to the Underworld, to be guarded by the monsters of Gaea. Darkness for Hades means invisibility, not seeing, not coming out into the light, no cancellation of Lethe, no truth. One might wonder if Erebus is not to be preferred, if one might choose, given the totally evasive and ungraspable region of Hades in all its terror. But Hades is there, quite utter and divine, forever canceling absence in his dark and elusive way.

Zeus' element is Aether. That is not to be forgotten. Aether, daughter of Night, granddaughter of Chaos, not the child of Gaea or of Uranus or of Cronos. As far as I know,

Erebus and Night were the only children of Chaos. For Nothing at All, Chaos did a lot, giving as it did the element of Hades and, through Night, the element of Zeus. But Zeus' element is once removed from Chaos, and the distance between Aether and utter darkness must itself be considered divine. Aether is not mortal light, and though related to Day, is not the same as the light of Day. That light vanishes and comes back, it is suffused with Night, circumscribed by it, and reflects the mortality of human beings. Aether, to the contrary, is as pure as Hades' darkness is utter, clear luminousity, ever light, total absence of darkness, clean separation from Mother Night, but grandchild of Chaos nonetheless, as awful for people in its purity as Darkness is in its density, but in a totally different way. Zeus could see as far as he wanted in it. Vision was not obstructed. It neither held things up nor weighted them down. All that is in Aether appears. Its touch is manifestness. No closure, no hiddenness, no necessity, no requirements, not even one principle of order. Old and condemned Chaos, once removed, smiles absently in the no order, no destiny, no history, no person, no good, no evil, luminous and absolute indifference of Aether, Zeus' element.

But Zeus is also Gaea's son, who defeated Cronos, the victor over Chaos' victor. He gathers and produces wonderfully. Eos, Helius, Silene, and Caephalus, the dawn's cold wind, are evoked and ordered divinely to keep people in light. And Eos and Caephalus together gave people the morning star of hope, in the direction of light, as the cooling breeze announces the rising, cloud-reddening illumination. But Zeus also brought together, in Aether, gods and goddesses, not for the sake of people, but for divine fellowship. In Aether, where there is no dawn or darkness, there was no natural order at Zeus' arrival at Olympus. Only absolutely uncompromised light. Chaos gave no order.

Zeus' situation is not enviable, given its history. Uranus angered and overworked Gaea. Cronos was a tyrant, selfish and alone, and Gaea would not tolerate his self-protective, ingesting refusal of a chancey kingdom and of growth and expansion. She did not like for her begotten to be closed off and held captive, and she was already giving Zeus (who had the Titans imprisoned) trouble when he emerged as King of heaven. Aether gave the conditions for divine sight, but nothing else. No guidelines or protection. In this unimpeded luminousity, the gods, now great and wonderful in their victory, gathered. And Zeus had to figure out how to rule with no precedent and with considerable danger.

What did the gods do in their element? Among many other things, they partied, counseled, were angered, were envious, sang, danced, had entertainment by the Graces, made love, gave birth, ate, listened to the Muses sing, thought, held games, were worried, were eloquent, recalled things, built, were jealous, cultivated, tended, were violent, were deceitful, were creative, were fearful. Olympus was not an abstract place, but a place where much that we think of as finite and fallible went on. Limited orders were forever forming, new alliances were made. There were reconciliations and agreements, friendships and complicated forms of opposites. And through all this ran old Chaos' indestructible heritage through the parentage of Night: immutable, mysterious, marble-like, unbending Fate that Zeus had to live with and respect. Grandfather of Fate, Chaos, was omnipresent, imprisoned or not. Zeus might have control of mortal's lives, but he was in a universe he did not make with an element that was foreign to his own lineage, with a company of deathless, headstrong gods who would pay him only so much attention. The element, Aether, and the company of gods were absolutely present with anything Zeus might do in the direction of order, and we must not forget that Fate and Aether combine at Olympus to mean that orders of divinity, and consequently of mortals, occur in directions and in luminousity that are absolutely indifferent to even the God of sky, contracts, oaths, and the protection of guests. What Cronos set in motion, Fate and the Light of Night, are immutable in the place where Zeus rules.

The elements of the brothers, Hades and Zeus, have the same parentage and are not related at all to Hades and Zeus. I suppose one could think of mortal light, Day, as between Darkness and Aether. But however they relate, they are in the same cosmos, and we have to think of this cosmos as one with their radical difference. Their sameness needs also to be noted. It is named as absence of order, as impenetrableness, as mystery, as most utterly other vis à vis the human. And they are both where the gods are, even though they are not related to those gods who indwell Darkness and Aether. They are each elements of the presence of life. They each cancel their grandfather Chaos by defining places. They occur as the depth and vault of Gaea. In Aether, Zeus could see to Hades, who dwelled in a kingdom which eliminated all Aether. Aether always made visible—the opposite of forgetfulness. They are the same in the sense that neither is mortal, neither is a kind of energy, and that the immortality of both together is reflected in the mortality of a Day's passage.

When we interpret this situation of the gods and the difference and sameness of Darkness and Aether as expressing aspects of the realm of awareness, we are put in touch with a world of a remarkably wide and variant range. Particularly when we do not collapse the situation into an order dominated by any one part or group of the parts. Chaos is remembered in both concealment and illumination. Being alive is remembered in being deathly. Totally incomprehensible movement (Fate) is remembered in the highest and most divine orders, of which we are not the authors. The nonpartiality of growth, nurturance, fecundity, and life itself is remembered in the process of continual emergence and overthrow of the greatest of powers. Even sleep, forgetfulness and deterioration recall death loss of brightness, passage of all lumination. The nonorder of simple, unpolluted clarity for sight means also the strength of ordering, the community of divines, the escapades, fights, and lives of the greatest powers, the present distance of utter darkness. The very presence of Hades (as well as Persephone, Charon, and particularly Dionysus) means that Darkness is endurable and dwellable. We are in a cosmos, a region in which the whole is implicated in the parts and in which the parts immediately reflect each other in their relations and discontinuities. Above all, in the situation of the gods, we are able to see that awareness is a region of relations, organically related, and not subject finally to explanation, but subject to description.

I am paying particular attention to the presence of Aether and Darkness in this account of cosmological extremities. I am assuming that these mythological relations reflect fundamental and given states of the realm of awareness, and that by reflecting these reflections we draw closer to our own immediacies and see them more clearly. Our therapeutic sensibility will also be affected as we find out what is at stake in an individual life as one lives out denials and acceptances of these outer regions of the human cosmos.

1.   Aether and Darkness are the progeny of Chaos, once removed. They are not engendered by Uranus, Cronos or Gaea.

This most remarkable insight in the myths shows that hiddenness and luminosity, in their utterness, are not produced by any ordering direction. They do not reflect personality or intentionality or a cosmic plan. Although Uranus, with his power of generation, overcame Chaos, Night and her children remained, unrelated to all powers of decay and growth that were to emerge. Manifestness and hiddenness do not mean anything, although they constitute the boundaries of the world and are the elements associated with the highest and deepest dimensions of reality. They are both timeless in the sense that they have no structure or movement. That does not mean that they occur without reference to time or movement or structure. It means that with all time and differentiation occurs an element or aspect, pervasive and ever and utter, that is not the same as what goes on or as the going on itself, a freedom, if you will, that is no choice, no identity, and no history.

These regions are violated as I make anything of any sort finally definitive of my being or the being of the world, such as identity, substance, what-I-want, definiteness itself, a virtue or all virtues, or volition. Aether and Darkness are present as not-identity, not-substance, not-what-I-want, not-definiteness, not-a-virtue, not-all-virtues, not-volition. They are what I fear most if I define my life by identities. Aether is where I can seem to fly endlessly and worldlessly. Darkness is where I can cease to see, grow, remember, etc. Each in other words, can be remembered or forgotten in how I live. And each can mean absorption and loss of world. But together they are the regions that give place for all that is divine and free of human constriction. They are present as the awful regions that mean awe, wonder, self-transcendence, depth, profundity, inspiration for us in our particular ways of being aware. As the grand-progeny of Chaos they are free of everything that happens in their realm. They are never seen as objects or subjects or things or images. They are utter. And they mean for human identities an incomprehensible endlessness that has not begun and that is present, but on no terms, exactly.

2.   Aether is the element related to Fate in which Zeus takes counsel.

Zeus is the father of the Fates of human being. As the grandchildren of Cronos they draw thread from a distaff, wind it, and cut it off. They have control over the time of birth, life, and death. But Fate is someone else. It was born of Night, too. It decrees, and Zeus has nothing to do with that. Fate does not mean anything that mortal minds can grasp. Fate is the "It is done" or "It is to be done" quality of experience in which one knows that he has no say, and not because someone else is more powerful, but because others are in the same decree. Surely a descendent of Chaos, with no perceptible overarching intuition or wish, but ever-present in human experience. It both provides structures of life and passes out of human comprehension, and it is not informed by the interests of human personality and character.

Zeus has interests and can be influenced by particular, human concerns and gifts as well as by human beauty. He

protects, and I suppose that he needs to protect, divine preroga-
tives. He is terrible in his power as far as individual mortals are
concerned, but he is always having to do something. Aether has
nothing to do. Fate does things, but without interest as far as
I can tell. But Zeus is a ruler—a passionate, working, protect-
ing, seeking god. He establishes. He is capricious and irrational.
But he wants order among the gods. He wants order among
people (he *will* have hospitality, for example). Even when he is
doing just what he feels like doing, for no good reason, a person
can see what he is up to and what is going on. His order is
fallible, and he is always punishing, shoring up, taking sides,
and repairing the damages. His divinity is found in his ordering
power.

That power occurs in Aether, which is not a power, and
is compromised by Fate, which has no known relation to ordering and generating powers and has plenty of relation to Chaos.
The very element of Zeus' sight (and hearing too, I assume)
offers no nurturance for what he sees, wants, or plans. And
Fate's iron decrees do not reflect his capacity for planning,
much less his interestedness and passion. Fate and Aether do
reflect each other in the absence of purpose, concern, personal
meaning, and character. I suppose that means that in the acceptance of inevitability one draws closer to the pure light of
divinity in its absence from all personal intent.

In this absence Zeus also finds an unestablished region that
means that the very condition of his divine perceptivity and
sensibility make inevitable the contingency of all specific (divine) relations and situations. His unending activity reflects this
nonfamilial element that does nothing and thereby relativizes
all his doings. Pure luminousity, in its absence of meaning,
means to us the light of everything as it is and the nonnecessity
of all orders. Just as Fate does with its ungrounded decrees.

3.   Day, the light of mortals, alternates with Night, her
mother. Night, reclaims her regency regularly vis à vis her
daughter. Day, aligned with Helios, Eos, and many other dei-
ties, has a daughter's power. But she is never free of her mother.

Aether seems to have total freedom in its unaltering, pervasive luminousity. It is constant and reflects Night in its absence of content and incomprehensibility. That is a reflection of total independence. But Day dawns and dies. Her light, which gives us our perceptivity, comes and goes. She and Night together are the elements of mortality. Day means that our sight fails, even as she means that all things are visible for us only for a time. She gives no order except in being born and dying. She always means Night, who has an encompassing power: Night is not born; she is found there in the depth of day—always there, a primordial absence. Night is in an order, but she escapes it in the sense that she will be present when this order ceases or when Order is gone. Even Gaea has no power over Night.

Being in Day and Night, mortals are limited moments in the progeny of Chaos. Best not look for meaning in that. Meaning happens in Day and Night with their support, to the extent that one is not ensnared in Fate. Mortals reflect, limitedly, the directions of the gods, in the weaker sister of Aether. Being free is being in light and darkness and doing what one finds worth doing in living reference to the company and history of those who are to die. If I expect Aether in Day, I shall be terribly confused by dawn and twilight. No joy, no serenity. If I live as though day leads to Aether and not to Night, I shall be repeatedly confounded by Night (and by Day as well); I shall be depressed in Night, instead of living with her daughters Sleep and Dream before Day reborns in the gift of Caephelus and in the bright distance of the morning star. The hopes and rests and directions and meanings of mortals happen only in the realm of no-hope, no-rest, no-direction, and no-meaning.

The elements are not to be denied in our being. They are our place, our region, even when they are not our specific place and have no meaning in particular.

4.   The elements of Hades and Zeus do not weep or laugh.

Through the myths I have been hearing aspects of awareness, which go far beyond personality, character, and individual identity. The elements of Utter Darkness and Aether are not objects of speculation or names for something outside the range of awareness. They name kinds of occurrences that are outside the range of our creating, ordering abilities. They name dimensions of all events which cannot be had, objectified, or comprehended. With all orders—ontological, social, or psychological —Utter Darkness and Aether are density and clarity that cannot be achieved or lost or incorporated by an order. They name those most awesome dimensions, usually forgotten and avoided, that are with, but totally free of the most intense and important passions and powers of reality. They name the non-powers of awareness that are ever and utter and appear to us as boundless in themselves, but bounded by each other. They refuse resolution or reduction. They are the elements of pure sight and pure hiddenness with which we share intimacy in being utterly different from them. They are reflected in the light of day and darkness of night, in circumscribed insights and nightmares, in thinking and confusion, in elucidation and oblivion. On our owning their presence depends our alertness with divinity and with the mortal freedom of our being. I shall not be free to live and die until I countenance the utter differences of Hades' and Zeus' elements.

We have already noted some of the things that go in these elements or regions of occurrence. We have noted too that the Cosmos involves them both in their radical difference. If I fail to live out of this difference, I shall most probably "humanize" everything, even Night (into relative darkness, missing the quality of darkness itself), Chaos (into uncooperativeness, ignorance, bad upbringing, and so forth), Cronos (tick-tock, tape measures, and dots on a line), and Lethe (repression, bad memory, or psychological blockage). If I give one dominance over the other, losing again part of Old Chaos' progeny, I will not see the manifestness of darkness or the hiddenness of Aether. Either the underworld or the highest regions will dominate my way of being with things, such that Gaea tends to mean to me total obscurity or mystic luminousity. She is both at once and will not be without sky-horizon or inner darkness.

This at-onceness is the center of our final emphasis. The difference of the elements of Zeus and Hades is not the last word. Hades and Zeus are great gods in elements not of their own making. How they are together is part of how (the meaning of) being human is in Day and Night, and these elements of the soul are not affective or intuitional or passionate at all. They are Utter Darkness and Pure Light, without tears and without a smile.

5.   Hades and Zeus are brothers; Darkness and Aether have the same parentage. The oneness of the Greek Cosmos, with its overpowering diversity of divinities, each of whom is far greater than human character, will not be denied. The pervasive Darkness that is Hades' realm, and the pervasive Light that is Zeus' realm are as related as are Zeus and Hades. Coming from two different parentages, the four relate like royal, intermarried families. They are related deeply in their histories —their being, as we know it, involves a tellable story of power, reign, murder, conspiracy, defeat, creation of kingdoms, and peaceable conjunction. That Chaos, through Erebus, becomes a place through Hades, and that Chaos, through Night, becomes a region of sight through Zeus is terribly remarkable. As remarkable as seeing that is never resolved into what is seen, as light that is so deeply related to darkness that in being light darkness is revealed, and in being darkness light is revealed.

The cosmic nature of the whole story means each of the divinities, and the place of each, manifest all the others in their relatedness. And the reflection of these divinities and realms in all our lives means at once a cosmos of infinitely related differences. Nietzsche (1965) teacher of classic literature, forever in service of Dionysus and Apollo, speaks out of this world of the soul:

> You higher men, what do you think? Am I a soothsayer? A dreamer? A drunkard? An interpreter of dreams? A midnight bell? A drop of dew? A haze and fragrance of eternity? Do you hear it? Do you not smell it? Just now my world became perfect;

midnight too is noon; pain too is a joy; curses too are a blessing; night too is a sun—go away or you will learn:a sage too is a fool.

"Have you ever said Yes to a single joy? O my friends, then you said Yes too to *all* woe. All things are entangled, ensnared, enamored; if ever you wanted one thing twice, if ever you said, 'You please me, happiness! Abide, moment!' Then you wanted *all* back. All anew, all eternity, all entangled, ensnared, enamored—ah, then you *loved* the world. Eternal ones, love it eternally and evermore; and to woe too, you say: go, but return! *For all joy wants—eternity.* (p. 323)

Chaos with definiteness. Night with light. Aether with Utter Darkness. And always at once.

The at-onceness of the Cosmos of related eternal differences means that we are with each other always in the reflection of the whole. When the whole is not reflected in a dominance by one or more of the parts, a usurpation occurs that will not long be tolerated by the Cosmos itself.

FREEDOM AND FANTASY

I have read these mythical relations as an account of how human being happens in a related universe far beyond its compass or meaning. Their power is in their indirectness; to be literal with them is always to miss them as myths. Their power to describe how things are, as well as their evocative and suggestive power, is in their non-literal manner. I believe that is because "what" these myths describe is not "objective." They give account of the happening of things in an "at once" that pervades even the most fundamental elements of all real things. Myths consequently have their meaning for human understanding in how they are appropriated, never in literal application. One must live with them, as one might live with a dream, until the Gods began to interact, as in a waking dream, alive and present without our guidance. Only then, I believe, will the full power of the myths of our tradition become consciously efficacious for the therapist; not as a pattern for pathology or health, but as a region of powers with which we dwell, sane or not.

Freedom with such powerful determinants? Hades found his freedom and his space of life in his element, Utter Darkness. And Zeus, in Aether. These non-orders, non-matters were the regions, the place qualities in which these Gods could make their mistakes, establish their domains, suffer, and perhaps even die. I do not mean to suggest that we are like Hades or Zeus or both together. They are not like persons. They are powers considerably in excess of all human character. I do mean to suggest that Utter Darkness and Aether, in the lineage of Chaos who countenanced no order, named the freedom of these two Gods, and that like them we humans have our freedom, our "element." It is found in, shall I say "mything"? Or in free imagining? Or in countenancing with fantasy? Or in the naming of things as they have to be? I mean to say all those things. Our "element" is the orderless region of dreaming, fantasizing, concocting, seeing, imagining, intuiting. I say "orderless" because the range of orders and worlds that can take place in this most awesome region appears unlimited. Who has counted the number of dream orders that happen in dreaming? Does the region of fantasy tell us how to put things together? Do myths, as such, teach us right and wrong? They thrive on contradiction, battles of orders, differences among Gods.

What is my life like when there is little imaginative psychic movement? Intelligent, perhaps, distracting, involved with things, but banal. Attentive to detail or spacy, responsible, or separated from claims, but flat behind the surface. The absence of much psychic movement is like an absence of enlivening meaning or lively images in addition to everything that is going on. At an extreme, it is that dead sense that gives backdrop to whatever a suicidal person does. In a more ordinary way, the absence of psychic movement is lived as an absence of imagination, as a vague boredom with everything, as a feeling that nothing is deeply arresting, as not being very moved by anything. In that absence, I do not get inside different ways of seeing or different way of being and find how to be in those differences. I live a straight out identity of my own, no matter how devious or how upright, without being able to experience that identity from different postures and in different ways of being. I tend to be literal about everything. I like the finality of certainty. I want non-ambiguity. Fantasy seems the opposite of truth. Dream seems the opposite of reality. And you seem vaguely distant behind whatever closeness we may achieve. When there is little imaginative, psychic movement in my life, I live as though I were not free.

Our freedom is found as we open to the region of fantasy without guarantees of stability, of life with multiple goals, this region of fecundity that supports nothing for long that we hold dear, but engenders yet dearer, as well as more dreaded, things. We may also come to our element as we dwell with the myths, finding ourselves strangely free as we imagine the inevitable and discover that we are ourselves of an element that casts doubt on even the most inevitable things of all.

REFERENCES

Nietzsche, F. W. *Thus spoke Zarathustra,* W. Kaufman, Transl. New York: Viking, 1965.

chapter 11

THE RIDDLE OF CHANGE

Kenneth L. Phillips, M.A.

Everything in the universe, from human relationships to high energy particle interactions is participating in a ceaseless process of change guided by simple, yet universal patterns. From the beginning of philosophical thought in ancient China, nearly 4000 years ago through current research in high energy physics and molecular biology, one basic question is being posed: "How do phenomena change?"

DNA, found in 1944 to be the "genetic substance" in which basic biological information is transmitted from cell to cell, achieves its remarkable control of cellular change using a code identical in structure to the I Ching, the profound Chinese classic of 4000 B.C. Modern subatomic physics in positing that mass is no longer associated with a material substance adopts a concept of change more akin to Lao Tzu than Newton. Astrophysics is developing models of "Black Holes" in outer space where mass and therefore gravity-like forces become so dense and strong that not even light or radio waves can escape. These important large-scale phenomena in outer space are often described in terms similar to those used by C. G. Jung, R. D. Laing, and others, in attempting to describe critical states of change in the inner space of our own psyches.

Although everything is in a state of continual change and metamorphosis, passing through periods of integration/disintegration, maturing/decaying, expansion/contraction, etc., the trend of Western science and medicine toward superspecialization increases the probability that redundant research may be carried out in more than one field at one time. The key concept leading to an important breakthrough in one field may already exist elsewhere. In areas such as medicine and the allied healing arts, the lack of interdisciplinary cross-pollenation of ideas can even be dangerous.

If everything is in a state of continual change, then "crises" either in personal relationships or physical processes occur as a result of resistances to change. A crisis may be one's reaction to the termination of a relationship, or a subatomic event which appears unpredictably or uncontrollably. Avoiding crisis becomes a matter of discovery—unraveling the nature of the basic change being resisted. This discovery may take place within the realm of the unconscious, within an electron microscope, while listening to music—literally at any time, and in any place. Most important though is one's willingness and openness to the universe as the stage upon which the cosmic dance of change takes place.

The idea of universal patterns of change is the cornerstone of Eastern thought. The Chinese view of change is a dynamic one. All change stems from the Great Ultimate, or Tao, which manifests "Chi," or energy. Yet all change results from the interaction of opposites, symbolically referred to in Eastern thought as YIN/YANG. Tao is a cosmic process of flow and change, thus the way to be is to follow the flow of the natural processes of the cosmos. The interaction of opposites in the Chinese sense means that the two poles of change are dynamically related to each other. The famous "Tai" symbol states this elegantly (Figure 11–1). Opposites are not exclusive, but inclu-

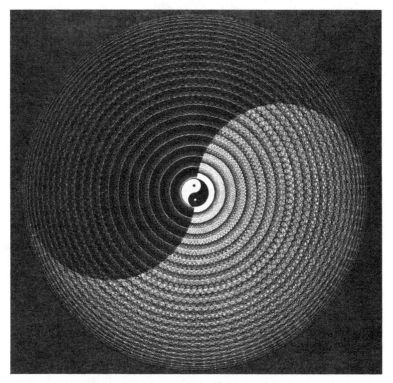

Figure 11-1   Tai symbol of YIN/YANG

CREDIT: String Art by John Eichinger

NOTE: original negative available from John Eichinger, P.O. Box 1104, Los Gatos, CA. 95030

sive of one another. There is always some light in the dark and some dark in the light. We are neither exclusively male or female, but rather more influenced by the male, yang energy, or the female, yin energy. Within Chinese philosophy, a concern for the practical application of ideas has always existed. Lao Tzu applies the relatedness of opposites to daily life in the *Tao Te Ching:*

If you would have a thing shrink.
You must first stretch it;
If you would have a thing weakened,
You must first strengthen it;
If you would have a thing laid aside,
You must first set it up;
If you would take from a thing,
You must first give to it.

THE EVOLUTION OF THE BOOK OF CHANGES

No collection of ancient writing has come so close to being forced into extinction so many times as the *Book of Changes.* Prior to 3000 B.C., Fu Hsi, the legendary first ruler of China was on the bank of the Yellow River, pondering the origin of the universe when a magic tortoise climbed out of the water. On the tortoise's shell was inscribed a pattern of symbols which Fu Hsi interpreted as a spontaneous response to his questions about the way of the universe. From the markings on the turtle's back, Fu Hsi constructed the Ho T'u, or *Yellow River Map* (Figure 11–2). Subsequently, Fu Hsi rearranged and added further elemental and seasonal attributes forming the eight "Kua" or trigrams as shown in the Lo Shu (Figure 11–3). Fu Hsi taught an entire code of ethics based upon the archetypal significance of the eight trigrams (Figure 11–4). For centuries these teachings were passed along verbally to a select few in the form of simple phrases which one now finds at the beginning of each of the 64 hexagrams of the I Ching. Originally these simple teachings were recorded on tortoise shells, as well as human and animal bones. Some say that dots, like those used in the River Maps were used, though no evidence to support this has ever been found. It was thought that the I Ching teachings had oracular properties. Oracular teachings were usually inscribed on bones or tortoise shells with the intention of casting them into a fire until cracks developed. An interpretation would then be made, based upon the formation of the cracks.

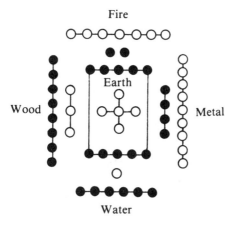

Fire

Earth

Wood

Metal

Water

Figure 11-2   The Ho Tu-Yellow River map

SOURCE: Wilhelm/Baynes (transl.), *The I Ching* or *Book of Changes,*
(Princeton: Princeton Univ. Press, 1951), p. 309.

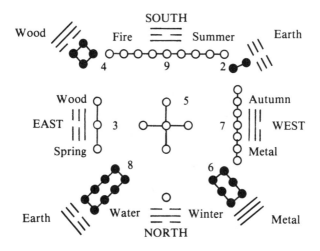

SOUTH

Wood   Fire Summer   Earth
         4   9   2

Wood   5   Autumn
EAST   3   7   WEST
Spring   Metal

        8   6
Earth   Water Winter   Metal
              NORTH

Figure 11-3   The Lo-Shu writing from the river Lo

SOURCE: Wilhelm/Baynes (transl.), *The I Ching* or *Book of Changes,*
(Princeton: Princeton Univ. Press, 1951), p. 310.

233

Figure 11-4 Table of Trigram (KUA) Attributes

Name	Ch'ien	K'un	Chen	K'an	Ken	Sun	Li	Tui
Family Member	Father	Mother	Eld. Son	Mid. Son	Yng. Son	Eld. Dtr.	Mid. Dtr.	Yng. Dtr.
Primary Attribute	Creatv	Rcptv	Arousing	Danger	Kpng Still	Penetration	Clarity	Joyusness

	(1)	(2)	(3)	(4)	(5)	(6)	(7)	(8)
Symbols	Tiger, Horse, Lion	Cow, Mare, Ant	Eagle, Dragon, Swallow, Ccds	Pig, Rat, Fox, Bat	Dog, Bull, Ox, Lprd., Mouse	Cock, Ckn., Crane, Snake, Worm, Unicorn	Pheasant, G. Fish, Crab, Shrimp, Oyster, Turtle	Sheep, Birds, Simians, Deer, Elk
Season	Aprch Winter		Apprch Spg. & Fall	Winter	App. Spring	App. Summer	Summer	Autumn
Physiognomy	Skull & Head	Abdomen	Vcl. Sys.	Ear	Hand	Leg	Eyes	Mouth
Internal Repres.	Mind	Stomach, Spleen, Lwr. Rg.	Feet, Liver	Sex organs, Kidney, Urn. Sys.	Back	Nervous system, Rsp. Sys.	Blood, Heart	Speech, Organs

SOURCE: W.A. Sherrill & W.K. Chu, *Anthology of I Ching*, (Boston/London: Routledge & Keagan Paul Ltd., 1978) pp. 218-227.

Bamboo strips replaced the bones and shells around 1700 B.C. and could accommodate more information. It is thought that this was the origin of Chinese writing, one line to a bamboo strip, written from top to bottom. The Chinese "alphabet" is also attributed to Fu Hsi; like the hexagrams, Chinese characters are composed solely of lines and strokes.

While imprisoned by the last emperor of the Shang Dynasty in 1132 B.C., King Wen began amplifying the short capsule statements, adding important commentaries based upon the interaction of the pairs of trigrams. Since there are eight trigrams:

Chien	Sun	Li	Tui	Ken	Kan	Chen	Kun

there is a total of 64 possible combinations forming 6-line hexagrams. A solid line (—) represented the Yang, male, projective, creative, etc., force, whereas the broken line (– –) represented the Yin, female, receptive, passive force. All of the hexagrams can therefore be expressed in terms of YIN-ness and YANG-ness, ranging from the first hexagram,

Chien: ——— to K'un: – –

No. 1   No. 2

First came No. 1, the Creative, and then came No. 2 the Receptive, thus the Creative and the Receptive are the primal opposites out of which everything evolves.

King Wen's son, the Duke of Chou furthered his father's superb work by writing explanations of the significance of each line of each hexagram: 384 in all. These meanings applied when the oracles indicated that a line was "moving," signifying that it changes to its opposite. In the example below, the first and fifth lines are moving. The lines are always numbered from the bottom up:

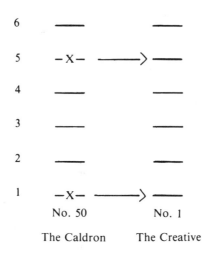

King Wen and the Duke of Chou are largely responsible for the form and content of the I Ching as it exists today, and without doubt, along with Lao Tzu and Confucius, are the most important figures in early Chinese philosophy.

Later, during the 6th century B.C. Kung Fu Tzu, known in the West as Confucius, wrote important commentaries on the *Book of Changes,* while during the same period, Lao Tzu wrote the beautiful *Tao Te Ching.* Within his own life Confucius got a late start in writing commentaries on the I Ching. Toward the end of his influential existence as the great teacher he wrote, "If I had further years to my life, I would devote them to the I

Ching . . . " and later, "Give me a few more years to study the I Ching and I could have a good philosophy of the mutation of human events." Confucius' commentaries contain a Machiavellian flavor and have been interpreted as a guide to good government.

Lao Tzu's *Tao Te Ching* reaffirms the spiritual elements of the I Ching; thus the religious philosophy of Taoism may also be traced back to its origins in the I Ching.

Today's proliferation of religions and philosophies of all kinds might well be compared to the period of "Warring States and 100 Philosophy Schools," in that both periods produced a considerable literature commenting on most major traditions of the time. Most people were confused in deciding just what to believe. This resulted in spiritual shopping expeditions and frequent shifts of allegiances, due to all of the choices.

This freedom came to an abrupt end in 213 B.C. when Emporer Ch'in Shih Huang Ti, as part of his effort to unify China, pronounced that all recorded history was to begin with the period of his reign. He ordered the famous "burning of the books," in which the state library, estimated to have contained some half-million volumes was totally destroyed except for a few volumes which conformed to state-approved policy. Though the basic I Ching was not destroyed, all of Confucius' works, including the highly regarded commentaries on the Book of Changes, were. The continued existence of the I Ching and the comparatively small amount of early scholarship which still survives today is due to nomadic gypsies who refused to abide by Chin's mandate and continued to pass these writings among themselves. Eventually they fell into the hands of scholars once again, during the ensuing Han Dynasty. Ultimately, many of the philosophies died out, perhaps as many of today's will, but when the spiritual dust finally settled, Confucius' work survived and became most influential in Chinese life. During the Sui dynasty, approximately 600 A.D., a civil service examination system was implemented of which the six Confucian classics were the basis.

It would appear that the West's first encounter with the I Ching was in the 17th century when Jesuit missionaries in China became fascinated with the book. When they wrote back to Europe that they were devoting all of their efforts to its study, they were ordered to cease and return home. They refused, and were labeled "insane and heretical." They were never heard of again—what became of their work remains a mystery.

In the 17th century Gottfried von Leibniz developed a system of binary mathematics which, because of its simple ability to represent any quantity in terms of zeros and ones, (i.e., 1, 2, 3, 4, 5 becomes 1, 10, 11, 100, 101) became the basis for the operation of digital computers, and an important step in the evolution of number theory and formal logic. Binary numbers or "base-two counting" is now taught to school children as part of the "new math." When Leibniz came upon the I Ching, and discovered the "Fu Hsi" sequence of hexagrams in particular (Figure 11–5), he realized that the 3 years spent developing his binary number system had been a duplication of effort, thanks to the Chinese of hundreds of years before. Leibniz observed that if a YANG, solid line was viewed as a zero, and a YIN, broken line as a one, then the hexagrams of the I Ching represented the integers 0 through 63. Since Leibniz was known to have had a saturnine disposition, it is not surprising that a great depression followed his encounter with the I Ching.

Leibniz during the first half of the 1880s presented a series of lectures on the significance of the I Ching's wisdom. These thoughts have recently been published in a small volume, *Discourse On the Natural Theology of the Chinese*. (1977)

A strong case may be made for a Taoist approach to the education of researchers and scientists. Such training would focus on the study of patterns of detail, rather than the details of patterns. I'm reminded of a saying I came across almost daily during my last year in high school. Enroute to school in the early mornings I would often purchase doughnuts to take along with me. They would be placed in a waxy paper bag on which was printed the shop's name as well as a slogan to the effect,

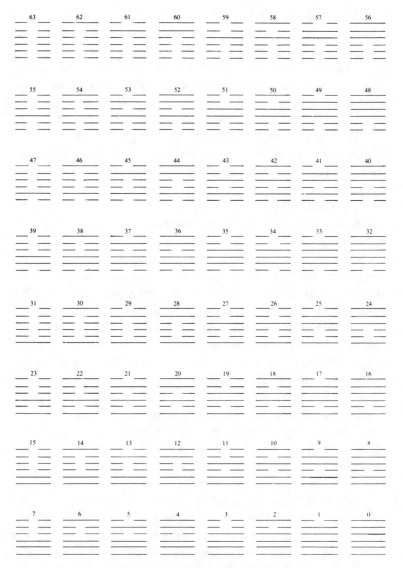

Figure 11-5   The Fu Hsi sequence

SOURCE: Gardner, Martin, *Mathematical Games,* Scientific American, (January, 1974) p. 122

"As you pass through life, keep your eye on the doughnut, and not upon the hole." The store should have been called the Taoist Doughnut Shop, but it was not.

C.G. JUNG'S ANALYTIC PSYCHOLOGY AND CHANGE

No Western school of thought comes as close to understanding human behavior in the manner of the I Ching as the Analytic Psychology School of C. G. Jung. True, Jung was Freud's most creative student, and the first to become disenchanted with the limitations and scope of psychoanalysis as Freud envisioned it, but to state merely that Jung left Freud because of disagreement over the role of sexuality, does not do justice to either man. Jung never took the position that sexuality was unimportant, but rather asserted that there were other dynamics of the psyche, such as the need to create, to grow toward balance and wholeness of the self, which were equally important as Freud's drive states. Jung further described the unconscious as being composed of two principle components: the personal unconscious, containing the complexes Freud so eloquently wrote of, and the collective unconscious, a transpersonal reservoir containing patterns of symbols and emotional experiences he termed "archetypes."

Jung was as much anthropologist as psychologist, philosopher, and theologian. He was fluent in a multitude of languages, including Swahili, and discovered in his travels through Africa that similar, if not the same patterns of symbols appeared in the dreams of Africans living in the bush as he had observed in his patients, first when he worked with Eugen Bleuler at the Burgholzli Hospital in Zurich as well as later while working with Piere Janet, Sigmund Freud, and in private practice.

Freud was largely unreceptive to Jung's notion of an unconscious which rather than acquiring its contents from personal experience, was the psychic residue of man's evolutionary development and the consequence of repeated experiences and feelings over many generations. Jung realized the great importance which ancient myth, symbol, and religion must play, if one is to accept his hypothesis of a "collective unconscious." His *Collected Works* fill 19 volumes most of which are devoted to some of the finest scholarship existant in the fields of mythology, art, dream theory, alchemy, gnosticism, psychology of religion, as well as empirical investigations of paranormal phenomena. Perhaps one could loosely draw the analogy that Jung was to Freud as King Wen and his son were to Fu Hsi: enormously gifted students of great teachers. Such relationships rarely last too long, but usually bear valuable results—such was the case in both instances. Jung's association with Freud lasted only 6 years.

Jung's notion of "archetype," universal patterns of experience, is much like the I Ching's notion of Change. The 64 hexagrams of the I Ching are as equally transpersonal and universal as Jung's archetypes. The same processes of change which comprise the 64 hexagrams of the I Ching may be located in the sources Jung found so important: myths, dreams, fairytales, artwork, and even theories of modern physics.

The idea of universal patterns of change did not make its first appearance in the West with Jung. The pre-Socratic Greek thinkers such as Pythagoras, Heraclitus, and Aristophanes all believed that a universal "harmony of the spheres" existed. Modern physics has grappled with this same question in attempting to describe a "unified field theory," or set of laws of change which apply to all events regardless of their order of magnitude.

Jung had an in-depth familiarity with the I Ching and could sit down on the floor and recite each hexagram and the commentaries associated with the lines. This he did on more than one occasion to the disbelief of some of his colleagues. In 1949, Jung wrote the forward to the Wilhelm/Baynes edition of the I Ching, which is the most sensitive translation available in English today.

Of particular interest to Jung was the oracular property of the I Ching. Historically, two methods of obtaining knowledge in response to a question upon which one meditates has survived, one using three coins, and another, older method which uses 50 stalks of yarrow or other suitable wood. By tossing either the coins or the yarrow stalks, one obtains a sequence of numbers which in turn reveal if each of the six lines of an evolving hexagram are YIN (– –), YANG (__), YIN and moving (-x-), or YANG and moving (–O–). One tosses the coins, for example, six times while meditating on some question of great personal importance.

Interestingly, for a considerable period of time the process of composing questions for the I Ching oracle became a highly evolved artform, though today the I Ching is often inappropriately regarded as either a "collection of magic spells" and rejected outright as nonsense, or as a direct line to some hidden fortune teller, and relied upon for frequent answers to mundane questions. Jung realized that the I Ching was neither of these, and immediately recognized that nowhere else was his concept of "synchronicity" [1]more directly at the base of events than in the oracles of the I Ching. Even limited experience with the I Ching will suffice to demonstrate its uncanny ability to seize the nature of the moment!

Before studying the I Ching, Jung found it curious that such a culture capable of great intellectual and artistic advances literally thousands of years ahead of Europe, never relied upon, or even attempted to develop what in the West is called science. Our science has been based upon the principle of causality. Recently this has begun to change, largely due to observations made by physicists which have shown that our once thought to be universal laws are merely *statistical* truths, all of which have exceptions. When dealing with nature, these exceptions occur by chance. The effect of chance in natural events is so pervasive that the case where events follow some specific law in all details is very much the exception.

The idea behind the I Ching oracle clearly is that "chance"

has meaning because what happens in a given moment in time inevitably possesses the entire quality of the moment. The universe is contained in a drop of water, but in the case of the I Ching, the drop of water is a moment in time. The hexagram is a means of describing the essential nature of the moment in time in which it was cast. The ancient Chinese looked upon the Tao, the Way of the Universe, in terms quite similar to those which only recently have become accepted in physics. Just as the physicist now accepts the statement that descriptions of subatomic events must include the effects of the observer, the dynamics of chance and change upon which the I Ching is based interact directly with the "subjective, i.e., psychic conditions" of the questioner, just as it takes into account the momentary totality associated with the drop of time at which the coins or yarrow stalks are thrown.

Jung attempts to demystify the notion of synchronicity by stating that it is a view of change "diametrically opposed to causality." Synchronicity views the intersection of events happening at the same moment in time, and same location in space as having meaning exceeding mere chance. Yet he willingly concedes that this perception is equally dependent on the state of the observer. Perhaps the classical case is that of walking down the street thinking to oneself about a particular acquaintance when suddenly he or she comes around the next corner.

On the surface, one might be tempted to ask, as I was, "What's the difference between a synchronicity and the occurrence of a highly unlikely event?" The answer clearly is one of *experiencing* the coincidence of events in some drop of time as meaningful. If your best friend were rounding the corner just as you were thinking of him or her and you were so wrapped up in thought that you did not see him, then clearly an unlikely event took place whereas a synchronicity did not.

Synchronicities for sure are a special case of change when they occur, but the principle upon which Jung's idea is based tells us that the process of change is not as independent of the observer as one might otherwise think. It is the interdependence of the psychic state of the questioner and the ability of the I Ching to sum up the feeling tone of a given moment in time that is at the bottom of the I Ching's remarkable oracular ability.

CHANGE IN THE BIOLOGICAL WORLD—TOWARD A UNIFIED THEORY

Though considerable progress has been made in physics toward understanding universal dynamic processes of change, this is not typical of the other branches of Western science. Generally, the explanation of phenomena is limited by "scientific method" to observations, explanations, and conclusions based solely upon components of the event in question. Yet, some leading researchers acknowledge the importance of a general systems approach to biological problems for example.

Biologist, Lancelot L. Whyte (1965) speaks of "the rules of ordering which must be satisfied (to within a threshold) by the internal parts and processes of any cellular organism . . . " He suggests that such rules may be expressed in terms of "coordinative conditions" defining the "network of the relations of atoms, ions, molecules, organelles, etc." comprising a viable life form. Such a map of dynamic relationships between the various complex systems within life forms may be either of the form of properties which apply at all levels of structure or alternatively, a set of "ifs"—"hierarchies of conditions." Clearly, Whyte's idea of "coordinative conditions" is equivalent to both the I Ching's postulation of 64 universal principles of change, Jung's transpersonal "archetypes," and the "general systems" or "unified field theory" approach taken in physics.

Returning to biology, many hold the view that the manner in which we think, conceptualize, and even perceive deep archetypal structures has its origin in molecular processes which are at the center of what we commonly refer to as "evolution." In particular, it is argued that such mental patterns of cognition, categorization, perception, and learning are the artifacts of the dynamic process in which DNA determines the basic structure and function of the organism. This means that the manner in which we think, intuit, feel, and dream, to some degree, is a representation of the basic organization of our organism.

With this assumption held in mind, Jung's work, which to a large extent asks the question, "what are the structures of religion, myths, dreams, rituals, phantasies, and oracular processes?" makes a great deal of sense. If the organization of our psyche and its rituals represent the organization of the physical systems and processes which support it, then the study of ancient practices and beliefs which have survived for thousands of years, such as the I Ching, should reveal valuable information. In addition, conscious participants in these traditions would be in a position to intuit a great deal concerning the nature of the physical universe.

Several years ago, while in graduate school studying psychology, I was required to take a course on "Behavioral Genetics." The course was loaded with statistical studies and biochemical discussions some of which I found less than fascinating. In discussing the mechanisms whereby certain disorders effecting the central nervous system are inherited, or are the result of errors in the DNA transcription process, the professor started to demonstrate the case for sterilization of those afflicted with these terrible conditions. My own inner reaction to this was to pay no further attention. My mind began to wander off, to what subject I cannot recall—probably to the artichokes a kind friend had promised to bring for dinner after class—when my attention was suddenly seized by the hard tap of something on the blackboard. My eyes flew involuntarily to the diagram on the black slate and in disbelief, observed a chart identical to one I drew years before as part of my private study of the I Ching. Immediately, I experienced a feeling of electrical excitement run through my body, and set about putting all the pieces of this puzzle together.

In describing the DNA molecule and the process to which it is central, we answer the question, "What makes a liver cell reproduce new liver cells and a muscle cell, more muscle cells?" What guides the complex process of cellular evolution and change so that complete disorder does not prevail in the biological systems comprising our bodies?

Most cells, the neurons of our central nervous system being the most blatant exception, have a generally similar architecture comprised of a nucleus containing chromosomes, surrounded by nourishing cytoplasm, both of which are contained within a cell wall. Cells which either perform highly specific functions in complex organisms, or may be one of only a few cells in more primitive life forms have a nearly infinite variety of special characteristics in addition to the cell wall-cytoplasm-nucleus structure. Some cells have means of propelling themselves, others have entire metabolic systems as an evolved sort within them, etc. The process of cell reproduction is at the base of our question about cytodifferentiation, as it is technically called.

Prior to the division of the cell body in reproduction, a precise distribution of the chromosomes within the nucleus takes place according to a five-part process called mitosis. Part of this process entails a splitting down the middle, by the chromosomes prior to the formation of a new cell in the last phase. Before the new cell can go its way, clearly its chromosomes must contain all of the information that have those in the old cell.

During the first stage of mitosis (called interphase) the chromosomes are in a thread-like form which sometimes may be seen through a light-powered microscope, though electron microscopes reveal much more. Usually they have a diameter of from 200–300 Angstrom units. An Angstrom is one ten-millionth of a millimeter, the strands are therefore inconceivably small.

What are these spaghetti-like fibers made of? Electron microscopes cannot even peer into this realm of minuteness, but evidence indicates that each strand has a core which is coiled and only 35–60 Angstroms in diameter.

Again, we must ask, "What are the cores of the chromosome fibers made of?" The answer is "nucleo-proteins," that is, nucleic acid affixed to proteins. In 1944 nucleic acid was found to be "deoxyribonucleic acid," referred to as DNA. In the early 1950s J.D. Watson and F.H.C. Crick began developing a model of DNA's structure which hypothesized that just as these paragraphs are composed of sentences, in turn composed of words, DNA was best considered composed of long sequences or sentences of building blocks called "nucleotides," each of which always consisted of a sugar molecular, a phosphate, and most importantly, one of four possible "bases."

Four types of nucleotides were suggested, each having a different base: ADENINE, GUANINE, CYTOSINE, and THYMINE. (Simply noted as A,G,C, & T.) In 1962 Watson and Crick were awarded the Nobel Prize for their 1953 model, since during the ensuing years their hypothesis was fully substantiated.

The helix is held together by hydrogen bonds between the pairs of bases. Thymine always bonds with adenine, whereas guanine always forms links with cytosine. Three hydrogen bonds always form between cytosine and guanine and two between adenine and thymine. The sugar and phosphate molecules are part of the outer spiral.

As we said before, prior to the cell dividing, DNA replication must take place so that the valuable information contained in the DNA sequences may be passed along to the newly forming cell. The strands in the double helix separate and through a "replicating enzyme" catalyze the construction of the internucleotide linkages using two triplets (of three bases) on one strand of DNA, at a time, as a template. Though not all the details of this mechanism are currently understood, several early hypotheses have been rejected. The work of Arthur Kornberg, recipient of the Nobel Prize in 1959, figures prominently in the advance of knowledge in this area.

For our purposes, it is important to bear in mind that a multitude of chemical arrangements could be established and replicated. The sequence of thousands of "A-G-C-T" bases, reordered into all possible combinations along the helix seem to have a random, or near random order. Ultimately, the sequence is transcribed into the newly forming cell via two triplets at a time, each consisting of three bases, or six bits of information. Almost every triplet of mRNA, the "messenger" employed in the transfer process, corresponds to an amino acid. The triplets of bases correspond to an amino acid. The aminos determine protein formation, which in turn determines the function and capabilities of any cell.

Most triplets produce an amino acid whose abbreviated name appears following the brackets in Figure 11–6. Notice that a few triplets give rise to "initiators" and "terminators." These are thought to be STOP and START commands, which have particular logical connections. For example, "STOP IF," "START AND," etc. Clearly an entire biochemical language exists here, seemingly much like the languages used to guide complex processes in computers.

At this point the structural analogy appears. The ancient Chinese, in developing their calculus of change, adopted a code in which Change, regardless of the scale of magnitude in which it guides events, is symbolically represented by clusters of six lines in which each line may be of four types, representing combinations of the archetypal opposites YIN/YANG, either in a state of rest of change: YIN (– –), YANG (__), YIN changing (–X–), and YANG changing (–O–). This format of six elements each being either Yin or YANG permits 64 possible combinations. The meaning of the hexagram is derived from

		U	C	A		G		
First letter	U	UUU ⎫ Phe UUC ⎭ UUA ⎫ UUG ⎭ Leu	UCU ⎫ UCC ⎪ Ser UCA ⎪ UCG ⎭	UAU ⎫ Tyr UAC ⎭ UAA Ochre (terminator) UAG Amber (terminator)		UGU ⎫ Cys UGC ⎭ UGA (terminator) UGG Tryp		U C A G
	C	CUU ⎫ CUC ⎪ Leu CUA ⎪ CUG ⎭	CCU ⎫ CCC ⎪ Pro CCA ⎪ CCG ⎭	CAU ⎫ His CAC ⎭ CAA ⎫ GluN CAG ⎭		CGU ⎫ CGC ⎪ Arg CGA ⎪ CGG ⎭		U C A G
	A	AUU ⎫ AUC ⎬ Ileu AUA ⎭ AUG Met (initiator)	ACU ⎫ ACC ⎪ Thr ACA ⎪ ACG ⎭	AAU ⎫ AspN AAC ⎭ AAA ⎫ Lys AAG ⎭		AGU ⎫ Ser AGC ⎭ AGA ⎫ Arg AGG ⎭		U C A G
	G	GUU ⎫ GUC ⎪ Val GUA ⎪ (initiator) GUG ⎭ (initiator)	GCU ⎫ GCC ⎪ Ala GCA ⎪ GCG ⎭	GAU ⎫ Asp GAC ⎭ GAA ⎫ Glu GAG ⎭		GGU ⎫ GGC ⎪ Gly GGA ⎪ GGG ⎭		U C A G

Third letter

Figure 11-6   The Genetic Code (64)

Please note that the number of nucleotide combinations is 64 the same number as that of the total of hexagrams in the I Ching.

SOURCE: Eldon J. Gardner, *Principles of Genetics,* (New York; John Wiley and Sons, 1975), p.85.

the composite of the symbols attributed to the two trigrams of which it is formed. For example:

SUN The Gentle, Wind

KUAN, Contemplation

K'UN The Receptive, Earth

No. 20

The process of cellular evolution likewise is regulated by a code identical in structure to the 64 hexagrams of the I Ching, except that in the "Messenger RNA Codons," each trigram or triplet is comprised of one of four *bases,* rather than YIN or YANG lines, moving or at rest. Here too, 64 mRNA codons exist (see Figure 11–6).

THE NEW AGE AND CHANGE

Usually when the details of the I Ching/DNA correspondence or any of many other such similarities I have observed in studying Western science and Eastern traditions is presented at conferences, great surprise is the general reaction. Among the growing community of interest in Jung's work, perhaps his notion of "archetype" is of the greatest interest. The observation of such patterns between seemingly unrelated fields is not synonymous with the discovery of something profound or rare. If the universe were *not* built upon such universal patterns, that would be a surprising finding! Explaining subatomic particle interactions, DNA transcription, and the hexagrams "conflict" and "peace" would indeed be impossible tasks if they were in no way related.

My goal has not been to present a rigorous, scientifically detailed exposition of how biochemistry is related to Chinese philosophy, but to share an experience—a mode of thought and discovery which, as our continued existence depends increasingly upon the solution of global problems such as energy, food and education, must begin to occupy a more prominent role in our collective consciousness in the future than it seems to at present. Subtle effects of advanced technology and psychology may be severely limiting our ability to solve problems which are rapidly reaching critical states. Computers, although a great boon to efficiency, require the statement of problems in terms which may not, ultimately, be productive of general systems solutions. High speed communications technologies tend to inhibit forethought and reflection on just what is being said. Can we really *communicate* at 9,600 bits per second? Will we succeed in eliminating such age-old diseases as cancer and arthritis when we fail to recognize the inclusive relationship between our bodies and our emotions? What is the effect of a multi-billion dollar industry thriving off the management of symptoms on the outcome of this critical question? The ancient myths tell of mortals who by not expressing certain emotions were turned to stone as punishment for wishing to hide something from the omnipotent gods. Is this not of interest in view of the biochemical process involved with most forms of arthritis, where "stones" form in the joints?

The future demands a form of consciousness in which we relate to the universe as we now relate to our own bodies and close relatives. Boundaries of all sorts will have to be pushed outward, if not eliminated all together. Scientists will have to befriend mystics, at least intellectually. "Believers" will have to accept their skeptical bretheren as less than heathens. Politicians will have to learn to relinquish the power they cherish, but actually have never had. Through approaching the universe as an interconnected network of meaningful, ordered events, balance will be maintained among the interplay of the "The Creative" and "The Receptive"—the archetypal forces of Change.

NOTES

1. Synchronicity is a concept that formulates a point of view diametrically opposed to that of causality. Since the latter is a merely statistical truth and not absolute, it is a sort of working hypothesis of how events evolve one out of another, whereas synchronicity takes the coincidence of events in space and time as meaning something more than mere chance, namely, a peculiar independence of objective events among themselves as well as with the subjective (psychic) states of the observer or observers (see foreword by C. G. Jung, *The I Ching Book of Changes,* 1950).

REFERENCES

Baynes, C., & Wilhelm, R., Transl. *The I Ching book of changes,* Princeton, N.J.: Princeton University Press, 1950. (Foreword by C. G. Jung).

Jung, C. G., Collected Works, Vols. 1–19. *Bollingen Series XX,* Princeton University Press, 1957–1970.

Leibniz, G. W. von, *Discourse on the natural theology of the Chinese,* Transl. H. Rosemont, Jr. and D. J. Cook. Monograph #4, Soc. for Asian and Comparative Philosophy, University of Hawaii Press, 1977.

Whyte, L. L., *Internal factors in evolution,* New York: Braziller, 1965, p. 33–36.

chapter 12

DEVELOPMENT AND TRANSCENDENCE

Ken Wilber

Everywhere we look in nature, said the philosopher Jan Smuts (1926), we see nothing but *wholes*. And not just simple wholes, but hierarchical ones: each whole is a part of a larger whole which is itself a part of a larger whole. Fields within fields within fields, stretching through the cosmos, interlacing each and everything with each and every other.

Furthermore, said Smuts, the universe is not a thoughtlessly static and inert whole—the cosmos is not lazy, but energetically dynamic and even creative. It tends (teleonomically) to produce higher- and higher-level wholes, evermore inclusive and organized. This overall cosmic process, as it unfolds in time, is nothing other than *evolution*. The drive to ever-higher unities, Smuts called *holism*.

If we continue this line of thinking, we might say that because the human mind or psyche is an aspect of the cosmos, we would expect to find, in the psyche itself, the same hierarchical arrangement of wholes within wholes, reaching from the simplest and most rudimentary to the most complex and inclusive. In general, such is exactly the discovery of modern psychology. As Werner (1957) put it, "Wherever development occurs it proceeds from a state of relative globality and lack of differentiation to a state of increasing differentiation, articulation, and hierarchic integration." Jakobson (1974) speaks of "those stratified phenomena which modern psychology uncovers in the different areas of the realm of the mind," where each stratified layer is more integrated and more encompassing than its predecessor. Bateson (1972) points out that even learning itself is hierarchical, involving several major levels, each of which is "meta" to its predecessor. As a general approximation, then, we may conclude that the psyche—like the cosmos at large—is many-layered ("pluridimensional"), composed of successively higher-order wholes and unities and integrations.

Now the holistic evolution of nature—which produces everywhere higher and higher wholes—shows up in the human psyche as *development* or *growth*. That is, a person's growth, from infancy to adulthood, is simply a miniature version of cosmic evolution. Or, we might say, psychological growth or development in humans is simply a microcosmic reflection of universal growth on the whole, and has the same goal: the unfolding of ever higher-order unities and integrations. That is one of the major reasons that the psyche is, indeed, stratified. Very like the geological formation of the earth, psychological development proceeds strata by strata, level by level, stage by stage, with each successive level superimposed upon its predecessor in such a way that it includes but transcends it ("envelops it," as Werner would say).

Now in psychological development, the *whole* of any level becomes merely a *part* of the whole of the next level, which in turn becomes a part of the next whole, and so on throughout the evolution of consciousness. Take, as but one example, the development of language: the child first learns babbling sounds, then wider vowel and consonant sounds, then simple words, then small phrases, then simple sentences, and then extended sentences. At each stage, simple parts (e.g., words) are integrated into higher wholes (e.g., sentences), and, as Jakobson (1974) points out, "new additions are superimposed on earlier ones and dissolution begins with the higher strata."

Modern developmental psychology has, on the whole, simply devoted itself to the exploration and explanation of the various levels, stages, and strata of the human constitution—mind, personality, psychosexuality, character, consciousness. The cognitive studies of Piaget and Werner, the works of Loevinger, Arieti, Maslow, and Jakobson, the moral development studies of Kohlberg—all subscribe, in whole or part, to the concept of stratified stages of increasing complexity, integration, and unity.

Having said that much, we are at once entitled to ask, "What, then, is the *highest* stage of unity to which one may aspire?" Or perhaps we should not phrase the question in such ultimate terms, but simply ask instead, "What is the nature of some of the higher and highest stages of development? What forms of unity are disclosed in the most developed souls of the human species?"

We all know what the "lower" stages and levels of the psyche are like (I am speaking in simple, general terms): they are instinctual, impulsive, libidinous, id-ish, animal, ape-like. And we all know what some of the "middle" stages are like: socially adapted, mentally adjusted, ego integrated, syntactically organized, conceptually advanced. But are there no higher stages? Is an "integrated ego" or "autonomous individual" the highest reach of consciousness in human beings? The individual ego is a marvelously high-order unity, but compared with the unity of the cosmos at large, it is a pitiful slice of holistic reality. Has nature labored these billion of years just to bring forth this egotistical mouse?

The problem with that type of question lies in *finding* examples of truly higher-order personalities and in deciding exactly *what* constitutes a higher-order personality in the first place. My own feeling is that as humanity continues its collective evolution, this will become very easy to decide, because more and more "enlightened" personalities will show up in data populations, and psychologists will be forced, by their statistical analyses, to include higher-order profiles in their developmental stages. In the meantime, one's idea of "higher-order" or "highly developed" remains rather philosophic. Nonetheless, those few gifted souls who have bothered to look at this problem have suggested that the world's great mystics and sages represent some of the very highest, if not the highest, of all stages of human development. Bergson said exactly such; so did Toynbee, Tolstoy, James, Schopenhauer, Nietzsche, and Maslow.

The point is that we *might* have an excellent population of extremely evolved and developed personalities in the form of the world's great mystic-sages (a point which is strongly supported by Maslow's 1971, studies). Let us, then, simply *assume* that the authentic mystic-sage represents the very highest stages of human development—as far beyond normal-and-average humanity as it itself is beyond apes. This, in effect, would give us a sample which approximates the "highest state of consciousness." Furthermore, most of the mystic-sages have left rather detailed records of the stages and steps of their own transformations into the upper reaches of consciousness. That is, they tell us not only of the highest level of consciousness, but also of all the intermediate levels leading up to it. If we take these higher stages and add them to the lower and middle stages/levels which have so carefully been described and studied by Western psychology, we would then arrive at a fairly well-balanced and comprehensive model of the spectrum of consciousness. I have attempted this type of synthesis in a series of books: *The Spectrum of Consciousness* (1977); *No Boundaries* (1979), and *The Atman Project* (1979). A general and simplistic outline is given below.

THE LOWER REALMS

It is generally agreed, by Eastern and Western psychology alike, that the lowest levels of development involve simple biological functions and processes. That is, the lowest levels involve somatic processes, instincts, simple sensations and perceptions and emotional-sexual impulses. In Piaget's system, these are the sensorimotor realms (see Gruber & Vonèche, 1977); Arieti (1967) refers to them as instinctual, exoceptual, and protoemotional; Loevinger (1976) calls them presocial, symbiotic, and impulsive. To the Hindu Vedantin this is the realm of the *anna-* and *prana-mayakosa,* the levels of hunger and emotional-sexuality (those are precise translations). The Buddhist calls them the lower five *vijnanas,* or the realm of the five senses. The chakra psychology refers to them as the lower three chakras: the *muladhara,* or root material and pleromatic level; *svadhisthana,* or emotional-sexual level; and *manipura,* or aggressive-power level. This is also the lower three *skandhas* in the Buddhist system of psychology: the physical body, perception, and emotion-impulse. It is also Maslow's lowest two needs, physiological and safety needs.

Now the body-ego or body-self[1] tends to develop in the following way: It is generally agreed that the infant initially cannot distinguish self from not-self, subject from object, body from environment. That is, the self at this earliest of stages is literally one with the physical world. As Piaget put it, "During the early stages the world and the self are one; neither term is distinguished from the other. . . . [The] self is still material, so to speak . . ." (Gruber & Vonèche, 1977).

That initial stage of *material oneness,* which Piaget called "protoplasmic," I call *pleromatic* and *uroboric.* "Pleromatic" is an old gnostic (and Jungian) term meaning the material universe—the *materia prima* and *virgo mater.* "Uroboros" is a mythological motif of the serpent eating its own tail, and signifies "wholly self-contained" and "not-able to recognize an other."

It is out of this primordial fusion state that the separate self[2] emerges, and the self emerges first and foremost as a body, a body-self. The infant bites a blanket and it does not hurt; he bites his thumb, and it hurts. There is a difference, he learns, between the body and the not-body, and he gradually learns to focus his awareness *from* the pleroma *to* the body. Thus, out of primitive material unity emerges the first real self sense, the body-ego. The infant identifies with the body's sensations and emotions, and gradually learns to differentiate them from the material cosmos at large.

Notice that the body-ego, by differentiating itself from the material environment, actually *transcends* that primitive state of fusion and embeddedness. The body-ego transcends the material environment, and thus can perform physical *operations* upon that environment. Toward the end of the sensorimotor period (around age 2), the child has differentiated the self and the not-self to such a degree that he has a fairly stable image of "object constancy" and so he can *muscularly* coordinate physical operations *on* these objects. He can coordinate a physical movement of various objects in the environment, something he could not easily do as long as he could not differentiate himself from those objects.

Let us note that triad: by *differentiating* the self from an object, the self *transcends* that object and thus can *operate* upon it (using the tools that constitute the self at that level—at this stage, the sensorimotor body).

At this body-ego stage(s), then, the self no longer is bound to the pleromatic environment, but it *is* bound to, or identified with, the biological body. The self, as body-ego, is dominated by instinctual urges, impulsiveness, the pleasure principle, involuntary urges and discharges—all the id-like primary processes and drives described so well by Freud and others. For this reason, we also call the body-ego the "typhonic self"; the typhon, in mythology, was half human, half serpent. In physiological terms, the reptilian complex and the limbic system dominate the self at this stage.

Eventually, however, true *mental* or conceptual functions begin to emerge out of, and differentiate from, the body-ego. As language develops, the child is ushered into the world of symbols, ideas, and concepts, and thus is gradually raised above the fluctuations of the simple, instinctual, immediate, and impulsive body-ego. Among other things, language carries the ability to picture things and events which are *not immediately* present to the senses. "Language," as Robert Hull (1972) put it, "is the means of dealing with the non-present world."

By the same token, then, language is the means of transcending the simply present world (language, in the higher realms of consciousness, is itself transcended, but one must go from the preverbal to the verbal in order to get to the transverbal; we are here talking about the transcendence of the preverbal by the verbal, which, although only half the story, is an extraordinary achievement). Through language, one can anticipate the future, plan for it, and thus gear one's present activities in accordance with tomorrow. That is, one can delay or control one's present bodily desires and activities. This is, as Fenichel (1945) explains, "a gradual substituting of actions for mere discharge reactions. This is achieved through the interposing of a time period between stimulus and response." Through language and its symbolic, tensed structure, one can postpone the immediate and impulsive discharges of simple biological drives. One is no longer totally dominated by instinctual demands, but can to a degree *transcend* them. This simply means that the self is starting to differentiate from the body and emerge as a *mental* or verbal or syntactical being.

Notice again: as the mental-self emerges and differentiates from the body (with the help of language), it *transcends* the body and thus can *operate* upon it using its own structures as tools (it can delay the body's immediate discharges and postpone its instinctual gratifications using verbal insertions). At the same time, this allows a sublimation of the body's emotional-sexual energies into more subtle, complex, and evolved activities.

At any rate, a fairly coherent mental-ego eventually emerges (usually between ages 4 and 7), differentiates itself from the body, transcends the simple biological world, and *therefore* can to a certain degree operate on the biological world (and the earlier physical world) using the tools of simple representational thinking. This whole trend is consolidated with the emergence (usually around age 7) of what Piaget calls "concrete operational thinking," i.e., thinking that can *operate* on the world and the body using concepts.

By the time of adolescence, another extraordinary differentiation begins to occur. In essence, the self simply starts to differentiate *from* the representational thought process itself. And because the self starts to differentiate itself from the representational thought process, it can to a certain degree *transcend* the thought process and therefore *operate* upon it. Piaget calls this—his highest stage—"formal operational," because one can operate on one's own formal thought (i.e., work with linguistic objects as well as physical ones), a detailed operation which among other things, results in the 16 binary propositions of formal logic. But the only point I wish to emphasize here is that this can occur because consciousness differentiates itself from syntactical thought, thus transcends it, and hence can operate upon it (something that it could not do when it *was* it). Actually, this process is just beginning at this stage—it intensifies at the higher stages—but the overall point seems fairly clear: consciousness, or the self, is *starting* to transcend the verbal ego-mind. It is starting to go transverbal.

(To touch bases with other researchers, the verbal ego-mind is known in Mahayana Buddhism as the *manovijnana,* in Hinduism as the *manomayakosa,* in Hinayana Buddhism as the fourth and fifth *skandhas.* It is Freud's ego function of secondary process thinking. Arieti's language and conceptual levels, Loevinger's conscientious and individualistic stages, Sullivan's syntactic mode, and Maslow's self-esteem needs. It is also the fifth chakra, the *visuddha-chakra* or lower verbal mind, and the lower aspects of the sixth or *ajna* chakra. These are very general but very significant correlations).

Now as consciousness begins to transcend the verbal ego-mind, it can integrate the ego-mind with all the lower levels. That is, because consciousness is no longer identified with any of these elements to the exclusion of any others, all of them can be integrated, i.e., body and mind can be brought into a higher-order holistic integration. This stage is referred to as the "integration of all lower levels" (Sullivan, Grant, and Grant 1957), "integrated" (Loevinger, 1976), "self-actualized" (Maslow, 1971), "autonomous" (Fromm, 1941, Riesman, 1954). My favorite descriptive phrase comes from Loevinger's statement of Broughton's work: his highest stage, stage 6, is one wherein "mind and body are both experiences of an integrated self." This integrated self, wherein mind and body are harmoniously one, we call the "centaur." The centaur, the great mythological being with animal body and human mind existing in a state of at-one-ment. The centaur is starting to go transverbal, but it is not yet transpersonal.

As I mentioned, both Eastern and Western psychology are in agreement as to the nature of all these lower levels, from pleroma to body to ego-mind. But the West has contributed a rather exact understanding of a phenomenon that is only vaguely understood in the East, namely, the process of dynamic repression. For what the West discovered is that as higher-order levels of consciousness *emerge* in development, they can *repress* the lower levels, with results that range from mild to catastrophic.

In order to take into account this process of dynamic repression, we simply use the Jungian terms "shadow" and "persona."[4] The "shadow" is the personal unconscious—a series of "feeling-toned complexes." These complexes are images and concepts which become "contaminated" by the lower levels —in particular, the emotional-sexual—and thus are (erroneously) felt to be threatening to the higher-order structure of the ego-mind. These complexes are thus split off from consciousness (they become shadow), a process which simultaneously distorts the self-concept and thus leaves the individual with a false self or inaccurate self-image (the persona or mask, which itself is a useful role-self, unless it is the *only* self one has, in which case the persona can always be shown to be constituted by a resistance to some shadow element). If the persona and shadow can be reunited, then the higher-order integration of the total ego can be established. That, in very general terms, is the major aim of orthodox Western psychotherapy.

So far, then, we have these major levels of increasing integration and transcendence: the simple and primitive fusion unity of the pleroma; the next higher-order unity of the biological body-self; then the mental persona, which, if integrated with the shadow, yields the higher-order unity of the total ego; and finally the centaur, which is a higher-order integration of the total ego with all preceding and lower levels—body, persona, and shadow.

THE INTERMEDIATE REALMS

With the exception of transpersonal psychology, the centaur level is the highest level of consciousness taken seriously by Western psychology. The existence of levels above and prior to the centaur is thus viewed by Western psychology with a jaundiced eye. Western psychiatrists and psychologists either deny the existence of any sort of higher-order unities, or—should they actually confront what seems to be a higher-order level—simply try to explain its existence as pathology, to explain it by diagnosis. Thus, for indications as to the nature of any of the higher levels of consciousness, beyond the ego and centaur, we have to turn to the great mystic sages, Eastern and Western, Hindu and Buddhist, Christian and Islamic. It is somewhat surprising, but absolutely significant, that all of these otherwise divergent schools of thought agree rather unanimously as to the nature of the "farther reaches of human nature." There are indeed, these traditions tell us, higher levels of consciousness—as far above the ego-mind as the ego-mind is above the typhon. And they look like this:

Beginning with (to use the terms of yogic chakra-psychology) the sixth chakra, the *ajna* chakra, consciousness *starts* to go transpersonal. Consciousness is now going transverbal *and* transpersonal. It begins to enter what is called the "subtle sphere." This process quickens and intensifies as it reaches the highest chakra—the *sahasrara*—and then goes supramental as it enters the seven higher stages of consciousness beyond the *sahasrara.* The *ajna,* the *sahasrara,* and the seven higher levels are, on the whole, referred to as the subtle realm.

For convenience sake, however, we speak of the "low-subtle" and the "high-subtle." The low-subtle is epitomized by the *ajna* chakra—the "third eye," which is said to include and dominate both astral and psychic events. That is, the low-subtle is "composed" of the astral and psychic planes of consciousness. Whether one believes in these levels or not, *this* is where they are said to exist.

The astral level includes, basically, out-of-the-body experiences, certain occult knowledge, the auras, true magic, "astral travel," and so on. Although this is the very lowest of the intermediate realms, it has today become something of a fashionable stupidity to regard this plane as an extraordinarily high state of being.

The psychic plane includes what we would call "psi" phenomenon, such as ESP, precognition, clairvoyance, psychokinesis, and so on. Many individuals can occasionally "plug in" to this plane, and evidence random or higher-than-random psychic abilities. But to actually *enter* this plane is to more-or-less master psychic phenomena, or at least certain of them, such as teleportation or levitation. Patanjali has an entire chapter of his Yoga Sutras devoted to this plane and its structures (which are *siddhis* or paranormal powers). I should also say that many researchers feel that the astral is higher than the psychic, and others feel that they are the *same body,* but the general points are as outlined above.

The whole point of the low-subtle—the astral-psychic—is that consciousness, by further differentiating itself from the mind and body, is able in some ways to *transcend* the normal capacities of the gross body-mind and therefore *operate* upon the world and the organism in ways that appear to the ordinary mind to be quite fantastic and far-fetched. For my own part, I find them a natural extension of the transcendent function of consciousness.

The high-subtle begins as the *sahasrara* and extends into seven more levels of extraordinarily high-order transcendence, differentiation, and integration. This is, on the whole, the realm of high religious intuition and inspiration; of symbolic visions; of blue, gold, and white light; of audible illuminations and brightness upon brightness; it is the realm of higher presences, guides, angelic beings, *ishtadevas,* and *dhyani-buddhas,* all of which are simply high archetypal forms of one's own being (although they initially and necessarily appear "other"). It is the realm of *Sar Shabd,* of Brahma the Controller, of God's archetypes, and of *Sat Shabd* and beyond these four realms to three higher and totally indescribable levels of Being. Dante sang of it thus:

> Fixing my gaze upon the Eternal Light
> I saw within its depths,
>   Bound up with love together in one volume,
>   The scattered leaves of all the universe. . . .
> Within the luminous profound subsistence
>   Of that Exalted Light saw I three circles
>   Of three colors yet of one dimension
> And by the second seemed the first reflected
>   As rainbow is by rainbow, and the third
>   Seemed fire that equally from both is breathed.

Keep in mind that that is what Dante *saw,* literally, with his eye of contemplation.

The psychiatrist Stanley Dean (1975) reports this:

> An intellectual illumination occurs that is quite impossible to describe. In an intuitive flash, one has an awareness of the meaning and drift of the universe, an identification and merging with

creation, infinity and immortality, a depth beyond depth of revealed meaning—in short, a conception of an over-self, so omnipotent. . . .

In Hinduism, this is the *vijnanamayakosa;* in Mayahana Buddhism, this is the *manas.* Aspects of this subtle realm have been
called the "over-self" or "over-mind" or "supra-mind," as in
Aurobindo and Emerson.

The point is simply that consciousness, in a rapid ascent,
is differentiating itself entirely from the ordinary mind and self,
and thus can be called an "over-self" or "over-mind" or "supra-
mind." It embodies a transcendence of all mental forms, and
discloses, at its summit, the intuition of that which is above and
prior to mind, self, world, and body—something which, as
Aquinas might have said, all men and women would call God.

But this is not God as an ontological other, set apart from
the cosmos, from humans, and from creation at large. Rather,
it is God as an Archetypal summit of one's own consciousness.
In this way, and this way only, could St. Clement say that he
who knows himself knows God. We could now say, he who
knows his over-self knows God. They are one and the same.

THE ULTIMATE REALMS

As the process of transcendence and integration continues,
it discloses even higher-order unities, leading, consumately, to
unity itself.

Beyond the high-subtle lies the causal region, known vari-
ously as the *alaya-vijnana,* the *anada-mayakosa, pneuma,* etc.
Again, for convenience, we divide it into the low-causal and the
high-causal.

The low-causal, which is revealed in a state of consciousness known as classical *savikalpa samadhi,* represents the pin-
nacle of God consciousness, the final abode of Ishvara, the
Creatrix of all realms. At this point, all the preceeding subtle-

realm manifestations begin to actually and literally reduce to modifications of Consciousness itself, so that one begins to *become* all that previously appeared as objective visions, lights, and sounds (this process begins at the high-subtle, but culminates here). In visualization meditation, this is the point that the *dhyani-buddha* or *yidam,* once created and evoked in the subtle realm, becomes one's own self, or rather, one's self dissolves into the God-Archetype. Blofeld (1970) quotes Edward Conze to illustrate: "'It is the emptiness of everything which allows the identification to take place—the emptiness which is in us coming together with the emptiness which is the deity. By visualizing that identification we actually do become the deity. The subject is identified with the object of faith. [As is said,] The worship, the worshipper and the worshipped, those three are not separate." At its peak, the soul becomes one—literally one —with God, with Ishvara, with Spirit, with the Dhyani-Buddha. One dissolves into Deity as Deity—that Deity which, from the beginning, has been one's own Self or highest Archetype. At this point, all of the archetypal forms of the previous stages (any *yidam, ishtadeva,* vision, light, etc.)—as well as one's own self —condense and dissolve into God, which here is as a subtle audible-light or bija-mantra from which the individual yidams emerged in the first place.

Beyond that point, into the high-causal, all forms are so radically transcended that they no longer even need appear or arise in Consciousness. This is total and utter transcendence into Formless Consciousness, Boundless Being. There is here no self, no God, no objects, no subjects, and no thingness, apart from or other than Consciousness as such. Note the progression: in the high-subtle and low-causal, the self dissolves into Deity; here, the Deity-Self dissolves into Formlessness. The Deity is reduced to its own prior ground. Blofeld describes this progression from a Buddhist view: "As the rite progresses, this deity enters the adept's body and sits upon a solar-disc supported by a lunar-disc above a lotus in his heart; presently the adept shrinks in size until he and the deity are coextensive [the subtle realm]; then, merging indistinguishably [the high-subtle], they are absorbed by the seed-syllable from which the deity originally sprang [the low-causal]; this syllable contracts to a single point; the point vanishes and deity and adept in perfect union remain sunk in the *samadhi* of voidness [the high-causal] .... " (Blofeld, 1970). This is described in much the same way by Hixon (1978) who presents the Hindu view, and it is widely and similarly described by all the traditions that reach this high realm. This state itself is *nirvikalpa samadhi, nirodh, jnana samadhi,* the high-causal—and the eighth of the ten Zen ox-herding pictures.

Passing through *nirvikalpa samadhi,* Consciousness totally awakens as its original condition and suchness (*tathata*), which is, at the same time, the condition and suchness of all that is, gross, subtle, or causal. That which witnesses and that which is witnessed are absolutely one and the same. The entire world process then arises, moment to moment, as one's own being, outside of which, and prior to which, nothing exists. That being is totally beyond and prior to anything that arises, and yet no part of that being is other than what arises.

And so, as the center of the self was shown to be God, and as the center of God was shown to be formlessness, so the center of formlessness is shown to be not other than the entire world of form. "Form is not other than Void, Void is not other than Form," says the Heart Sutra. At that point, the extraordinary and the ordinary, the supernatural and the mundane, are precisely one and the same. This is the tenth Zen ox-herding picture, which reads: "The gate of his cottage is closed and even the wisest cannot find him. He goes his own way, making no attempt to follow the steps of earlier sages. Carrying a gourd, he strolls into the market; leaning on his staff, he returns home."

This is also *sahaja samadhi,* the *Turija* state—the ultimate Unity, wherein all things and events, while remaining perfectly separate and discrete, are only One. Therefore, this is not itself a state apart from other states; it is not an altered state; it is not a special state—it is rather the suchness of all states, the water that forms itself in each and every wave of experience, as all experience (Wilber, 1977). By the same token, this is the radically perfect integration of all prior levels—gross, subtle, and causal, which, now of themselves so, continue to arise moment to moment in an irridescent play of mutual interpenetration. This is the final differentiation of Consciousness from all forms in Consciousness, whereupon Consciousness as Such is released in Perfect Transcendence, which is not a transcendence from the world but a transcendence into the world. Consciousness henceforth *operates,* not on the world, but as the entire world process, integrating and interpenetrating all levels, realms, and planes, high or low, sacred or profane.

This, finally, is the ultimate Unity toward which all evolution, human as well as cosmic, drives. And, it might be said, cosmic evolution, that holistic pattern, is completed in and as human evolution, which itself reaches ultimate unity consciousness and so completes that absolute Gestalt toward which all manifestation moves.

THE FORM OF DEVELOPMENT

Overall, the process of psychological development—which is the operation, in humans, of cosmic evolution—proceeds in a most articulate fashion. At each stage, a higher-order structure, more complex and therefore more unified, emerges through a differentiation of the preceeding, lower-order level. This higher-order structure is introduced to consciousness, and eventually (it can be instantaneous, or can take a prolonged time) the self *identifies* with that emergent structure. For example, as language emerges in awareness, the self begins to shift from a solely biological being to a syntactical self—the self eventually identifies itself with language, and operates *as* a syntactical self. Likewise, in advanced evolution, the Deity emerges, is introduced to consciousness, the self identifies as the

Deity, and operates from that identification. The point is that as each higher-order structure emerges, the self eventually identifies with that structure—which is normal, natural, appropriate.

As evolution proceeds, however, each level in turn is differentiated *from* the self sense. That is, the self eventually *disidentifies* with that structure (so as to identify with the next higher-order emergent structure). Or we might say that the self detaches itself from its *exclusive* identification with that structure. The point is that because the self is differentiated from the lower structure, it *transcends* that structure and thus can *operate* on that lower structure by using the tools of the newly emergent structure (operation *can* become manipulation, but that is a separate issue). As the body-ego was differentiated from the material environment, it could operate on the environment using the tools of the body-self (muscles). As the ego-mind was differentiated from the body, it could operate on the body and world with its tools (concepts, syntax). As the subtle self was differentiated from the ego-mind, it could operate on mind, body, and world using its structures (psi, *siddhi*), and so on.

Thus, at each point in psychological growth, we find: (1) a higher-order structure emerges in consciousness; (2) the self identifies its being with that structure; (3) the next higher-order structure then emerges, the self disidentifies with the lower structure and shifts its essential identity to the higher structure; (4) consciousness thereby transcends the lower structure and becomes capable of operating on that lower structure from the higher-order level; and (5) all preceeding levels can then be integrated in consciousness, and ultimately as consciousness. We noted that each successively higher-order structure is more complex, more organized, and more unified—and evolution continues until there is only Unity, ultimate in all directions, whereupon the force of evolution is exhausted, and there is perfect release in radiance as the entire world process.

A few technical points: using the terms of linguistics, we say that each level of consciousness consists of a *deep structure* and a *surface structure.* The deep structure consists of all the basic limiting principles embedded as that level. The deep structure is the defining *form* of a level, which embodies all the potentials and limitations of that level. Surface structure is simply a *particular* manifestation of the deep structure. The surface structure is constrained by the form of the deep structure, but within that form it is free to select various contents (e.g., within the form of the subtle deep structure, one may select a particular dhyani-buddha or yidam or ishtadeva as surface structures; what all of the forms of the subtle have in common is the deep structure of the subtle, namely, an *ishtadeva* is different from a *yidam,* and each yidam is different from all others, but all of them are equally *forms of the subtle level*). A deep structure is like a paradigm and contains within it all the basic limiting principles in terms of which all surface structures are realized. To use a simple example, take a ten-story building; each of the floors is a deep structure, whereas the various rooms and objects in each floor are surface structures. All body-selves are on the second floor; all verbal ego-minds are on the fifth floor; all yidams are on the eighth floor; God is on top and the building itself is consciousness as such. The point is that although all verbal egos are quite different, they are all on the fifth floor: they all share the same deep structure.

The movement of surface structures we call *translation;* the movement of deep structures we call *transformation.* Thus, if we move the furniture around on the fourth floor, that is a translation; but if we move up to the seventh floor, that is transformation. Many egos try to think about Buddha, which is merely translation, whereas what is required is a transformation: the fifth floor cannot see what is going on on the tenth, and probably should not try.

Two more technical terms: a *sign* is that which points to, or represents, or is involved with any element *within* a given level; whereas a *symbol* points to, or represents, or is involved with an element of a different level (either higher or lower).

Therefore, we say that *translation operates with signs, whereas transformation operates with symbols.* The word "g-o-d" is merely a sign if, while on the fifth floor of verbal-ego deep structure, I simply think about "g-o-d" or philosophize about what that word might mean, and refuse to identify it with anything higher than my present state of adaptation. "G-o-d" is especially a sign if I make the error of identifying it with anything that can be presently seen from the fifth floor. "G-o-d" is a symbol when it is understood, by the ego, to represent a transcendent being which cannot be fully understood without transformation to a higher state itself. And "G-o-d" visualized, as *yidam,* becomes an actual symbol of transformation which discloses that higher realm.

With all that in mind, we can say that each transformation upward marks the emergence in consciousness of a new and higher level, with a new deep structure, within which new translations or surface structures can unfold and operate. And we say that evolution is a series of such transformations, or changes in deep structure, mediated by symbols, or forms in consciousness (the lowest form being the body, the next being the mind, then the subtle, etc.). And most importantly, we say that *all* deep structures are *remembered,* in the precise Platonic sense of *anamnesis,* whereas all surface structures are *learned,* in the sense studied by Western psychologists. It is generally agreed that one does not learn to become a Buddha, one simply discovers or remembers that one is already Buddha. Just so, no one learns any deep structure, but simply discovers or remembers it prior to the course of learning its surface structure. You do not learn to have a body, but you do learn to play baseball with it—you discover deep structures and learn surface structures. Only this view, I have argued in the Atman Project, can explain emergence or psychological development.

Every time one remembers a higher-order deep structure, the lower-order structure is subsumed under it. That is, at each point in evolution, what is the whole of one level becomes merely a part of the higher-order whole of the next level. We saw, for example, that the body is, during the earlier stages of growth, the *whole* of the self sense—that is the body-ego. As the mind emerges and develops, however, the sense of identity shifts to the mind, and the body becomes merely one aspect, one part, of the total self. Similarly, as the subtle level merges, the mind and body—which together had constituted the whole of the self-system—become merely aspects or parts of the new and more encompassing self.

In precisely the same way, we can say that at each point in evolution or remembrance, a *mode* of self becomes merely a *component* of a higher-order self. For example, the body was *the* mode of the self before the mind emerged, whereupon it becomes merely a component of self. This can be put in several different ways, each of which tells us something important about evolution: (1) what is *identification* becomes *detachment;* (2) what is *context* becomes *content* [that is, the context of cognition and experience of one level becomes simply a content of the next]; (3) what is *ground* becomes *figure* [which releases higher-order ground]; (4) what is *subjective* becomes *objective* [until both of these terms become meaningless]; and (5) what is *condition* becomes *element* [e.g., the mind, which is the a priori condition and category of egoic experiencing, becomes merely an element of experience in the higher-order realms; as it was put in *Spectrum of Consciousness:* "One is then looking at these structures, and therefore is not using them as something with which to look at, and thus distort, the world."].

Each of these points is, in effect, a definition of *transcendence.* Yet each is also a definition of a stage of *development.* It follows that the two are essentially identical, and that evolution, as has been said, is actually "self-realization through self-transcendence."

And so proceeds evolution, transforming itself from unity to unity until there is only Unity, whereupon Brahman, in a shock of recognition and final remembrance, grins silently to himself, closes his eyes, breathes deeply, and throws himself outward for the millionth time, losing himself completely in his manifestation for the sport and play of it all. Evolution then proceeds again, transformation by transformation, remembering more and more, until each and every soul remembers Buddha, as Buddha, in Buddha—whereupon there is then no Buddha, and no soul. And that is the final transformation. When the Zen Master Fa-ch'ang was dying, a squirrel screeched on the roof. "It's just this," he said, "and nothing more."

NOTES

1. I am using body-ego and body-self interchangeably. Ego is related to self (small self or personal "I") in Eastern psychology.
2. Here self (lower case *s*) is being used interchangeably with ego.
3. I am using self in this instance interchangeably with consciousness.
4. In contrasting dynamic and Jungian thinking I intend only to make correlations between the two and not connections between the two.

REFERENCES

Arieti, S. *The intra-psychic self.* New York: Basic Books, 1967.

Bateson, G. *Steps to an ecology of mind.* New York: Ballantine, 1972.

Blofeld, J. *The tantric mysticism of Tibet.* New York: Dutton, 1970.

Dean, S., Ed. *Psychiatry and mysticism.* Chicago: Nelson-Hall, 1975.

Fenichel, O. *The psychoanalytical theory of neurosis.* New York: Norton, 1945.

Fromm, E. *Escape from freedom.* New York: Farrar, Straus, & Giroux, 1941.

Gruber, H., & Vonéche, J. *The essential Piaget.* New York: Basic Books, 1967.

Hixon, L. *Coming home.* New York: Anchor Books, 1978.

Hull, R. The psycho-philosophy of history. *Main Currents,* 1972, *29*(2).

Jakobson, R. Child language aphasia and phonological universals. Quoted in H. Gardner, *The quest for mind.* New York: Vintage, 1974.

Loevinger, J. *Ego development.* San Francisco: Jossey-Bass, 1976.

Maslow, A. *The farther reaches of human nature.* New York: Viking, 1971.

Patanjali, *The Yoga system of Patanjali.* (Transl. Houghton-Woods) Delhi, India: Banarsidass, 1972.

Riesman, D., Glazer, N., and Denney, R. *The lonely crowd.* Garden City, N.Y.: Doubleday, 1954.

Smuts, J. *Holism and evolution.* New York: Macmillan, 1926.

Sullivan, C., Grant, M. Q., and Grant, J. D., The development of interpersonal maturity, *Psychiatry.* 1957, 20, 373–385.

Werner, H. The concept of development from a comparative and organismic point of view. In D. B. Harris, Ed., *The concept of development.* Minneapolis: University of Minnesota Press, 1957.

Wilber, K. *The spectrum of consciousness.* Wheaton, Ill.: Quest Books, 1977.

Wilber, K. *No boundaries.* Los Angeles: Center Publications, 1979.

Wilber, K. *The Atman project.* Wheaton, Ill.: Quest Books, 1979.

Part IV

RESEARCH

chapter 13

VISUAL IMAGINATION AND DREAMING

Gerald Epstein, M.D.
George L. Hogben, M.D.

INTRODUCTION

Visual imagination is the ability to develop spontaneous visualizations of people, places, or events without simultaneous external stimulation by the objects visualized. Visual imagery seems to provide a method for investigating consciousness and psychological processes. Individuals using visual imagery often experience a clearer realization of psychological processes than with verbal association techniques.

Techniques for utilizing visual imagery have been used as an adjunct to verbal psychotherapy (Singer, 1974). The individual is instructed to visually imagine and explore settings thought to possess symbolic significance and to describe the resultant process. A partial list of these settings include: meadows, mountains, caves, and bodies of water. Most therapists select the symbolic situation to be explored (Leuner, 1969). Occasionally, visual fantasies that arise spontaneously in therapy are utilized.

In the course of the authors' work with a visual image technique the impression has been developed that the visual imagery process has an impact on the production of dreams. This chapter describes a visual image technique and reports characteristics of the subsequent dreams. Comparison of these dreams with the subjects' previous dream experience and our own clinical experience with dreams are used to understand the effect of the technique on dreaming.

METHOD

The experimenter determines the subject's favorite, or most significant currently used room, and asks the subject to imagine himself in that room. He is then asked to describe the room in detail to the experimenter with his eyes closed so as to shut out the distraction of external stimuli. After the subject has described the room to the experimenter he is then asked to clean the room in a certain fashion. As he does so he is asked to report any feelings and thoughts that occur. The experimenter tells the subject to clean the room from the top down. This means that he should begin with the ceilings, then to the walls (top), working his way down to the floor. *All* the articles contained on the ceiling and walls are to be removed and brought to the center of the room. For the purposes of cleaning high places he should furnish himself, in his imagination, with the necessary implements including a ladder. As he works his way down to floor level, all articles there should be brought to the center of the room. Books should be taken out of bookcases, their nature described, and then should be put in the center. If it is a bedroom, everything should be placed on the bed (providing *it* is in the center of the room to begin with). Instruct the subject that in the center of the room he shall have a container to hold all of the articles he intends to discard. The container can be a valise, trunk, barrel, carton, etc., especially one that he might find while cleaning up. After he has everything in the center of the room, instruct him to place what he does not want into the trash container. He should indicate what these things are that he is throwing away. He should be asked to wash the windows, vacuum the floor and carpet, clean the fixtures, and so forth, all of which he should do and describe. If the subject wishes to perform other activities such as painting the walls or polishing furniture, etc., he should be encouraged to do so. After he has all of his discards in the container (he might also throw out furniture which is placed in large containers) he should then put everything back in any way that he chooses. He is then instructed to take the container(s) to the doorway. He then comes back and cleans up the center of the room. Then he is asked to take the container(s) outside to a convenient location and either burn the container(s) completely or sink it in water, watching it until it disappears to the bottom. He then comes back, after describing his thoughts and feelings on watching the container burn or sink, looks again at the room, and describes how he feels. At this point the exercise ends.

RESULTS

This technique has been used by the senior author (G.E.) with 40 subjects. Thirty of these subjects were patients who performed this technique at the outset of the psychotherapeutic process. The other subjects were colleagues. The subjects were told that the exercise might enhance their personal awareness. Dreaming was not mentioned as an effect of the technique. A representative sample of three subject illustrations are presented below:

Subject 1

> A 50-year-old woman dreamed: "I am on a beach with my children and relatives. I am nude. In the background is the city of Cincinnati. I suddenly find myself in a big building that looks like a department store. Near the elevator I see a crippled old

man. I go up on the elevator. There seems to be many staircases going up and down. I find myself at a place that seems to be like a hotel. I go looking for my room and I make the wrong turn and I find myself at a staircase going to a place that I have never seen before." This dream was reported to have been in color, and to be quite intense. She commented, "I never had a dream like that in my life."

Subject 2

A man in his mid-30s reported the following dream: "I was sailing on a 12-meter sloop in the middle of the ocean against two other 12 meters. It was an Americas Cup race, which seemed unusual since there are only two boats in these races. The boat I was on was in second place. We were close to the first boat and quite far ahead of the third boat. I was very excited and was concentrating hard on getting ahead of the first boat. Suddenly, an enormous island with an enormous high mountain peak welled up out of the water between my boat and the first-place boat. Just as suddenly, I catapulted over the island and landed on the first boat. Then the island vanished, and the two boats were next to each other again. Next there was a great deal of confusion, and I landed back on my own boat. The race continued, and I had the feeling that I would catapult again onto the first boat." He went on to report that the dream was very unusual. "I felt very moved by the dream experience and had no trouble remembering it," he said. He went on, "I remembered the dream for the next couple of days. Although I enjoy remembering dreams and try to, I rarely recall them. Also, when I do, they just don't stick in my mind like this one. The events were also weird. I have had sailing races in my awake life. Maybe the outcome is slightly different from what happens when I race. But my dreams don't have such surrealistic things happen like mountains coming out of the water and then disappearing, or my leaping through the air to other boats. Also, the type of race stays close to what happens. In this dream there were three boats in what always is a two-boat race." This dream was reported as being in color and was said to be very "vivid."

Subject 3

A professional man at the age of 28 dreamed thus: "I am sitting in a large field. The sun is shining brightly and the sky is very blue. The field is empty except for a yellow haystack appearing in the middle of the field. This haystack is four to five stories high and I am amazed to see one that high. There are several people climbing on it. I find myself climbing on it. I am half-way up when I discover that it is too steep and I begin to feel some anxiety. Behind me is my girlfriend urging me up. I notice that I am wearing blue jeans and a red bandana is tied to my waist. I feel frightened about falling off and I fall to my hands and knees to keep my balance. I continue to climb, but I slide as I do so. I start to experience an uncomfortable feeling of falling. The scene suddenly shifts and I am at the base of the haystack. I walk around it trying to find a less steep route up." He was "struck" by the vividness and unusual quality of this dream experience. He said that he did not dream in color previously, nor did he ordinarily recall dreams well. He had no experience of the day preceding the dream or in a prior recent time before this dream that he could relate to account for the setting of the dream.

Thirty-eight of the subjects responded with dreams whose characteristics were experienced as unusual from their ordinary dream life. These dreams took place 24–48 hours after the completion of the visual imagination exercise. Several qualities seemed to differentiate these dreams from dreams ordinarily encountered by us in our own psychotherapeutic work.

1. Each of the 38 subjects who responded to the exercise with unusual dreaming described their dreams as "weird," "odd," or "fantastic." The subjects seemed to be responding to gross distortions in the formal characteristics of the environment they encountered within the dream experience. For example, Subject 1 was in a department store packed with multiple staircases, like a Pironesi print. Subject 2 saw a mountain well up from the ocean in front of his boat, and Subject 3 climbed a haystack five stories high. Department stores, mountains and haystacks are represented in dreams which occur during the course of ordinary dreaming. However, in ordinary dreams these elements seem to retain the formal structure usually per-

ceived in the waking state. The subjects did not experience the ordinary representations of the waking world in the post-visual imagination dreams.

The subjects said these dreams were "different." They described these dreams as fantastic: the events having a surrealistic cast experientially. The subjects felt the settings were strange and unfamiliar, but the dreams were not reported as being like nightmares. The strangeness did not deter the subjects from exploring these unfamiliar places; whereas, in ordinary dreams the dreamer usually shies away from settings that are strange and prefers not to explore them. The strangeness in these dreams is not generally accompanied by anxiety, but if anxiety occurs the dreams continue uninterruptedly. These dreams occur as those before awakening.

2. Most subjects experienced themselves as moving up and down or in a vertical manner for a good portion of the dream. This movement was experienced as being of a self-propelled sort rather than one of being passively acted upon.

   In all the dreams the dreamers were intimately involved in the action of the dream and not as participant observers, as often is the case in ordinary dreams. The dreamers were sometimes made uncomfortable by their behavior, but they did not shrink from entering into the experience. Their behavior was experienced as volitional rather than experiencing being acted upon by events.

3. The subjects sensed that the dreams were of extraordinary vividness. A number of subjects felt "moved" by the dream. For example, Subject 1 of the subject illustrations commented, "I never had a dream like that in my life." Another subject (not reported here) said, "It was a very odd dream. I don't recall a dream ever being that odd."

The experience of vividness, often used interchangeably with intensity by the subjects, was an ubiquitous
occurrence. That such an experience is not infre-
quently found in the usual course of a person's dream
life has been documented. That our subjects' responses
moved them to characterize these dreams as "the most
vivid I've ever had", sets them apart. This quality of
singling out a specific dream event with certainty was
quite striking.

4. The dreams are most often experienced in color, and
    they are of great color intensity.

5. The recall of the dream is usually very clear whether
    or not the subject regarded himself as a good or bad
    dream recaller—or even in those who claimed not to
    be aware ordinarily of having dreamed.

Discussion

The foregoing observations about the kind of dreams occurring after the visual imagination exercise (VIE) might allow
us to link the imaginative faculty and dreaming. Three ideas
might be considered in this connection:

1. One takes time out to do work that is not done ordi-
    narily in the course of everyday life. In effect, the
    subject momentarily dehabituates, by which is meant
    that he reverses his usual habit(s) of everyday life. A
    reversal of this behavior allows one to become open to
    the freshness of an experience. In so doing there can
    be a sudden and new recognition about one's present
    existence. This recognition will then, in the form of an
    aroused action, carry itself out in the dream existence.
    There are numerous ways to dehabituate and the VIE
    is but one.

2. One is "granted permission" to clean up the clutter. Generally speaking, in the relationship between therapist and patient the latter is "granted permission" to speak freely about whatever he wishes in an atmosphere of benign tolerance and acceptance. This is called the condition of "free association" (Epstein, 1976). In much the same way there is an opportunity offered to the patient to freely use his imaginative faculty which has been lying dormant. Here, then, a visual mode of expression is wedded to the lexical mode (Horowitz, 1970). The form selected in which to imagine freely has highly symbolic meaning. The room (or a house) has long been thought to be symbolic of the Self (Bachelard, 1969). In the VIE one is asked to clean out the clutter, clutter that keeps one at a distance from the Self. This specific task that can be freely done via imaginal action is readily performed by the patient. In effect a space is opened in which a new experience in the form of dreaming can emerge.

3. Imagination should be differentiated from fantasy. In Western culture, and by common usage in the English language, fantasy and imagination are used interchangeably. Both functions meet by dint of being considered to be "unreal." Such common statements as, "it's only your imagination," and, "that's just a fantasy," testify to the idea of unreality connected with these activities. However, imagination and fantasy differ in a number of significant ways.[1] In non-Western contexts the imagination is viewed as a real function with a real spatial setting, albeit of an immaterial nature. In this vein Henry Corbin, one of the most eminent Western scholars of Islamic culture wrote: "It must be stressed that the world into which these Oriental (Islamic) theosophers probed is perfectly real. Its reality is more irrefutable and more coherent than that

of the empirical world, where reality is perceived by the senses. Upon returning, the beholders of this world are perfectly aware of having been "elsewhere"; They are not mere schizophrenics. This world is hidden behind the very act of sense perception and has to be sought underneath its apparent objective certainty. For this reason, we definitely cannot qualify it as being imaginary in the sense of the word, i.e., an unreal, or non-existent. Just as the Latin word "origo" has provided us in French with the derivatives originaire (native of), original, originel (primary), the word image can give us the term imaginal in addition to the regular derivative imaginary. We would thus have the imaginal world as an intermediary between the sensible world and the intelligible world (Corbin 1972).

In the same vein the dream realm is a real world in which the individual exists. How does this phenomenon tie in with the notion of day residue as the initiator and instigator of dream activity? Although the main thrust of this paper does not deal with the notion of day residue, it can be said, that, regardless of the actual validity of that idea there seems to be another source related to the arousal of dream activity besides the postulated ones of external waking events and fantasy activity. On occasion some aspect of what is discovered in the cleaning exercise appears in some direct manner in the dream. This was true for subject 2 where he discovered a calendar with pictures of boats buried in one of the drawers he cleaned in the VIE. However, the content of most subjects' dreams are not reflective of what appeared in the cleaning exercise.

IMPLICATIONS

That imagination has a regulatory capacity and is part of an overall imaginative faculty is not an essentially new idea (McMahon, 1976). Prior to the advent of the Cartesian revolution in Western thought, the imagination was viewed in exactly the way described above. Imagination was seen then to have a physical location in the ventricles of the brain and was stimulated into action by the taking in of external sensory stimuli of the "objective" world (McMahon, 1976). It was in effect an immaterial function acting on a material substance (the senses). The imagination was then viewed also as the regulator of various sorts of imagery that an individual would experience such as visual hallucinations and dreams. The discontinuity occurred when Descartes succeeded in removing the imaginative faculty from medicine, where it was used as a way of treating people with both physical and/or psychological disorders. Descartes' division of life into the *res cogitans* and *res extensa* succeeded in removing imagination because this function was viewed by him as immaterial and thus not real. Medicine became, thereby, bound up with what was material and able to be grasped as a concrete reality by the five senses as its domain of operation.

Imagery as a viable source of important experience has begun to gain some respectability in the fields of neuropsychiatry and neurophysiology (Galin, 1974). The use of the VIE reported here is a derivative of the imagination and imaginative faculty. It represents a way to try and reestablish the imagination within the framework of experience that would become once again an accepted part of the experiences of life in general and medicine in particular.

NOTES

1. The following are some of the differences between fantasy and imagination:

Imagination	Fantasy
1. Unique experience	1. Repetitive action and feeling

2. Creative and informs concrete world	2. Habitual
3. Not wish fulfilling	3. Wish fulfilling
4. Takes place in imaginal realm	4. Concerned with matter and the concrete world
5. Loss of self centeredness	5. Self-centered

REFERENCES

Bachelard, G. *The poetics of space.* Boston: Beacon Press, 1969.

Corbin, H. Mundus imaginalis. *Spring.* New York: Spring Publications, 1972.

Epstein, G. A note on a sematic confusion in the fundamental role of psychoanalysis. *Journal of the Philadelphia Association for Psychoanalysis,* 1976, *3,* 54–57, 60–61.

Galin, D. Implication for psychiatry of left and right cerebral specialization. *Archives of General Psychiatry,* 1974, *31,* 572–583.

Horowitz, M. *Image formation and cognition.* New York: Appleton-Century-Crofts, 1970, see also Epstein, G. The experience of the Waking Dream in psychotherapy. In J. L. Fosshage and P. Olsen, Eds., *Healing, implications for psychotherapy.* New York: Human Sciences Press, 1978.

Leuner, H. Guided affective imagery. *American Journal of Psychotherapy,* 1969, *23,* 4–22.

McMahon, C. E. The role of imagination in the disease process. *Psychological Medicine,* 1976, *6,* 179–184.

Singer, J. *Imagery and daydream methods in psychotherapy and behavior modification.* New York: Academic Press, 1974.

INDEX